As I Walked Down New Grub Street

As I Walked Down New Grub Street

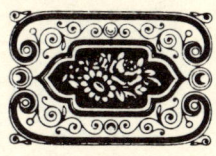

Memories of a Writing Life

WALTER ALLEN

The University of Chicago Press

The University of Chicago Press
Chicago, 60637

William Heinemann Ltd, London W1X 9PA

© 1981 by Walter Allen
All rights reserved
Published 1981

Published with financial assistance from the
Arts Council of Great Britain

ISBN 0–226–01433–9

Library of Congress Catalog Card No: 81–69852

Printed in Great Britain

to Peggy

I

By convention, the memoirist devotes his initial chapter to his forbears. Thus, on the second page of *A Little Learning*, Evelyn Waugh writes: 'None of my ancestors were illustrious. I can therefore be acquitted of vainglory if I follow the old fashion and preface my own history with some account of theirs.' Then, beginning a new paragraph with the words, 'My eight great-great-grandfathers', he recounts his family story for twenty-five pages, or roughly an eighth of his book, before succeeding in getting himself born.

I assume that I too had eight great-great-grandfathers but on my father's side I cannot trace my ancestry beyond his grandfather, who, I have always believed, was born in Tipton Workhouse, in South Staffordshire, and on reaching mature years, say seven or eight, was put to work in the coalmines. It is only comparatively recently that it has struck me that this may have been no more than a whimsical conjecture of my father's akin to his often-stated belief that we were related to the Bedfords, a belief based upon the fact that he was born in Great Russell Street, a notorious nineteenth-century Birmingham slum, and shared a taste for philosophical speculation with Bertrand Russell, whom he would refer to as 'your cousin Bertrand'.

For the most part, though, I still accept my father's story, for it offers considerable freedom of scope, as Eric Linklater pointed out to me. I can claim descent as it suits my fancy from the wicked aristocracy through a bastard line or from a sturdy peasantry despoiled of their heritage when those same wicked aristocrats enclosed the common lands in the eighteenth century.

Of my mother's family, I can speak with great confidence. The family tradition was that it had come down in the world. My maternal grandfather was said to be the younger son of a younger son. There were legends of a Welsh baronetcy, from whom he had expectations, in the not remote background. As a young man, he had come into a hundred pounds from somewhere and he passed his life in the vain hope of inheriting more. The unusual names current in the family seemed pointers to comparative grandeur: one of my uncles was christened Kinsey Beaumont, pretty expensive monickers for a man destined to spend his life as a labourer in a brass foundry. The grand relations could in truth be identified; as squires in mid-Wales and glass manufacturers, who tended to be Conservative members of Parliament, in the Black Country.

I doubt if there is a working-class family in England that does not cherish similar legends of aristocratic connections. Lower down the street where I passed my childhood there lived a family called Holte, the name for centuries until less than two hundred years ago of the lords of the manor of Aston, the district of Birmingham in which I was born. These Holtes, it was commonly believed, were the dwindled remnants of the family that had built the splendid Jacobean mansion – the original of Washington Irving's Bracebridge Hall – the city of Birmingham maintains as a museum in Aston Park, cheek by jowl with the ground on which Aston Villa plays football on Saturday afternoons.

Both my grandfathers died before I was born. I did not have much sense of Grandfather Thomas, but Grandfather Allen's presence was still vivid. His fourteen or fifteen sons and daughters were united in an intense reaction against him and his manner of life. He was illiterate and usually so drunk at weekends that he rarely went to work on Monday. On Tuesday he would be sacked for bad time-keeping. On Wednesday would come a telegram reinstating him, for he seems to have been a phenomenally skilful metal-worker. He could, for instance, solder aluminium, which was thought impossible, though one of my brothers, a metallurgist specialising in light alloys, had a specimen of Grandfather's craft that showed it could be done. He seems always to have been in work and to have earned good wages, though, because of his initial poverty, his lack of education, the size of his family and the scale of his boozing, he was always poor. He was – naturally, I am tempted to say – a Radical, and Mr Gladstone was the only god he recognised.

My father was a silversmith's engraver and designer and die-sinker. He had had a year or so at grammar school, long enough to give him the rudiments of Latin grammar and an insatiable thirst for learning. He painted water colours, for years was an ardent photographer and was a passionate player of the violin. It was not until I was at the

University that I realised that I had been brought up in surroundings much more than ordinarily cultured, for as a schoolboy I accepted uncritically the values of my peers, prominent among which was the belief that the good life consisted in belonging to a tennis club where you could get a decent game of bridge.

Not that ours was a literary culture. There were books in plenty but I don't remember any poetry or fiction among them. There was Plato's *Republic*, and More's *Utopia* and Marx's *Capital*. There was some Carlyle, a lot of Ruskin and Newman's *Apologia*. What I most remember, though, were the school textbooks which, spotted in second-hand book shops and junk shops, my father could not resist. As I recall him, at any time in his life he was going through the theorems of Euclid, the problems propounded in Hall & Knight's *Algebra* and the exercises in primers on heat, light and sound.

It was typical of him that he should celebrate his seventieth birthday by once again climbing Snowdon. He loved walking in Wales, and I was conditioned to accept Wales as the great romantic country, partly, perhaps, because they spoke a foreign language there, as you could actually hear them doing, though I remember being distressed by the 'buggers', 'fuckings' and 'sods' that seemed to interlard their entrancingly incomprehensible speech. As a young man, he had been one of the first members in Birmingham of the Independent Labour Party, for which he used to speak on soap-boxes at street-corners. He had a story of applying, sometime in the eighteen-nineties, for a street orator's pitch. 'What do you say you are?' the police inspector asked. 'ILP? Oh, cranks'. Later in life, his interest shifted, and he became preoccupied with philosophy, for which I believe he had real talent. His mind was full of so many things and was so open to new ideas that he could scarcely have failed to be the greatest single influence on me. He had one great adventure in his life. When he was nineteen he went to America to seek his fortune. He did not find it; he arrived at the same time as an economic depression and after some months he came back to Birmingham. But he never ceased to talk about it and he recalled the sights he had seen with a wonder I found very vivid and which fired me at an early age with the ambition to go to the United States.

Some of my father's brothers I knew hardly at all. It was my Uncle George I knew best, no doubt because he was the elder brother in whose shadow my father had grown up. To the casual observer they must have seemed very much alike, and I feel that in some ways George was a fanatical parody of my father. He too was a silversmith and a notably fine craftsman. He had his own little business, and twice a day, whatever the weather, he walked the three miles between his home and his workshop. His dress was always the same: a suit of dark grey broadcloth and a wide-brimmed black velour hat of a kind affected by nonconformist ministers. Inevitably, he was taken for some sort of clergyman. In fact, he belonged to a tiny Calvinist sect that worshipped in a tabernacle of corrugated iron. I remember him best for a conversation that occurred one day in early September in 1918, when I was seven. He was on holiday with us in North Wales and on a path above Barmouth estuary, a spot sacred to him because praised by Ruskin, he addressed me on the subject of John Stuart Mill. Reasonably enough, the name was new to me. John Stuart Mill, he warned me, was a Utilitarian and therefore a most wicked man whose example and precepts I was to shun as though they were the Devil's. I was much impressed by this admonition, in the light of which I remember the astonishment I felt a dozen years later when, as an undergraduate, I read Mill's autobiography. Had Uncle George, I wondered, ever *read* Mill? I couldn't ask him because by then he was dead.

All children, I imagine, identify themselves more with one side of their family than the other. I identified myself with my father's side. Despite its background of grandeur, I tended to be censorious of my mother's. They seemed to me a trifle raffish, unaware or regardless of the higher things of life. I do not have to say I was a dreadful little prig. When I became aware of the alleged differences between Celt and Anglo-Saxon I decided I was wholly Anglo-Saxon and saw my maternal uncles as irredeemably Celtic. They were all eminently bowler-hatted men, though Uncle Kinsey, whom I knew least well of the three, wore a bowler hat of the sort we called, wrongly I believe, a billycock. By that, we meant that his hat was older, seedier, greener, than a bowler hat should be. His moustache was more ragged and more drooping than his brothers', and he normally wore a silk muffler round his neck instead of collar and tie. He was a labourer and often out of work.

It was Kinsey who, in a memorable phrase, summed up my Uncle Andrew: 'One of these days our Andrew will give his arse away, and then what'll he do to shit?' The conduct of Andrew's life was governed by an unhypocritical, innocent benevolence, a benevolence of settled dignity and poise. In my memory, he had an eighteenth-century vastness of girth, and he moved in a ponderously formal world of his own. Whatever he said or did seemed to be somehow elevated to a loftier plane. Thus, sitting in his wooden armchair by the fire, he would take his gold watch out of his waistcoat pocket, scrutinise it searchingly, rise ponderously and announce to my aunt: 'Mother, I have to slip out for five minutes to see a gentleman.' The public bar of the pub round the corner was the last place his words and manner evoked.

Above the mantelpiece in his living room hung framed a most impressive enlarged tinted portrait-photograph of him in his regalia as Worthy Primo in the Royal and Antediluvian Order of Buffaloes. It is only fair, perhaps, to record that his sons irreverently called him the 'Glaxo baby'. His end was sad. He met a gentleman too many, who offered him a partnership in a scrap-metal business. It would be extremely lucrative, and all he had to do was to put some money into the business. Uncle Andrew borrowed left, right and centre, the gentleman took the money and was not seen again.

His elder brother Ted could not have been more different, dignity and formality apart. Of all my uncles on either side of the family he was my favourite. It was as his friend that my father had met my mother, and though temperamentally far removed from him, Ted had had, I am sure, a great influence on him. He was a particularly formidable autodidact, game to tackle any branch of knowledge. I remember him best as he was in the last years of his life. He would have been in his early fifties and was retired, for incipient blindness had forced him to resign from the Post Office service, in which he had climbed as high as anyone of his background could do at that time. He had entered as a messenger. At seventeen, a junior postman, he had gone to evening classes at the Midland Institute and passed first in the country in a nation-wide examination in metallurgy. He could never understand, not that he had come first, for to have done anything else was inconceivable, but why his success had had no sequel. 'They gave me a medal and a pile of books,' he'd tell me, 'but it never seemed to enter anybody's head to find the money to send me to college. I stayed a postman. They let me be wasted, boy.'

He went off on another bent. How, I do not know, but he became interested in the English language, mastered Anglo-Saxon and Middle English and did work for the Early English Text Society. Then, my father in tow, he went to classes in economics. When I compare them, I see that Uncle Ted was infinitely shrewder, more practical, more knowledgeable in the ways of the world than my father. Had the word been fashionable then, he would have rejoiced in being called a pragmatist, whereas my father was a romantic through and through.

They joined the ILP together, and Ted climbed high in the party. He would reminisce to me of his associations with MacDonald, Snowden, whom he always referred to as Philip, and Margaret Bondfield. He gave up his own political ambitions – he was several times offered parliamentary constituencies to fight – for a career in the Post Office. Every year, I remember, he and my aunt went on a continental holiday under the aegis of the Workers' Travel Association. Pleasure was combined with more serious pursuits; one year, they were inspecting municipal trading in Holland, another, welfare provisions in Germany. It was apropos the latter that I first heard of Herbert Morrison, whom my uncle had met on one of these family jaunts. 'Watch young Morrison, boy,' he urged me. 'He's the coming man.' I suppose that would have been 1927 or thereabouts.

Uncle Ted's manner was peremptory, brusque: he tended to bark. His customary greeting was: 'Well, boy, what have *you* been up to?' On his retirement, he was appointed a Justice of the Peace and became a Poor Law guardian. My brother Frank and I took great pleasure in a story told of him illustrative of his power and authority. He had stepped off the tramcar at the city centre and found that he had neglected to stuff his ticket in the used-ticket box, for he was still clutching it. Rather than commit an offence against the by-laws by throwing it into the gutter, he had continued to hold it till he met a policeman, to whom he said: 'Officer, please dispose of this for me.'

I have no notion what he earned. It cannot have been enormous but I suspect it was at least twice as much as my father did. His house and establishment always seemed a cut above ours. He lived pretty comfortably, and though it was modest, his house seemed to abound in small luxuries that I didn't think small. There was a sizeable gramophone and a collection of records which included, besides the obvious popular classics, Harry Lauder, Gracie Fields, Norah Blaney and John Tilly, in whom I especially delighted. There was also – and I have never seen another – a pianola, on which Uncle Ted used to 'play' Beethoven and Rachmaninov with considerable bravura. And there were books, far more than I had seen in any other private house.

I had a standing invitation to go round to supper after church on Sunday evenings. I answered, as accurately as seemed necessary, his routine questions about my progress at school and then looked over the books and magazines he had borrowed from the Birmingham Old Library. It was then that I first came across *Harper's Magazine* and the *Atlantic Monthly*, which he took out regularly. It was out of one of these that there arose what I interpreted as a considerable compliment. He called my attention to a short story by an English writer. 'Boy,' he said, 'If you couldn't write a better story than that, I'd be ashamed of you.' I purred but privately thought it unlikely I could. The story was by David Garnett.

Biography and memoirs were his favourite reading, I think, and he had a taste for Westerns. 'Boy,' he would pontificate to me, 'Zane Grey is doing for the American West what Scott did for the Border country.' After supper, he'd say: 'Go and find yourself a book, boy.' I'd wander round the house looking at his shelves. It was understood that these were not loans but gifts. So I came by my first Keats, both poems and letters, a collected Chaucer, Marlowe's plays edited by Havelock Ellis in the old Mermaid edition, a Tennyson, and, among many others and very early on, a compilation I pored over for years, a history of English literature by a man named Compton-Rickett which I have never encountered elsewhere. It was reprinted on recycled paper of the period of the first war. The critical opinions expressed were very much of their time, but the narrative was so lavishly illustrated by examples of verse and prose as to amount to an anthology drawn from the greater part of English writing. It is a book to which I owe a considerable debt.

I was the youngest of four brothers. Charlie, the eldest of us, I scarcely remember. He was twelve years older than I, was conscripted into the Army when I was six and killed at St Quentin in March, 1918. In photographs the facial resemblance to my father is striking, which is perhaps merely another way of saying that Charlie and I, too, were closely alike in appearance. I still have a copy of *Alice in Wonderland*, the inside cover embellished with a transfer of King Albert of the Belgians, which must have been added by me, sent for Christmas, 1917. My next brother, Bill, was nine years older, which was enough to make him remote. As a child, I felt he was somehow different from the rest of us, scarcely an Allen at all but recognisably a Thomas. He was just young enough to escape the war but suffered the full blast of the economic depression after it. I was closest to my brother Frank, for there were only four years between us. I was the kid-brother hanging on, identifying with him and reacting against him. For years I thought our boyhood and youth together were spent in a mutual competition in priggishness. I scarcely knew where the one of us ended and the other began.

II

When I was eleven I sat the entrance examination for King Edward's Grammar School, Aston, was awarded a 'free place' and so moved on from my elementary school. The fees my father did not have to pay came to thirteen pounds ten a year. Aston was one of a number of similar schools founded in the 1880s as offshoots of King Edward's, Birmingham, which we always called 'New Street', where it was situated. King Edward's Birmingham is a sixteenth-century foundation and, academically, one of the most distinguished schools in England. In my time, it was resolutely middle-class; doctors and lawyers sent their sons there to become doctors and lawyers in their turn. As of right, the boys went on to the old universities. The grammar schools were lower-middle class at best. In terms of the curriculum, I suppose the main difference was that at New Street Greek was taught, while at the grammar schools Latin was the best you could aspire to. I see now that they bore a relation to New Street similar to that of the provincial universities, Manchester, Birmingham, Leeds and the rest, to Oxford and Cambridge. It was difficult not to see them as in some sense a second-best, a sop to the underprivileged.

Which did not prevent us having a pretty good opinion of ourselves. We were a cut above, we thought, our strictly educational peers, the municipally established secondary schools. For one thing, our fees were higher by about thirty shillings a term. And then, were we not part, however recent our origin, of an ancient foundation? This was expressed in the school song, which was the school song to end all school songs, fruitier by far than E.M. Forster's in *The Longest Journey*. My memory of it is patchy, but I recall that we 'learnt the game of life In cricket's manly warfare and football's honest strife', and the refrain was unforgettable:

> Long live the name of Edward,
> Let all good fellows sing.
> Long live the name of Edward,
> Our Founder and our King!

We were taught to cherish those things that differentiated us, we believed, from the municipal secondary schools. The assembly hall was never to be referred to as 'assembly' or 'hall'; for us, it was Big School. And how proud we were of our leaded windows and bits of stained glass. And then, our rugger team. In retrospect, rugger dominated us completely. The members of the First XV were heroes not only to the other boys but also, it seemed, to many of the masters as well. We were inordinately proud that in the year I entered the school our Old Boys' team had no fewer than eight players in the North Midlands XV.

I took to it all like a duck to water, even though I was hopeless at rugger and never achieved a regular place even in my House third team. It wasn't until I had begun my third year at the school that a dreadful revelation was forced upon me. I discovered that to be a free-place boy was a shameful thing. The Maths master was known as Beaky. I see him now: the formal, rather old-fashioned clothes he wore, the gold tie-pin; the neurotic trick he had of holding his hand behind his back as he walked and opening and closing his fingers; the marionette-like strut; the oblong, lined face that seemed strung on wires like a cage beneath the skin. He had taught me Latin, the year before, but it was not until I went into Lower VB that he appeared to me as a personification of spiteful persecution. He persecuted with relish. His weapons were a ferocious sarcasm, against which boys were helpless, and a relentless cross-examination; and his main victims were free-place boys. I was terrified, of course, that one day he would pick on me, for I was bad enough at Maths. Daily, he inveighed against boys with free places, boys with maintenance grants, thieves all of them, he assured us, who stole ratepayers' money. We were, I understood, like the tenants of council houses, who notoriously used the bath to store the coal in. His chief victim was a boy who stammered, a quiet, gentle youth whom we all knew to be sensitive and thoughtful.

I was coming to consciousness of myself and of the school. In this, I was helped by the English master, whom we knew as Frank. We remained vaguely in touch with each other for thirty-five years, and throughout that time my attitude towards him was ambivalent, as I suspect his was towards me. Despite this, I am conscious of a debt to him. He was a local celebrity, prominent as an amateur actor and freelance journalist; for many years he was president of the North Midlands Rugby Football Union; and he had compiled many of the textbooks we used, the English grammar, the Latin grammar and the anthologies of verse. I am pretty sure that it was he, as one of the earliest Old Boys of the school, who had devised most of what passed as the traditions of the school.

It was Frank who wrote on my report at the end of my time in the Lower Vth, 'A boy with interests beyond his years. He must see that these do not interfere with school work.' That seemed to me pretty silly at the time and it still does. My hobby was writing little five-hundred-word articles for the popular literary weeklies of the day, *T. P.'s Weekly* and *John O'London's*, belles-lettres of a sort, things with titles such as 'Autumn in the Poets'. The payment, I recall, was a guinea and a half. I managed to sell half a dozen or so. They did me no harm, and even if the end was mercenary led me to read widely in the English poets.

In fact, Frank was a great encourager, and these things awakened in him some interest in me. He discovered some acting ability in me and took me along to the Playgoers' Club, which was run in connection with the Repertory Theatre, and I appeared in one or two of his productions, as Creon in Murray's translation of the *Medea* of Euripides and in an unspeakably bad play by John Drinkwater. At school, I played Macbeth and then Hamlet in his productions. He still seems to me to have been a notably good teacher of Shakespeare. His literary judgements were, I think, wholly conventional and of their time and where modern writing was concerned were generally wrong. But he had the gift of making books come alive, even for boys normally without interest in them. I recall a book we read with him which I would now think by and large almost grotesquely unsuitable for boys of the age we were. It was an anthology called, I think, *Selected Modern Short Stories*, and published in the World's Classic series. The stories were mainly from the nineteenth century. We all registered the appropriate frisson when reading Poe's 'A Cask of Amontillado' but I don't recall any of us were anything but bored by Henry James's 'Four Meetings' and 'Owen Wingrave'. They were, we learnt, 'psychological'.

But I remember the volume particularly because it was my first introduction to George Gissing. It contained his 'A Poor Gentleman', the story of a man of good family who falls in the social scale until he is living in an East End slum; but throughout he manages to keep his status as a gentleman by never ever pawning his dress suit. Frank characterised the story as 'morbid'. I cannot pretend I liked it but I found it oddly disturbing, and it was the beginning of a life-long fascination, in which there is a streak of aversion, with Gissing.

This anthology was important to me in much the same way as another book we read a year later, an anthology sponsored by the English Association and called *Poems of Today, Second Series*. I realised within a year or two how wretchedly poor and unrepresentative it was. The only concessions to the modern were a poem or two by Aldous Huxley, whom Frank said was 'too clever', and a piece of bad free verse by Robert Nichols. Nevertheless, it was *Poems of Today* that made me think I might become a poet myself and not, as I had thought till then, merely a newspaper reporter. It was more or less at this time that I wrote a sonnet which appeared in the school magazine and which Frank sent to *Public School Verse*. It was accepted, but before it could be published *Public School Verse* went out of existence. Five or six years later, its editor, Martin Gilkes, was to become a friend of mine.

Frank was a good teacher and a generous man; as I remember in two different examples. My close friend at this time was a boy named Norman Hicken. Our friendship began when we found ourselves making common cause: we discovered we were, so far as we could tell, the only two Socialists — more precisely, supporters of the Labour Party — in the school. That itself, in 1925, was fighting stuff; but no one willingly took to fighting Norman, for he was massive, the mainstay in the front line scrum. Some years later, I seem to recall, he played full back for the North Midlands team. There was no mistaking Frank's position. He was a traditionalist, from which it followed that he could only be a Tory and a strong Church of England man. Which didn't prevent his responding with a welcome interest to our eccentricities and holding the ring for us; and this was so even in 1926 in the week of the General Strike, when feelings ran high.

Norman, too, had interests beyond his years. These were in natural history, in butterflies and moths particularly. I realise now that he was a prodigy. I had no means of gauging his knowledge and I don't imagine anyone else had — biology was not taught at the school then — but I suspect it may well have been extraordinary. He was consumed by something I recognised as a passion. Regularly, you could read its manifestations in the weekly natural history column in the *Birmingham Mail*. They were always astonishingly precise in their detail, masterly records of observation. He left school at sixteen and went into the laboratories of the Dunlop Rubber Company and I lost touch with him, though heard of him from time to time. He was working for an external B.Sc. of London University and, that achieved, for a Master's degree. We ran into each other again in the very early Fifties, lunched together, as a consequence of which I spent a weekend with him and his wife in Surrey. He was different from what he had been as a boy only in that his personality now stood out, as it were, in bolder relief; he was more decisive and decided and also, I thought, more flamboyant, for he was successful and prosperous. I picked up the story of what had happened since I last saw him. He had gone on to read for his doctorate, but instead of embarking on anything useful, on anything that had a bearing on rubber technology, he had returned to the concerns of his boyhood. I remembered his interest even then in the caddis fly, a 'feebly flying, freq. nocturnal insect of the order Trichoptera, living near water', as the *Concise Oxford* has it. It was on the caddis fly that his doctoral thesis had been written. He gave me a published copy of it, illustrated with his own elegantly precise scraper-board drawings.

I rejoiced to see how his schoolboy interests had flowered and vindicated themselves. I found in this great reassurance. He was plainly well-heeled, as they say, but his opinions did not seem to have changed. He told me he was richer than he had ever dreamt it was possible for him to be. He enjoyed it, though I thought I detected in the enjoyment a trace of rueful embarrassment. All the same, it enabled him to indulge in his delight in fast motor cars and to send his daughters to one of the leading girls' schools in the country. For he had left the rubber industry and become an industrial biologist, a pioneer in the business of pest control. As his prosperity increased, he eased himself by degrees out of the day-to-day running of the business he had helped to build up and more and more lived the life of what I can only call a gentleman-biologist. Armed with the best cameras and binoculars, he went on safari throughout the world. He fulfilled what I suspect was a boyhood dream by visiting the Galapagos Islands. Increasingly, he devotes himself to nature conservancy and to writing on wild life, always illustrating his books with the scraper board drawings that he makes with such delicate accuracy. His career, it seems to me, has been truly admirable and enviable, at once romantic and remarkable.

But I have digressed from my theme of Frank's generosity of mind. More than ten years after the General Strike, when he had encouraged Norman and myself to put the case for the strikers, I was very moved to learn that he had taken into his house and maintained a number of

Basque children, refugees from Guernica and Franco's war in Spain.

It wasn't Frank, though, who urged me to read modern poetry. It was the art master, a man we called, for reasons unknown to me, Twisty Bill. Bernard Fleetwood Walker was to become in the course of time a Royal Academician. 'Read the Sitwells, boy,' he told me, and I did. In 1927 the Sitwells seemed very different poets from the Sitwells of twenty and thirty years later, after Leavis's and Grigson's demolition-job on them. I was greatly taken by Osbert's satires and Edith's *Ballet Russe* light verse; I remember buying *Gold Coast Customs* in great excitement.

Walker was the school's eccentric master, consciously so, I suspect. By our humdrum, provincial standards, his habitual dress was extravagant — the bow tie, the jaunty, not-quite-conventional trilby hat. He talked to us as no other masters did, calling us 'smelly fellows' and asking us conversationally, as he sat down beside us to inspect our work: 'Do you know you stink, boy?' Art was very much a junior form subject, which I was relieved to be rid of, for it was one of the many subjects I was bad at, and, considering my background, I thought I should shine at. It was when I was in the VIth Form that I really came to know him. I had become interested in modern painting and I took advantage of my new relative freedom of movement by wandering from time to time into the art room to talk to Walker. He knew I had ambitions to write and 'Be an art critic, boy', he would say. 'Be an art critic.' It was he who introduced me to the books of Roger Fry and Clive Bell and it was from him that I first heard of Wyndham Lewis and Nevinson and Paul Nash. He took me with him to exhibitions in the local galleries, one, I remember, of Cezanne. And I am indebted to him for a saying he used in times of tedium, such as writing comments on school reports: 'Let's say *bum* and throw a brick through the window.'

In 1926, I sat the school certificate examination. My results were not bad but also not such as to make them acceptable for university matriculation purposes, for I failed in maths, physics and chemistry. This meant I had to repeat the year. This was not as boring as it might have been, for I was developing in ways unrelated to school. Not entirely, for that year Blake's *Songs of Innocence and Experience* was one of the set books in the school certificate examination. It is, surely, the supreme volume of lyric poetry in English, and I found it, besides, devastatingly revolutionary in what it had to say. I recall my astonishment at the English master's tone of good-humoured condescension to some of the poems. In this form, it was not Frank and I could not understand how the master's response to Blake was so temperate, so tepid. He was always, it seemed to me, on the edge of dismissing Blake as a lunatic, whereas to me it was astonishing and wonderful that the Joint Matriculation Board of the Combined Universities could be so imaginative as to prescribe this little book as suitable for study by adolescent boys and girls.

I took Blake out of his context as examination material and appropriated him to my own purely private ends. It was the beginning of a spell when I was almost totally absorbed, it seems in retrospect, in a passion for books. I seem to have spent almost all my free time in the Birmingham Public Library, which became far more important to me than school. I had stopped writing my little articles for *John O'London's* and *T. P.'s* and was now ashamed of them, as I now despised the periodicals themselves. This contempt was quite misplaced, and now that they no longer exist one sees their value. They were rarely critically rigorous and they made it, achievement and the appreciation of achievement alike, seem a little too easy. But they were doing for literature much what Kenneth Clark has done for art in his television programmes. The same praise and the objections can be applied to both.

The first writer to intoxicate me, I suppose, was Shaw, though this had happened a year or two earlier. Within the course of three years, I must have seen at least half of his plays performed, for every July the MacDona Players, who devoted themselves entirely to Shaw, were at the Prince of Wales Theatre for a month, and I was in the gallery night after night. I thought his ideas enthralled me: I see now it was his rhetoric. By what now looks like inevitable association, I came on Wells, who I still think had the largest natural talent of any English novelist of the century. He did not, as we all know, always use it well, but he was a positive cornucopia of ideas, which he poured out in a ceaseless stream. And he had, too, an enormous capacity for fun. Almost certainly, he will look much greater in the future than he does now.

But it was Bennett who most excited me. *Clayhanger* was my favourite of his novels and it was the novel that first turned me to the thought of writing novels myself. In it, for the first time in fiction, I met a landscape, mental as well as physical, akin to my own in Birmingham. Out of seemingly unpromising material Bennett had made something beautiful; and the warmth and depth of his sympathies were immediately apparent to me. How vividly, indeed, one still remembers the account of Darius Clayhanger's childhood and the vignette of the 'oldest Sunday-school teacher in the Five Towns'. And side by side with the sympathy was the unflinching, stoic honesty. Bennett, I decided, was my man; and of all the men of my time he is still the one I would most like to have met.

Fifteen years later, I wrote a little book on Bennett. I made no effort to meet his friends or kinsfolk, but after it was published, I did as a result come into contact with some who had known him. I had, I remember, an appreciative, lively letter from his sister Tertia and I was invited to tea at Chelsea Square by the American painter Ethel Sands, a friend of Bennett and a protégée – this I did not then know – of Henry James. I met, too, Frank Swinnerton, who praised it generously in a review, and ten years after publication it evoked a charming letter from Siegfried Sassoon.

Desmond MacCarthy reviewed the book in two columns of the *Sunday Times*, continued his review in a long letter and invited me to dinner. He told me how Bennett had said to him: 'You know, Desmond, I am a n-nice man.' MacCarthy convinced me Bennett was indeed that. He contrasted him with Wells, with whom he had also been on friendly terms. He had reviewed a novel by Wells, found it bad and said so, whereupon Wells had not spoken to him for a month and afterwards had gone round London saying Desmond was drunk when he wrote the review. Bennett, whom he had also in his time reviewed adversely, took unfavourable criticism in his stride and bore no grudge. It was the magnanimity of Bennett that shone through MacCarthy's recollections.

After this meeting with MacCarthy, I began, without much success, to collect reminiscences of Bennett. L. P. Hartley told me of his one encounter with him. They had met at a tea party at Ethel Sands' and sat back-to-back in one of those curious French eighteenth-century pieces of furniture which are literally two chairs joined back to back. As he was about to leave, Bennett swivelled round and said to Hartley: 'We haven't had much to say to each other, have we?'

And Graham Greene told me of his meeting with Bennett. It was at a luncheon given by his publishers when Graham was still very much a new novelist. At coffee time the guests moved round and Graham found himself sitting side by side with Bennett. Waiters came round for orders for brandy, and Graham asked for one. When it was set in front of him, Bennett, who in some ways remained the Methodist he had been brought up to be, said, 'You won't get very far, young man, if you go in for that sort of thing.'

MacCarthy cherished the memory of Bennett, and I am grateful additionally to Bennett because it was through him I met MacCarthy. He was in his seventies, a legendary figure. We all know the story of how for years he carried round with him in his brief-case the manuscript of his book on John Donne, which he never finished. His creative talent was dissipated in wonderful conversation, for he was one of the wittiest and most brilliant of talkers. He had great difficulty in finishing anything, however slight, and he seems invariably to have finished his pieces of dramatic criticism for the *New Statesman* in the taxi on his way to the printers. I met him only twice, the second time soon before his death. It was at Frascati's restaurant in Oxford Street, where the PEN Club was holding a memorial dinner to Shaw. MacCarthy was President of the Club, and I was to be one of the speakers. We were called to dinner and mounting the stairs in conversation with me, MacCarthy grasped me by the arm and led me to a sofa on the landing. I was embarrassed because the occasion could not begin without Desmond and I reminded him that the dinner was due. 'That can wait,' he said. 'Tell me what you are doing now.' He would not let us go into dinner until I had satisfied him. One saw why he was a legend and why he was universally loved. For me he is summed up in a story about him told me by Kingsley Martin, who had been his editor for many years and who was devoted to him, though they had little apparently in common. Desmond, who came of an aristocratic Irish family and had been at Eton and Cambridge, was in his time a great frequenter of great country houses. After he discovered that Tolstoy, also an aristocrat and also in his time a great frequenter of great country houses, always carried his chamber-pot from his bedroom himself because he thought it demeaning to the chambermaid to expect her to do so, Desmond also insisted on emptying his own slops.

The centre of my extra-curricular activities was the City Public Library. In the Reference Library I read all the books of contemporary verse that piqued my interest. I remember an anthology, taken down from the shelves almost at random, that helped to canalise my interest was Henry Newbolt's *New Paths on Helicon*. There I first encountered poets like Pound and Herbert Read. I found Newbolt's book especially useful because, as his notes on the individual poets showed, he was almost as puzzled by them as I was. Knowing him only as the writer of 'Vitai Lampada', I was surprised that his attitude towards them was so generous and broad-minded. I found myself fascinated by Robert Graves's critical books and pamphlets, *On English Poetry, Poetic Unreason, Contemporary Techniques of Poetry, Pamphlet against Anthologies,* above all the book he wrote with Laura Riding, *A Survey of Modernist Poetry.* It was as though I believed — and perhaps I *did* believe — that there was a magic formula for the writing of poetry, and I was reading in a desperate endeavour to find it. Graves seemed to offer clues to the formula.

The Lending Library was the scene of my broader forays. I must have made myself a fearful nuisance to the staff, for I was always finding and pointing out errors in the catalogue; such as the attribution of *Time and Western Man* to D. B. and not P. Wyndham Lewis. All the same, they endured me; and one assistant, with whom I became friendly and who was interested in the contents of books as well as their covers, which is not invariably true of librarians, slipped me under the counter, as it were, a copy of the just-published *Lord Raingo* before it was put on the shelves.

On all sides I found books that fascinated me, found them by something like a sense of smell, a gift which good publishers have for manuscripts coming in from the blue, good editors and good critics too. So I came across writers like David Garnett and Richard Hughes with his collection of stories *A Moment of Time* and men of a generation earlier like J. D. Beresford, whose Jacob Stahl trilogy excited me. Later, I realised it was one of the many Edwardian descendants of *The Way of All Flesh* and I have never dared look at it again, for fear it is not as good as I thought it was when I was sixteen.

In the novel my great unaided discovery was Lawrence. That was in 1927, and it was seeing his novels in the Library that first made me aware of his name. The very look of the books, those dark-brown squarish Secker volumes, intrigued me. I would pull one out, peep inside it, read a page or two and put it back, as though consciously deferring the excitement I sensed in it. *The Rainbow* I came across in the most improbable place, a tiny commercial circulating library dedicated to women's romantic fiction housed in a shop near where we lived that sold knitting wool. I took it out as quickly as I could, furtively, rather as though buying a packet of contraceptives. I bore it home as it were in my bosom; I knew, though how I do not know, that it was forbidden stuff, and I kept Lawrence to myself as a secret at least until my undergraduate years.

For me, Lawrence remains the greatest *English* writer of the century. I still marvel at the range of literary forms he commanded. One doesn't think of him as a virtuoso, but he was; novelist, poet, short-story writer, travel-writer, literary critic and, as the final revelation when his plays were put on at the Royal Court, very nearly a great dramatist. What primarily excited me was what had initially excited me in Bennett. His upbringing and social background were close enough to mine to make it almost inevitable that I should identify with him. He was a working-class boy with no advantages except his talent. More than that, he was a miner's son. I knew no miners, but miners were my working-class heroes. There were no coal pits actually in Birmingham itself but there were two about three miles away in what was semi-rural country between Birmingham, West Bromwich and Walsall to the north-west. I do not think this country can ever have been comparable in beauty with the country round Eastwood, but it was the scene of my favourite country walks for some years, and, wet or fine, I'd make the five-mile circuit of the two pits most Saturday nights. I was enchanted by what seemed to me the beauty of this region in which farms were dominated by the headstocks of the pits. The long smouldering pit-mounds and the pools of pumped-out water flanking them gave the countryside character that I felt it would have lacked if left wholly to farmers. I particularly valued it at night and in the rain, for then I found in it things I had seen only in the paintings of the French Impressionists glimpsed in my father's old copies of the *Studio*: such as steam rising from a railway engine passing under a bridge and dissipating into the mist. It was the scene of the sonnet that had been accepted by *Public School Verse*.

So I was conditioned to admire Lawrence, and the admiration and the wonder he aroused in me were akin to those I felt for Blake. Lawrence too was like dynamite. He died when I was an undergraduate, and his dying was the first real shock of death I had known. 'The day of his death was a dark cold day.' It was as though the sun had gone out. Auden told me later he had felt the same.

I made a pilgrimage to Eastwood and the Lawrence country soon after I went down from the University. BBC Midland Region was showing some interest in a proposal I had made for a talk on Lawrence. My guide was Walter Brierley, who lived at Ripley near by and had written a moving novel called *Means Test Man*. He was an unemployed miner whom I had met through John Hampson. I think I may have supplied the title for his novel. In Eastwood he introduced me to Councillor Willie Hopkin, who kept a shoe shop in the High Street. He had been one of Lawrence's earliest friends and, I believe, at one time his Sunday school teacher. He was the advanced man of Eastwood, was devoted to the memory of Lawrence and had cast himself rather in the role of the St Peter of the Lawrence Heaven. He led me into the parlour behind the shop, indicated a chair and told me to sit down, I obeyed. 'Young man,' he said, 'you're sitting in the same chair as Katherine Mansfield and Middleton Murry, Aldous and Maria Huxley, Koteliansky, four American professors and two French professors sat in.' Thus he put me in my place.

That trip to the Lawrence country had no material result, but at the end of the war I wrote a feature programme on Lawrence for BBC Midland Region. Professional actors in those days were not expected to be able to cope with regional accent other than Mummerset, and amateur actors from Nottingham were drawn upon for the programme. One of them, a man of about seventy, played the parts of Walter Morel and Lawrence's father. After the broadcast I found myself standing side by side him in the lavatory. He said: 'I knew him, y'know.' 'You knew Lawrence?' I exclaimed, much excited. 'What was he like?' He thought. 'He wore a rum bugger,' he said.

Lawrence was not the only major contemporary I discovered in the Birmingham Public Library. On the poetry shelves I found a thin book bound in thick brown unaesthetic public library binding. When I first took it off the shelf I opened it gingerly, as though it might explode. It bewildered me but I took it from the shelves the next time I was in the library and at last I gathered courage to borrow it and take home. It perplexed me because for one thing, though the work of a poet with an Anglo-Saxon name, some of the poems were written in French. And the poems in English were hardly poetry as I had been taught to understand it. The book was *Poems, 1914–1925* by a man named T. S. Eliot.

I have always thought of him as *Mr* Eliot. When I went to London I ran into people who referred to him as Tom Eliot: I soon realised this did not always mean that they had met him. I saw him many times, so often indeed that it seemed to me that if you had your being in central London you could not *not* see him, for he was part of it. I sat opposite him in tube trains. I saw him in theatres, I stood behind him in a queue to buy stamps at Holborn Post Office, I saw him in restaurants in Soho, I recall I was once in the lift with him at Notting Hill underground station. In 1938 and 1939 I went on occasion at lunchtime to a pub called The Friend at Hand behind Russell Square tube station for the express purpose of seeing Mr Eliot come into the saloon bar, carrying his rolled umbrella and wearing his gent's city clothes and black trilby hat. Without speaking a word to anyone, he would drink his double whisky before going to his lunch engagement. Towards the end of the Fifties, at a late-night party at the Savoy

Hotel I saw him dancing with his young wife. And soon after this I met him. He invited me to have tea with him in his office at Faber's, for I was thinking of writing a book on Wyndham Lewis, who had recently died. He was very cordial and gracious. He had known Lewis from the time he first arrived in England, and Lewis had told me with some pride that Mr Eliot went round to his flat every Thursday evening to read to him, for these were the years of Lewis's blindness. I was after information. Mr Eliot was an amiable sphinx. 'You know,' he said, 'I never felt I really knew Lewis.' That was all he would vouchsafe. It was a wonderfully baffling meeting.

Weekly, I entered in a log the titles of the books I'd read. I have long lost that book and regret it: I would very much like now to know exactly what I did read in those days. I was writing poetry too. I aimed at a poem a day, for there seemed merit in quantity, and the more I wrote the prouder I was. Those that seemed suitable I sent to Mr Eliot at the *Criterion*. They were bound to appeal to him, I thought, so well it seemed to me I had caught the rhythms of his own verse. Regularly he returned them without comment. As a young poet I was totally unsuccessful, though once or twice I got encouraging notes from Murry at the *Adelphi*. For a day or two, his remarks seemed as good almost as an acceptance, for he had actually gone to the trouble of scribbling on a rejection-slip his opinion of my verses.

During these years, however, it was for Robert Graves that I cherished my deepest personal admiration. I knew that, no matter how intense my regard for Lawrence and Eliot, I could never aspire to being like either. Part of their fascination, indeed, was the fascination of otherness. Not that I was conscious of any kind of resemblance between myself and Graves; that would have been the wildest self-deception. In some sense, though, I felt him to be an exemplar, someone who compelled me to say, If I weren't myself I'd like best to be Robert Graves.

I knew one or two of his poems before I met his criticism, but it was through his criticism that I really came to his poetry. I valued the criticism for a number of reasons. More than any I had yet come across, it seemed to grapple with the fundamentals that went to the making of a poem. I was impressed by the insistence on the physical nature of poetry and by Graves's determined rooting of it in the poet's psychological being. All this was, as it were, in the cause of something else, something summed up in the foreword to his collected poems of 1938, where he divides into five parts his 'struggle to be a poet in more than a literary sense'. What especially fascinated me was his account of the third stage of struggle, when 'the poetic self has become the critic of the divided human self. Poetry is not a mere mitigation of haunting experiences: it is an exorcism of physical pretensions by self-humbling honesties.'

No doubt I would have come to the poetry even if I had not known the criticism. Every Saturday lunchtime, my father brought home the *New Statesman*, which he handed to me. I always turned first to the book reviews and one Saturday morning in 1927 I saw a review entitled boldly and baldly 'A Major Poet'. It was by Arnold Bennett and was written in Bennett's style of downright assertion. He had discovered a major poet and was telling us in no uncertain terms. The poet was Robert Graves, the occasion the publication of *Poems: 1914–1926*. Bennett's quotations explained and justified his excitement. I got together seven shillings and sixpence and next Monday after school went into the city and bought the book, the covers of which were mottled in various shades of grey.

It was the first book of poetry I had bought on my own initiative and, though later I sometimes worshipped elsewhere, erecting shrines to Eliot and Auden particularly, Graves remained my favourite contemporary poet for the next forty years. I valued the witty muscularity of his expression and the gnomic nature of so many of the poems, which were at once homely and mysterious, and in a curious way I never succeeded in defining for myself, very English. I found I could use his collections as a *sortes Virgilianae*. I was entranced by lines like these, for instance:

> To go in no direction
> Surely as carelessly
> Walking on the hills alone,
> I never found easy.

And, greatest quality of all, was a rock-bottom honesty, and obstinate refusal to be anyone but himself. It was an integrity won from great struggle. There shone through everything he wrote 'features Resolute and unchangeably your own'.

I found these, too, the defining qualities of *Goodbye to All That*, which I read very soon after it was published in 1929. Almost fifty years after my first reading of it, I am more sure than ever I was that it is one of the great autobiographies of our time. For me, Graves was a seminal influence.

In 1927, I finally passed the School Certificate examination at matriculation level and went into the Sixth Form, where I came to know and value the head master, whom we knew as Joe or, sometimes, the Old Man. He seemed in his academic gown an enormous man. He was, in fact, six feet two and very broad; as a boy at New Street he had been a famous cricketer and Rugger player. To all appearances, he was a very formal man, but I guessed that this was largely a matter of appearances because, before I was in the Sixth or had any first-hand knowledge of him, I had seen him twice almost break down under emotion at morning prayers; once on the death of Asquith and then when announcing the death of a master at the school who had been a close friend from boyhood. I never learned anything about his background but I see him now as a man who in the course of living found himself being forced reluctantly to move towards opinions not quite orthodox. A year before I went to the school he had done away with the OTC, an action that at that date could have stemmed only from principle. Then, boys were sent to him to be beaten. This he loathed and a year or so after I left, refused absolutely to do. He was a very sensitive man, one for whom the misery of the world was misery, and he compelled himself to live within very tight curbs, as it were. Daily, he led us in prayers, the Lord's Prayer and the General Confession, which, since I was not an Anglican, initially I found bewildering, but, though he never allowed it to appear publicly, he was a fierce unbeliever.

In my two years in the Sixth he seemed continually discovering new writers and new ideas. Some of them were not new even to me, and perhaps that added to my appreciation of the excitement engendered in him and which he felt bound to communicate. It was on his lips that I first heard Hardy's line: '. . . if way to the Better there be, it exacts a full look at the Worst.' Hardy was his great enthusiasm, a recent discovery, the poetry and novels alike, and it is with Hardy that I have come to associate him, for he too, I think, was a simple, conservative man who would have been glad, if it had been possible, to hold conventional opinions. I remember talking to him about Shaw, whom he had come to delight in, admitting a late conversion, for he had for years uncritically accepted the Shaw that was presented by the press, whom he found distasteful. And I was personally delighted with his enthusiasm for a very early poem of Graves's, 'Star Talk'.

Being in the Sixth was an emancipation for me. I found the syllabus for the Higher School Certificate examination exciting, Donne and the metaphysical poets particularly. I took the examination after a year instead of the more normal two and passed top of the school, an achievement that carried with it the school leaving exhibition to university. But Joe persuaded me to stay another year and sit for an Oxford scholarship, which I did.

Before this, however, I had an adventure unexpected, wholly pleasurable and rewarding. I had entered for a competition organised in Britain by the *Daily Express* and styled, I think, an International Oratorical Contest. It was open to schoolboys between the ages of sixteen and eighteen; you wrote an essay of a thousand words on a British statesman and, if it was thought good enough, you 'orated' it before a panel of judges chosen by the *Express*. If you won, you gained the prize of fourteen days in Washington, D.C. That was what fired me. The oratorical contest took place at the *Express* office one afternoon in early July, 1928, and I got the day off from school to attend.

I had been to London only once before, five years earlier with my parents on a day-trip to the British Empire exhibition at Wembley. That wasn't much help to me now, but I knew exactly what I wanted to do before going to the *Express* in the afternoon. From Euston I made my way easily enough to Harold Monro's Poetry Bookshop, which was just off Great Russell Street, opposite the British Museum. When I entered, Monro was lolling in a swivel-chair, reading, his feet on the desk in front of him. There seemed yards and yards of him. The shop was empty, and he did not look up when I entered or address a single word to me while I was there. He was the first poet I had set eyes on in the flesh and I recognised him from press photographs. He seemed prodigiously tall, wore horn-rimmed spectacles and had a clipped military moustache; he had been an officer in the Army during the war and in appearance at least was a typical guardee.

By now, he must be almost forgotten as a poet, but in the middle Twenties he was a considerable figure. Typical of his work is a sonnet sequence I read called, I think, 'Week End', celebrating the joy of leaving London on Friday afternoon for one's country cottage. Quintessentially Georgian it must seem now; but he also wrote a few poems that show him on the edge, as it were, of the Modern Movement. And through his ownership of the Poetry Bookshop and his quarterly, *The Chapbook*, he did valuable work for writing.

As I looked round the shop, it dawned on me that I hadn't realised there was so much poetry in existence. In desperation, I went over to the shelves containing Benn's sixpenny poets. I wasn't interested in them, for I could get them easily enough in Birmingham, but they did put me at my ease, as it were. They led me to another series of pamphlets of similar size, published by a firm called Simon &

Schuster I had never heard of. I pulled one out and found it was a series of American poets. The one I held was *Selected Poems* by a man named Conrad Aiken, also unknown to me. I turned the pages and read a poem called 'The Morning Song of Senlin', which began:

> It is morning, Senlin says, and in the morning
> I shall think of God as I descend the stair.

I was much intrigued. I seemed to have met similar rhythms in Eliot, in 'Prufrock' and 'The Portrait of a Lady', though for some reason I thought it was Aiken who had influenced Eliot and not the other way round. Aiken and Eliot were, in fact, contemporaries at Harvard and, as Van Wyck Brooks shows in the chapter in his autobiography on Eliot's Harvard, shared common properties in the verse derived from the Harvard ambience of the day. When I had read 'Morning Song of Senlin' I knew something important had happened and I did not wait for more. I took the pamphlet over to Monro at his desk and plonked down my one-and-sixpence, which Monro pocketed in silence and without looking up.

Thereafter, through the years I followed Aiken. Until a few years before his death, he was much underrated both in the United States and in Britain, existing, as he seemed to, in Eliot's shadow. This is a total misreading. He wrote many volumes of verse, almost the first novels to be influenced by *Ulysses*, some of the best short stories of our time, and some first-rate literary journalism. I never met him, though, as I now know, I could have done so easily enough, for until the second world war broke out, he lived at Rye, in Sussex. He covered tennis at Wimbledon for the *New York Times*, I believe, and he was the mentor and close friend of Malcolm Lowry.

At the *Express* building I learnt from the receptionist that of the half dozen of us who had been short-listed, five were named Allen, a fact that throughout the afternoon gave rise to much merriment and intermittent confusion and in me, after the initial consternation, the realisation that I bore one of the half-dozen commonest English surnames. I was taken to the top floor and ushered into Hannen Swaffer's office. Swaffer had been deputed to look after us young men and put us at our ease. He did so. He must be forgotten by now, but in the Twenties, Beaverbrook apart, his was the name perhaps most immediately associated with the *Express*. He was dramatic critic and a vigorous controversialist on behalf of spiritualism into the bargain. He was not short of arrogance. He told us how he put the fear of God into London theatre managers. If – and at that time I must admit it was – it was a little like seeing Shelley plain, it was a pretty pinchbeck Shelley. He was a tall, thin man who, in my memory, looked like the conventional notion of a Nineties poet. He was dressed in black and wore a high collar like a band of linen round his neck and a black stock. His hair, for those days, was notably long. I don't think it is merely my shaping imagination that supplies the scurf that liberally spattered his shoulders. What I am certain of is that he was the first chain-smoker I encountered before I met Wystan Auden. He lit one cigarette from the butt of the previous one and tossed the smouldering end negligently out of the window into Fleet Street below, where I pictured them dropping on to and burning holes in the flowered hats of the ladies passing below.

Even if he was scarcely prepossessing, Swaffer entertained us. My competitors in the oratorical contest I remember hardly at all, though one was a Westminster boy togged out, to my goggle-eyed surprise, in topper and tails and carrying a rolled umbrella; another I associate with Nottingham High School. When we were all assembled, Swaffer took us down to the boardroom, where we were introduced to the other judges: the editor of the day, who I think was R. D. Blumenfeld, Leslie Hore-Belisha, not yet a cabinet minister or even an M.P. but the paper's parliamentary correspondent, and the business manager, a man named Plummer, who seemed to me absurdly young for the job. Years later, when I was on the *New Statesman*, I was to know him quite well. By then, he had become Sir Leslie, was a Bevanite M.P. and a director of the Statesman Publishing Company.

These men could not have been nicer to us boys. They took the task of judging and choosing seriously; they did not condescend or patronise but treated us as equals who were engaged with them in what was, at that moment, the most important job in the world. I found this enhancing. Before I left the *Express* I knew I had not won the contest. I cannot think I was not disappointed, but the disappointment I don't remember, for it had been an exhilarating day. I had seen a poet, discovered another and a better, and had a glimpse of the great world, which had proved a warmer and friendlier place than I had expected. It was all ironically different from my experience of Oxford a few months later.

I was the first boy of the school ever put in for a scholarship at one of the ancient universities, and what chance the masters thought I had of winning one I do not know, though I suspect that most of them were almost as much in the dark as I was, and my ignorance of Oxford may be gauged from the fact that I thought Balliol, where I was to sit for the scholarship, rhymed roughly with 'bally fool'. In those days, there was only one scholarship in English at Oxford. The set books were six Shakespeare plays, Milton's English poetry, six of Johnson's *Lives* and *Culture and Anarchy*. The plays and the *Lives* were not entirely new to me, but most of the Milton was. Since no one from the staff could be spared from his other teaching to coach me, I had to master them myself as best I could. I could only have been miserably unprepared, though I was confident as I have never been since.

On a cold, raw, early December day I made the journey to Oxford. It was the early days of vacation and there were still some undergraduates up; I have the impression now of tall, self-possessed young men, most of them blond with college scarves round their necks and of gramophones with horns playing in college windows. I was put in rooms occupied in term by a man I knew was the son of a former Lord Mayor of Birmingham. In his autobiography *Pack My Bag*, Henry Green comments on the lack of comfort at Oxford after Eton: I was amazed that one person could possess two such rooms for his sole use. I felt awkward and embarrassed, very much an intruder. I examined the books on the shelves. They told me nothing: brown limp volumes of Plato and the Greek tragic poets in Greek, which I didn't understand, some Jane Austen and Kipling, representative works of E. V. Knox and A. P. Herbert.

My self-confidence was shrinking. I didn't know what to do; for some reason, I expected someone to come and look for me, someone I would be accountable to. I was unused to freedom. I was hungry; it was drizzling outside, and I was cold, and though the fire was laid I did not light it for fear of offending. I roamed Balliol in vain, and for my three days' sojourn Balliol remained a college without water-closets. Percipiently, the City of Oxford had placed public lavatories in the Broad just by the college gates, and to these I repaired when it was necessary.

I went to the Cadena for tea and probably had herring roes on toast, for that was my current notion of high living. I bought a packet of Players' cigarettes, and my self-esteem rose when a charming young man came over from a nearby table and asked me for a light. By the time I returned to Balliol, my self-esteem had guttered. It was dark now, and the gramophones were louder. Forlorn and cold, in desperation I lit the fire and crouched over the unimpressive flames, reading Knox and Herbert, neither of whom I found remarkably funny. The scout arrived, and I felt I had done wrong in lighting the fire. He was a brusque, bustling man, very neat in an Army way, and he called me

'Sir', which I feared was sardonic. I felt he had sized me up. I was getting hungry again but I was too shy or gauche to ask him when dinner was served or where.

The evening dragged on, the room never became warm, the gramophones mocked. I was very hungry but dared not go to a restaurant again, for my tea had proved more expensive than I'd expected. I wrote two falsely cheerful letters. I felt as a child must feel on its first night in hospital among the dazzling, sterilised whiteness and the bright impersonal nurses.

I must have found Hall in time for breakfast next morning, for I remember no more problems about meals. But the isolation, or the sense of it, persisted. It was a lack of grace in me, but it was inescapable. As I recall, there were over a hundred candidates in for the examination and, as I eyed them, they seemed to know one another intimately and half Balliol besides. In the five or six meals I ate in Hall I think I spoke to only one boy and then because he spoke to me first. He was a tall, handsome youth with a scar down his left cheek. He wore a grey flannel suit and was at Shrewsbury, which was the name of the house I'd been in at my elementary school. I liked him enormously but I was tongue-tied and could say nothing more than yes and no. I must have seemed insufferably churlish.

I was miserably conscious and bitterly ashamed of the envy and rancour I felt. I had not known I possessed them. And I was intimidated by my surroundings, by the hall with its enormous open fires, the like of which I had not seen before, by the portraits of the College worthies that look down from the walls, Matthew Arnold with his prim and supercilious air among them, by the bright young dons who supervised the examination, some of whom seemed scarcely older than the examinees. As for the examination papers, they terrified me. I could see they were much more intelligent than any I had met before and demanded a wider and more accurate knowledge than I possessed.

The ordeal ended, I left Oxford on the first possible train. Next morning, Joe eagerly studied the papers and approved my choice of questions. I did not tell anyone how wretched I had been. Weeks later, Joe showed me a copy of the *Manchester Guardian* containing the results: the scholarship had been won by a man already at Balliol. Joe said he would write and find out my marks. If he did, he had pity on me, for he never told me.

For years, I could not remember that episode in my life without squirming. No doubt it was a salutary experience, for it compelled a truer estimate of myself. All the same, I wish it had been less painful or I had been more prepared for it. As it was, it exacerbated a sense of class and class-privilege that I have never wholly freed myself of. For me, men on strike always have justice on their side.

It also conditioned for good my responses to Oxford, which have remained ambivalent. When I went to live as a writer in London in the Thirties, I was struck by the way it was assumed that I was a university man, meaning by that of either Oxford or Cambridge and, in my case it seemed, Oxford rather than not. It became a point of honour to assert that I was a graduate of Birmingham, thank you, for the assumption that I must be of Oxford seemed to me only another example, conscious or not, of the snobbery of the English. This, I see now, was absurd. Even I, who had a vested interest in such matters, knew of only one other writer among my immediate contemporaries who was a product of a provincial university. That was Rayner Heppenstall from Leeds. My friend Henry Reed was still unpublished and unknown. And before us? Gissing, Lawrence, Brett Young, Herbert Read cannot exhaust the list, but the names of the others do not come precisely trippingly to the tongue. Even in the Thirties, if a young English writer had a university education, you more or less had to assume that the university was either Oxford or Cambridge.

Nowadays, the assumption is much less safe and is made much less automatically. All the same, though it will not speedily be shaken, one may still regret the Oxford and Cambridge domination of the English educational system. In a very real sense, the other English universities will always be second-best, even though no Oxford man, not even the youngest, smuggest and most stupid, can touch a Harvard graduate in his built-in belief that his college is the finest, the noblest, the greatest in North America and that to have been elsewhere is necessarily to have failed to know the best. Staggering as the arrogance of Harvard men can be, it is still relatively harmless, since the United States is a vast country in which Harvard, for all its being a place of enormous distinction, is merely one among other institutions of comparable distinction, the University of Chicago, Johns Hopkins, Yale, the University of California at Berkeley, the University of Virginia, the University of North Carolina at Chapel Hill, to pick out names almost at random. But England is a tiny country, and Oxford and Cambridge were its only universities for seven hundred years. The ambience is one that the sensitive and imaginative will always seek out, and this apart, they are still pre-eminent as centres of teaching and learning. Others – Manchester, Sussex, the rest – abide our question. Like Arnold's Shakespeare,

Oxford and Cambridge are free.

Of the two, I have always felt closer to Oxford, as the more sympathetic, possibly because it was the choice of my childish partisanship on Boat Race Day. Towards Cambridge I can be cool as towards a market town deep in the Fens and even find it a trifle provincial and priggish. I have been much more frequently to Oxford and have always had more and closer friends there. My attitude to it of love-and-hate seems enshrined now in a visit I made in the summer of 1955 to Christ Church, as the guest of the young Norman St John-Stevas, whom I had met at about this time on the Society of Authors' committee under Sir Alan Herbert that was looking into the law relating to obscenity. St John-Stevas was then a law student at Christ Church. My visit proved a mixed delight. Dinner was enjoyable; I sat next to J. I. M. Stewart, who was the English don in the college and had come in to dine that evening in order to meet me. That was gratifying. After dinner, we adjourned to the Senior Common Room, if that is its proper name, for the ritual drinking of port. St John-Stevas suggested that we should ignore the port and continue drinking claret, which we did. When we had finished the bottle my neighbour, who was Roy Harrod, urged me to have some port. It was, he said, very good. But the port had been three times round the table, and — presumably because ritual demanded it — I found three glasses in front of me.

I was chivvied by an absurd old man who was a superannuated Fellow. He was, I learned, a great Oxford character, the equivalent, in other words, of a licensed buffoon. His one excuse was his age. He was absurdly solicitous on my behalf; insultingly so, for I could see that I had become his butt. Had I, he asked me, ever known anyone who had been at the House? I said I knew a novelist named Green who I believed had been at the House. He doubted whether this was possible; he could not think of any novelist named Green who had been at the House; though, come to think of it, there was a young man named Greene with a final -e at the House at the present time reading, if he remembered aright, physics, and his father, he believed, was a novelist called, he believed, Graham Greene. This — triumphantly — was doubtless the man I had been thinking of! No, I replied, Graham was a Balliol man; I was thinking of a man named Henry Green; and then I had laboriously to explain that Green was not his real name but a pseudonym; his real name was Yorke, Henry Vincent Yorke. I further explained that Henry Yorke had gone down from Oxford without a degree. This demanded a searching of the college records. Cursing myself for having been so stupid as to get myself involved in this discussion, I awaited the old man's return. He was more triumphant than ever. No such name was on the college books. My mistake, I began to be aware, was nothing short of fraudulent.

I have since discovered, from Anthony Powell's memoirs, that Henry Green was indeed not at the House.

Later in the evening, Lord Cherwell, Churchill's scientific adviser, Professor Lindemann, came in. He was always called Prof. He was a Student — that is to say a Fellow — of Christ Church and lived there, though, because he was a vegetarian, he rarely dined in Hall. But he made a point of visiting his carousing colleagues nightly. A very tall, severe-looking man with a domed bald head. My aged and unwelcome mentor beckoned to him. 'Prof., I want you to meet our guest Mr Allen. Mr Allen writes for the *New Statesman*.' 'A paper I do not read,' said Cherwell and turned away. Never was I so magnificently snubbed, and the old man watched with glee.

Next day I ran into E. R. Dodds in Cornmarket. 'What are you doing in Oxford?' he wanted to know. I told him I had been staying at Christ Church; I had forgotten his Chair was established there. 'Why didn't you let me know?' he said. 'I'd have come into dinner. I dine there very infrequently.' I could see why.

Against this, and in fairness, I have to remember the pleasant times I have had in Oxford and the friends I have there. And I recall that the day after that dinner at the House I met Asa Briggs at Worcester College for the first time.

But I am anticipating. My last months at school, after my Balliol trip, were unstrenuous and unremarkable. On the result of the Higher Certificate examination I gained an entrance scholarship to Birmingham University. That really settled my immediate future.

III

In the Michaelmas term in 1929 I entered Birmingham University, as an undergraduate in the Honour School of English. It was a split university, literally. The campus, at that date a daring Americanism I first encountered on the lips of the Vice-Chancellor, a man my Uncle Ted assured me was a 'bloody old woman – he talks too much', was at Edgbaston and housed only scientists and commerce students. I was at Mason College, a sham-Gothic building in the middle of the city, which, in my memory, stinks permanently of gas. Mason – Sir Josiah Mason – was a nineteenth-century industrialist and philanthropist. There was a statue of him in Chamberlain Square – 'Squirt Square' to us, because of the fountain – opposite the College. He is represented in Victorian dress sitting in a chair under which are rolls of what looks uncommonly like wallpaper but are, I assume, the deeds of the University.

Mason College was the seat of the Faculties of Medicine, Law and Arts and the Department of Education, and, like the University, was itself split, for the rear half of the building was sacrosanct to medicos and dentists, a race apart. There was a medical school in Birmingham for the best part of a hundred years before the University, and medical students tended to behave as though the University did not exist. In any case, their first loyalty went inevitably to the hospitals where they were taught. They were, I think, physically different from us in the Arts faculty, bigger, burlier, and they spoke with a markedly different accent. They were public school almost to a man, and the difference in size and physique was a class difference.

The law students were similarly public school and middle-class. If I knew rather more of them than I did medical students, who greatly outnumbered them, it was because they made a practice of debating, and I too for a time patronised debating. Men from public schools were distinguishable from the rest of us not only in physique and speech but by dress. For the most part, we Arts students wore what had once been our best suits, sacred to Sunday: medical students and lawyers, and the engineers and commerce students at Edgbaston as well, followed the conventional uniform of Oxford and Cambridge undergraduates, flannel trousers, sports jackets with leather-patched elbows, long flowing scarves. The girls were almost all middle-class, were scarce among the medicals, absent from the lawyers, and in a slight majority in the Faculty of Arts. They were a natural prey of men from the other faculties, with whom we could not compete either financially or in the social graces.

For most of us in the Faculty of Arts, as for students in the Faculty of Science in Edgbaston, the University was what is called in New York a subway university: living at home either in Birmingham itself or in nearby towns of the Black Country, we came in by train or tram for the first lecture and left, more likely than not, immediately after the last, though a few, of whom I was one, contrived to stay all day. Collectively, we were known as brown-baggers, from the attaché-cases in which we carried our books. It was a pejorative expression; at the various meetings for freshmen indoctrination we were passionately urged not to be brown-baggers, appeals effective enough to have prevented me for the rest of my life from willingly carrying attaché-cases or brief-cases, innocuous and even reasonable as these are for transporting books and papers.

For me, Birmingham at first was very much a second choice. I was disappointed and disillusioned that none of my coevals seemed to have heard of Eliot or read Lawrence. Then I discovered that if I wished, as I did, I could have more or less free range of the university magazine. The dramatic society too provided for me. Before my first year was through, I had written and produced an extremely bad one-act play, a pastiche of Synge. For the most part, I enjoyed myself hugely at Birmingham, and even after I had gone down it was close to the centre of my life until I went to London. I was conscious from the first of moving in an atmosphere of freedom. The lecturers struck me as astonishingly unlike schoolmasters. One had at least the illusion of talking to them as an equal, and if one asked a serious question one got an honest answer. It was from their example that I learnt what is meant by disinterestedness, which must be an element both in scholarship and good writing. They were mainly Oxford graduates. In my time, the English School at Birmingham was very much an offshoot of the Oxford English School. There had only been three professors in the history of the School, the first Churton Collins, who is honoured by Eliot in an essay in *The Sacred Wood* and must always be thought of with respect because he incurred the enmity of Edmund Gosse, and the second Macneile Dixon, the author of a book on tragedy who went back to Scotland after only a year or so at Birmingham.

The professor in my time was Ernest de Selincourt, who was also Professor of Poetry at Oxford. I am obviously prejudiced against him and I realise from what I have learnt about him from men who knew him better than I ever did and whom I hold in high regard that I am unfair to him. He gathered round him an excellent staff, and perhaps he was even advanced for his time. In Birmingham, English literature went on at least until 1890 and even after, for though the twentieth century was ignored, Robert Bridges, on the strength of *The Testament of Beauty*, was given special dispensation and was lectured on. At Oxford, by contrast, English literature was all over by 1830, and when it was proposed in 1949 that its life should be extended officially to 1890, the suggestion was turned down, I was told, after C. S. Lewis pointed out that the novels of Dickens had not yet been edited nor their texts established definitively.

De Selincourt was a great scholar. He had discovered and edited the 1805 manuscript of *The Prelude*; he had edited Spenser and Keats besides. But great scholars are not invariably appreciated by young men, and I found de Selincourt antipathetic, a frigid bore. He was quite astonishingly devoid of *bonhomie*. When I too, late in life and unexpectedly, became Professor of English in a British university I had an uneasy feeling that if de Selincourt had been the real thing I couldn't possibly be. The backbone of the English syllabus was de Selincourt's lecture course on the history of our literature. For a span of three years, every Tuesday and Thursday morning for an hour, he read remorselessly from a manuscript book which did not seem to have undergone emendation or revision in the score of years he had been delivering the lectures. He doggedly pursued the course of English from Chaucer, with whom it all began, to A. E. Housman, with whom it all but ended. He left, as they say, no stone unturned, and not to be mentioned in de Selincourt's course was not to be in English literature. For every writer in it he had his word and for every writer mentioned there was a saving grace. Was the subject-matter distasteful, as that of, say, *'Tis Pity She's a Whore*? Well, at least Ford showed 'keen psychological insight'. The high point was when he came to William Browne of Tavistock, words treasured and handed down through generations of students so that when he came to the crucial passage everyone was chanting in unison: 'And now we come to William Browne of Tavistock, a minor poet not without a certain charm of his own. Giles and Phineas Fletcher, on the other hand . . .'

Bridges apart, there seemed no contemporary writer of whom de Selincourt approved. I did once hear him say a kind word for Edmund Blunden, but generally his comments were derogatory, as on Joyce: 'I don't want the contents of the water closet flung in my face.' Once, when Virginia Woolf was mentioned, I heard him expostulate: 'But the woman's mad', in such a way as to leave me puzzled, for I knew nothing of her private life. It never struck me he meant the words to be taken literally. Of the relatively young he indicated disapproval by significant sniffs, as in 'Mr (*sniff*) Aldous (*sniff*) Huxley (*sniff*) says . . .' or 'Mr (*sniff*) T. (*sniff*) S. (*sniff*) Eliot (*sniff*), whom some of you young gentlemen profess to understand and admire.'

In my final year I was in the Professor's tutorial class. It was regarded as a great honour; it meant you were thought to be a possible First. One morning, *apropos* of nothing it seemed, he said to me: 'Tell me, Mr Allen, do you admire the poetry of Mr (*sniff*) W. (*sniff*) H. (*sniff*) Auden (*sniff*)?' The sniffs warned me, but I still had to admit I did. 'And would it surprise you, Mr Allen,' the rejoinder was triumphant, 'to learn that Mr (*sniff*) Auden (*sniff*) got a third at Oxford, and a bad third at that? I know, because I was the external examiner.' What I said, if anything, I have forgotten, but I could only think, as I do now, that the University of Oxford had made rather a fool of itself.

I did not get a first and I was chagrined and ashamed. The morning after the lists were put up I ran into one of my lecturers, Mrs Dodds. She said: 'Oh, Mr Allen, I'm sorry you missed a first, but you didn't know enough.' It seemed a fair comment. I was chagrined precisely because I felt that if I had worked harder and exercised greater self-discipline I would have got a first. Later that morning, I passed de Selincourt in the corridor. He did not acknowledge me.

But I was lucky in my other teachers, one of whom, A. M. D. Hughes, who was reader and succeeded de Selincourt in the Chair, was outstanding. I was fortunate because from the beginning he was my tutor. When the war broke out he was a lector at Kiel and he'd been struck down by blindness in the internment camp. He was born, I think, in Hereford and came of Welsh stock. He had a greater eloquence in the fullest sense of the word, which takes in not only diction and sonority of voice but also quality of what is being said, than anyone I have ever listened to, and it was an eloquence as commanding when he was talking to three young men in a tutorial as when addressing a crowded lecture theatre. He was riveting and inspiring and never more so than when he was quoting from Shelley's *Prometheus Unbound*. In tutorials, he was courteous and understanding; one had the sense of being with a scholar who delighted in sharing his knowledge and passion. When we disagreed with him or failed to see the point he was urging on us he would say, after everything else had been said, 'Well, here we come to an impasse.' He made an impasse sound a fine and honourable place to come to. He had a wonderful loftiness of mind and a complete disregard of himself which for me is fixed in an image I have of him as I often saw him, blind, disdaining help, plunging into the Birmingham's traffic to cross the road. He was knocked down by a vehicle more than once, but that did not deter him.

I have always supposed he was a Platonist, possibly because I have never heard the case for Platonism argued more persuasively than by him. I recall him maintaining in a tutorial that beauty of body, beauty of face, were themselves evidence of beauty of soul. It was an idea I had not met before and, if true, seemed to be another example of the blatant injustice of things, which was something I was unwilling to admit. I was not converted to Platonism but I do not find it difficult to believe that Hughes's own beauty, which was one of utterance and of something indomitable in his stance, was evidence of the beauty of his soul. And from time to time, I have felt this of others too, notably of Joyce Cary.

His blindness prevented Hughes writing the books he had in him, and what he published gives, it seems to me, only faint indication of his distinction. When appointed to the Chair at Birmingham, he had only three years to go before retiring, but he was not then entirely lost to teaching, for when war came he went back to his old college at Oxford, St John's, where he taught John Wain. At Birmingham, he continued lecturing on occasion throughout his life, and he lived to be a hundred.

Whenever I did anything that seemed to him notable, he saluted it by a note that was generous and affectionate. All his life in Birmingham, he lived in the garden village of Bourneville, and I like to remember how eloquently he cursed Cadbury Brothers, who made him cut his front-garden privet hedge to a prescribed height and allowed no public house to sully their estate.

I remember the rest of my teachers with pleasure and affection. John Waterhouse, who later left university teaching to become music critic of the *Birmingham Post*, became a close friend. I missed being taught by Helen Gardner, who joined the staff a year or two after I went down, but I came to know her and am indebted to her for many kindnesses. She was probably the leading English scholar of her generation. It was from her that I first heard the famous story of how, interviewing a schoolgirl for admission to the Oxford English School, she had asked her what she most enjoyed in poetry, to receive the rebuking answer: 'Poetry isn't to be enjoyed; it's to be evaluated.'

And two other people of distinction I narrowly missed being taught by. I wasn't to know until twenty years later that one of the applicants for the lectureship John Waterhouse got was Eric Linklater. He was then assistant to the Professor of English at Aberdeen and, I guess, still undecided about his career. At fifteen he had enlisted in the Black Watch and after the war had set out to be a doctor but had ended with an Arts degree. He had then spent two years in Bombay on the *Times of India*. He was salmon-fishing in the remote Highlands when a telegram finally reached him from Birmingham summoning him for interview, but the date of the interview was already passed. He went, instead, to Cornell as a Commonwealth Fellow and thence to the writing of *Juan in America*.

This he told me one evening in the early Fifties, and when we realised that if he had gone to be interviewed he might well have taught me, we both became very excited. I think thereafter he saw me as in some sense *in statu pupillaris* to him. I did not see him often or know him well but I found myself very fond of him. He reminded me, I don't think quite absurdly, of my uncle Ted. He was short and stocky, with a high domed bald head and a clipped military moustache, and he cultivated a brusque manner and a military bark. He might, indeed, have appeared as a Home Guard officer in the television serial *Dad's Army*. He posed as a very old-fashioned, very high Tory, and while I do not doubt this was genuine enough, I also do not doubt that in part it was adapted to comic ends, for no man had a keener sense of the ridiculous than Linklater.

He was more like Peacock than anyone else of his time, more truly Peacockian, I think, than either Norman Douglas or Aldous Huxley. I do not think he was in any real sense a novelist but he was a born writer and a wickedly witty man who revelled in *jeux d'esprit*. He found the novel a convenient form for his gifts, which were those of the eighteenth century. He cultivated satire and high spirits, pursued paradox and set parody in flight. What he would have been like as a teacher I can only guess but that he was a man of real literary learning his books show.

I last saw him in Edinburgh in the early Sixties. I had gone there with my producer, Halvor Olsson, to interview some Scottish writers and artists for the BBC North American Service. We had spent a most rewarding afternoon recording Hugh MacDiarmid and were sitting round afterwards drinking the Corporation's whisky. I said, seemingly casually, that Linklater was coming in at six; perhaps, if he had nothing better to do, MacDiarmid would care to wait and see him? The suggestion was mischievous; I could not imagine two men more different from each other. MacDiarmid responded enthusiastically: he hadn't seen Eric since just after the end of the war and would love to see him again.

Eric arrived and greeted MacDiarmid, whose presence must have been totally unexpected, with comparable enthusiasm. I was much relieved. They sat down each with his glass and reminisced about their last meeting. They had quarrelled, and the subject of their quarrel was whether or not Britain should enter Europe. At that time, 1947 or 1948, MacDiarmid was all for, Linklater all against it. Now, as they recalled the quarrel, they began to quarrel again, again over the matter of Britain's entry into Europe, but this time it was Linklater who was for it, MacDiarmid resolutely against it. I thought it best to break up the party and decided it was time to record Linklater. MacDiarmid left, inviting us to join him afterwards in the Abbotsford. In the event, Linklater swept Halvor and myself off to dine with him in the best restaurant in Edinburgh.

The other man I missed was William Empson. When he left Cambridge under a cloud he had sought refuge at Highfield, Philip Sargant Florence's house near the campus at Edgbaston. Florence was Professor of Commerce, an American who had spent most of his life in England and had been educated at Rugby and Cambridge. Highfield was a vast house in its own grounds inhabited not only by Florence and his family but by a miscellany of guests and transients. Most English left-wing intellectuals and American left-wing intellectuals visiting Britain must have passed through Highfield between 1930 and 1960.

According to the story, Empson arrived at Highfield for a weekend, with a toothbrush and a pair of pyjamas, and stayed for six months. Indefatigable in good works, Florence hoped to get Empson a job in the English Department and persuaded de Selincourt to come to tea and meet his protégé. Empson greeted him by telling him he had just read the most wonderful book, which he urged him to read.

'And what is that?' de Selincourt asked. *The Sexual Life of Savages* by Bronislaw Malinowski,' Empson replied. There was no job for Empson in the English School at Birmingham.

On the evidence of *Seven Types of Ambiguity*, which had its genesis in a Cambridge undergraduate essay for I. A. Richards, Empson must have been the most sheerly brilliant young man in English studies of the century. I cannot see him in the Birmingham school at all, but if he had been and one had been there at the time, how exciting it would have been.

In my time, the Birmingham school had its weaknesses, shared with all other English universities. I particularly regret the way Old and Middle English, always called 'Language', was regarded. It was at once over- and undervalued. It was compulsory, which seems to me absurd rather than not. But it was treated in such a way as scarcely to exist as literature. It was turned into a philological and grammatical grind, and the poetry, 'Beowulf', for instance, and the great heroic 'Malden' fragment were made mere pedantic exercises.

Other things were simply different from what obtains now, neither better nor worse necessarily. The novel was still barely respectable. In my three years, the only novels to which I was specifically directed were *Tom Jones* and Jane Austen's. In the final year, we had to choose what was called a 'special period' to be examined in, and I opted for the nineteenth century. I read no end of Carlyle and Ruskin, for which I am duly thankful, but it astonishes me now to realise that fiction was totally ignored. On second thoughts, not totally; we were required to read *Erewhon*, but no Dickens, no Thackeray, no Trollope, no George Eliot, no Hardy.

The hierarchy of novelists as generally received was different, too, as I can illustrate from a conversation I had with one of my lecturers. I was greatly excited by a book I had been reading extra-curricularly, for American literature as such was not recognised. The work that fired me was *Moby Dick*, and I suspect I wanted to find out whether my enthusiasm was respectable. *Moby Dick*, I learnt, was highly approved of; and then the lecturer turned our talk round to Conrad. One can see how her mind was working. Conrad, she assured me, was a very valuable kind of novelist, for young people especially, for he was a bridge between stories written for juvenile taste, such as *Treasure Island*, and serious reading-matter. Though I assumed I would one day write novels myself, I did not seriously read in the English novel before 1890 until I was required to teach it in an American university in 1935.

One of the weaknesses of the Birmingham English School in my time stemmed simply, I think, from the fact that it was an offshoot of Oxford. Cambridge was where the innovatory work was being done, and all that I missed. It wasn't till after I'd gone down that I discovered the existence of I. A. Richards, for instance. I regret having been deprived of *The Principles of Literary Criticism* as a student or of *Science and Poetry*, which very much excited me. I can only think that I came across Richards from references in articles in the *New Statesman*, *Spectator*, *T.L.S.* or *Listener*, papers to which, it seems to me, I owe as much as I do to my formal education.

What I now see as an event of major importance in my life occurred at the beginning of my second year, though at the time it seemed no more than a casual flattering, ego-boosting accident. At five o'clock on the first Monday of the Michaelmas term of 1930 I went into the refectory for a cup of tea. The evening before, at the Birmingham Film Society, which I had just joined, I had seen *We From Kronstadt*, my first Russian film, and it seemed to me wonderful; I was prepared in my excitement to believe it was the best film ever made anywhere. I sat down with my tea at a table by the window and was looking abstractedly at the rush-hour traffic below when I heard a voice I did not know say: 'You don't mind if I join you?' I looked up and saw it was Professor E. R. Dodds. I did not see how he could know me, for he was Professor of Greek and I did not do Greek. I was conscious that distinction was being conferred upon me and I am sure that consternation akin to near-panic must have gripped me. He sat down and asked me what I thought of last night's film, and it dawned on me he was president of the society.

In a university like Birmingham, tilted as it was to the 'useful' and technological, the very subject Dodds professed gave him a special aura: to the uninitiated, Greek even more than quantum physics is esoteric lore. I remember Dodds asking me, more than forty years after we first met, what we did about Greek in the new university where I was professor. I told him. He said rather wryly: 'Ah well, Greek studies won't die out completely. Every university will have to have at least one lecturer in Greek if only to explain the classical references in *Paradise Lost* and *The Waste Land* to the English specialists.'

That autumn afternoon in 1930, I had the impression of an intensely silent man schooled to keep himself to himself. I knew he was a poet and had indeed read his book of verse, *Thirty-Two Poems*, in the Birmingham Reference Library and decided they were too much of the Celtic Twilight for my taste. Three or four years after I went down, he succeeded Gilbert Murray as Regius Professor of Greek at Oxford. The appointment, I assume, was in the hands of Baldwin, the Prime Minister, and it was so surprising in some circles as to be turned into a scandal. I surmise it was Maurice Bowra who was generally expected to get the chair. The *Daily Mail*, that bastion of all that is best in Greek studies, was especially roused to fury. Among other things, the appointment was an insult to the King, for Dodds was not even a British subject. A Belfast man of Protestant stock, he had opted for Irish citizenship when Ireland was partitioned and always thereafter, I think, travelled on an Irish passport, even when going abroad for Britain during the war. Moreover, he was not only not a subject of the King, he was one of the King's enemies, for he had been a member of the Irish Republican Army, which in those days in fact was fighting not the British primarily but the Free State. Dodds, like many Ulstermen, loathed the Ulster establishment. When he saw in the *Times* in 1967 the report of my appointment to the Chair of English in the New University of Ulster he wrote and told me I must be mad. He looked very Irish, so much so that it would not be difficult to produce a description of him equivalent to that of the Irishman of caricature. He was a small man with a large head and a wide mouth. His smile was slow and melancholy. He did not like his Christian names and his wife referred to him as The Master or Himself or, sometimes, as Mick. I always addressed him as Professor.

His autobiography, *Missing Persons*, a work of great distinction, draws a speaking likeness of him. He was a man of great intellectual austerity and, among other things, the discoverer and mentor of poets. It was to Dodds in his early Birmingham days that Dr G. A. Auden showed his undergraduate son's verses, and Dodds in turn showed them to Eliot, who published *Paid on Both Sides* in the *Criterion*. It was Dodds who brought MacNeice to Birmingham as a Classics lecturer and, many years later after his death, became Louis's literary executor. It was from the Dodds's drawing room, which opened on a conservatory, that MacNeice one Christmas saw snow falling seemingly against roses. Dodds was especially proud that he had known the four men whom he regarded as the best English poets of his time, Yeats, Eliot, Auden and MacNeice, and that two of them had been his intimate friends.

More or less from the afternoon he first spoke to me, I thought of Dodds as a kind of patron. Both from him and Mrs Dodds, whom I came to know a week or two later, throughout the years I had sympathy, kindness and encouragement. Mrs Dodds was a lecturer in the English School and was much feared by us all, for she was truly formidable and her tongue caustic. I found myself in her seminar on eighteenth-century prose and I recall a young woman student bursting into tears when, having ploddingly reported her findings on Sterne or it may have been Goldsmith, Mrs Dodds said; 'Oh, Miss So-and-So, you've made a horrible hash of that, haven't you?' My own relief may be imagined when she said, after I had read a paper on Johnson's criticism, 'Mr Allen, you've written a model seminar essay.' No praise has ever been sweeter.

It was after Auden's first book, *Poems*, was published in 1930 that Mrs Dodds took unto herself the role of his proof reader and corrector of the press. The volume had appeared with a poem, obscure in itself, containing a stanza that baffled everybody:

> To accept the cusions from
> Women against martyrdom.
> Yet applauding the circuits
> Of racing cyclists.

Cusions? What were cusions? The mysterious word fascinated, and it would not surprise me if poems by very minor Thirties poets were even now discovered containing the word. But it was not Mrs Dodds's way to put up with mystery, and she challenged Auden, bade him explain cusions. It was, he admitted, a misprint for cushions. After that, until he left for America, she supervised his proofs, and he left the checking and sorting of the poems in his anthology *The Oxford Book of Light Verse* entirely to her, while he took a summer holiday before going off to China with Isherwood.

During the war, when I was in Bristol, the Dodds invited me to spend my annual week's holiday with them in Oxford. I was working in a factory all day and patrolling as an air raid warden most nights. I was much cosseted. In the afternoons Dodds punted me along the Cherwell, or is it the Isis? They were living in a house in the High. They had, I remember, a parrot and two small dogs, terriers, I seem to think, of a Scottish breed. As comes out clearly in *Missing Persons*, animals were consciously adopted surrogates for the children they failed to have and whose absence they greatly regretted. Both were enthusiastic, green-fingered gardeners, and watching Mrs Dodds tending her flowers in their small garden and listening to them talking of the paintings they had bought, it was borne in on me that they moved in a sensuous world of which I had little first-hand knowledge.

It was at this time that Dodds told me that after Birmingham he found Oxford an unreal city, and as he makes clear in his autobiography, he regarded his years in Birmingham as the happiest of his life. And though I doubt whether Birmingham realised it, Dodds was a splendid man for such a city to have in its midst. How he became to be president of the Film Society I do not know, but he was at the centre of interest and activity in the arts in the city. It was in the Film Society more than anywhere else that young artists came together. It was through Dodds that I first met them. Very soon after I graduated, he invited me to a dinner he gave in a private room in the Burlington Restaurant to a group of young men whose mentor in some sense he was. Most of them were clerks in local government or industry. There were perhaps ten guests, among them the sculptor Gordon Herickx, who worked as a stonemason, Stanley Hawes, who became a documentary film director and worked first in Canada and then in Australia, the painter John Melville and his brother Robert, who became a distinguished art critic and whom I last saw a glimpse of in a television film about the British Surrealist movement; he was meditatively and seemingly absent-mindedly kicking a violin along a gutter in a street near Waterloo Station.

Dodds died in his eighty-sixth year. I last saw him a month or two before he died. He had spent Christmas in London and the day after Boxing Day he visited me. I had not seen him for perhaps eighteen months – he usually looked me up on his rare excursions to London – and I thought he looked very old and tired. I was much moved that he should visit me. As a mutual friend wrote to me after his death, to have seen Dodds in his last years was to understand something of what Addison meant when he said, 'See in what peace a Christian can die.' And this is invalidated in no way by the fact that neither Dodds nor our friend was a Christian.

My most vivid non-literary memory of my undergraduate years is of being briefly, marginally and farcically caught up in the politics of the day. I was one of a tiny circle who shared much the same interests. We were not all students of English, for one or two were metallurgists. Our common God was Aldous Huxley, the Huxley of *Antic Hay* and *Point Counter Point*. We were sparked into activity or, more accurately, minor demonstration, by the news that Harold Nicolson would fight in the next general election as New Party candidate in the parliamentary constituency of the Combined English Universities, for those were the days when university graduates had an additional electoral vote by virtue of their status as graduates. Nicolson was an attractive figure, a witty and graceful writer, a felicitous broadcaster, an evidently civilised man. I particularly admired his book *Some People*. He was editing a weekly called *Action*, which had been founded by Mosley as the organ of the New Party. Mosley, as MP for the nearby constituency of Smethwick, had been a presence in my consciousness throughout my adolescence. Flashingly handsome, gallant as his war-record showed, by birth an aristocrat, he was a charismatic personality adored by his working-class Socialist constituents . A minister in MacDonald's government, he resigned in 1930 in protest against their unemployment policy and founded the New Party. This attracted a number of minor intellectuals, of whom Nicolson was one and another the member for Aston, John Strachey, whom I had seen and heard speak many times at street-corners standing in his little Morris Cowley car.

So we, who were not yet graduates and therefore could not vote, decided to found a branch of the New Party in the university. We put up posters announcing its existence and had the satisfaction of seeing them torn down personally by the Pro-Vice-Chancellor, a grim surgeon named Sir Gilbert Barling. I do not remember that we did anything else but, as founding members of the University branch, were co-opted on to the Birmingham committee of the Party. The Chairman was Strachey, whom I was to know years later when he was chairman of the Society of Authors. He too was a civilised man. He had a distinguished political career, and his polemical books, *The Coming Struggle for Power* especially, were enormously influential, while during the war when he was an air raid warden and later an officer in the RAF he wrote some excellent short stories and reportage. At those meetings at the Society of Authors, I could never bring myself to remind him that we had met in quite other circumstances more than twenty years before.

The only occasion when we may be said to have been active was when there was a meeting in Birmingham Town Hall at which Mosley spoke. We attended. The Town Hall was packed, by a predominantly hostile audience made up largely of people from Mosley's constituency who, having adored and applauded him in the past, now believed he had betrayed them. What especially impressed and dismayed us was the number of stewards lining the hall and flanking Mosley like a bodyguard. They were headed by the famous boxer Kid Lewis, and their job was obvious, to intimidate. Not that they succeeded. Mosley was a wonderful speaker, equalled at this time only, I suppose, by Lloyd George, Churchill and A. J. Cook, the miners' leader, but it was very plain that he was being allowed to speak only by courtesy, as it were, of the Secretary of the Birmingham branch of the Communist Party. When he had finished, we looked at one another, said nothing and left. In the downstairs bar of a pub in Temple Street, we formally dissolved the Birmingham University branch of the New Party and went on to get sorrowfully drunk. When we emerged at closing time and walked into New Street I was suddenly flung into a shop doorway by a policeman. His action, my fuddled mind registered, was kindly, for there in the street before me was a large crowd chasing Sir Oswald, encircled by bodyguard, back to his hotel.

Next morning, we learnt from the papers that Mosley's distinguished supporters, Strachey, Nicolson, Osbert Sitwell, Cyril Joad, had all simultaneously resigned from the Party. They too could recognise Fascism when they saw it, and it was some consolation to know that we were not the only ones to have been duped.

I still find myself bemused by this episode of my youth. There should be a moral to it, but if there is I have been unable to extract it. I have occasionally, as in some sense a warning, told the story to young people. Their reaction is always the same. How naive we were, to have been beguiled by Mosley. Didn't we know *anything* about Fascism? The short answer is: In any real sense, nothing at all. To the untravelled Englishman in 1930, Fascism was no more than a vaguely comic opera movement of histrionic Italians, and Hitler was yet to be seen as anything like the menace he was to become before the decade was half-way through. Moreover, the racist element in Fascism, which came out of Nazi doctrine, had scarcely emerged.

In 1930, we knew nothing and could have known nothing of how Fascism was to manifest itself and we were stupefied by what was only one of the ingredients that brought it into being, the spectacle of mass-unemployment on a world-wide scale. The age was seen as either an age of apocalypse, as in Yeats's poem 'The Second Coming', or in the grip of obscure malaise, as in Auden's question, 'What shall we say of England, this country of ours where no-one is well?' Authority, the need for bold measures to remedy ills that democratic government seemed from its very nature not to be able to cure, was attractive, and once democracy had lost its credence it is scarcely surprising that serious men could switch from one extreme to another almost overnight. Extreme views were expressed as it were unperceived, as the case of Auden, who reviewed for Nicolson's *Action*, shows. There is a long poem by him in Michael Roberts's influential anthology of the Thirties *New Country* containing these lines:

> And all of the women and most of the men
> Shall work on the land and not think again.

So far as I know, the lines, which I quote from memory, aroused no comment at the time. I do not think the poem was republished in Auden's lifetime, probably because of the revulsion he felt against his beliefs of those years which led to his suppressing or altering a number of early poems. I suspect that *The Orators*, too, could now be made to appear a fascist or near-fascist extravaganza. The shock tactics Auden used in his verse disarmed criticism, of course, but, seen with hindsight, the first years of the Thirties strike one as a time when ideas that seem to us inherently Fascist were floating freely in the general consciousness and regarded in themselves as neither good nor bad.

I went down from the university in 1932. I realised later that probably the most important thing that had happened to me there was that I met Louis MacNeice. He had come to Birmingham in 1930, fresh from Oxford and newly married, as an assistant lecturer in Classics. As he wrote later:

> I came to live in this hazy city
> To work in a building caked with grime
> Teaching the classics to Midland students;
> Virgil, Livy, the usual round,
> Principal parts and the lost digammas;
> And to hear the prison-like lecture room resound
> To Homer in a Dudley accent.

In my second year, I was in his Latin prose class: we read Cicero's *de officiis* in a common boredom. He had published a first book of verse, *Blind Fireworks*, which I had not read, and a pseudonymous novel. I gazed at him as at a rare wild animal caged in a redbrick university and quite out of place there. Mistakenly, I assumed he was contemptuous of it. To me, he was a very exotic figure, and throughout his life there was something of the wild animal about him: he appeared to be always on the *qui vive*, about to shy. He was a *fauve* both in the literal sense and in the way the word is used in art history.

He was an extremely handsome, olive-skinned young man. He had the Irish lower lip and was at times very Irish, becoming more Irish, his accent ripening into a brogue, the more drunk he was.

But I didn't learn that till later. As we construed Cicero in utter boredom, it was the dandy in Louis that most struck me. Geoffrey Grigson somewhere calls him an exquisite, and, so long as the word is not taken to mean the epicene, it is at least partly apt. He did not dress in any way unconventionally; he wore the Oxford undergraduate's uniform of sports jacket and grey flannel trousers. But, it seemed to me, he did wonders with them, and never were the colours of jacket, shirt, tie and handkerchief more subtly matched and blended. He had a figure born to wear evening clothes, and, in a few years' time when his marriage was over, he would take off at the weekend for London and dances at the Dorchester. Later, I found he had strong views on clothes, both men's and women's. We were walking along Corporation Street once and stopped to look at a display of lingerie in a shop window. What he saw did not please him; he assured me that girls should never wear pale blue underwear. I was surprised by the vehemence with which he spoke; it was not a subject on which I had strong or settled convictions.

But the impression he produced of the exquisite was immediately contradicted by its opposite, for though he was an aesthete he was also in his own way a hearty. There was an air of the countryman about him, a suggestion of association with horses and dogs. I recall that it was said in the notice of his death in the *Guardian* that at times he looked like an Irish groom. This duality in him, of the aesthete and the man of the open air, he was very conscious of. The two sides debate with each other in the magnificent, early 'Eclogue for Christmas', with its splendidly sombre last couplet

> We shall go down like palaeolithic man
> Before some new Ice Age or Genghiz Khan.

He was essentially a man for whom the physical existed. He delighted in games. When he was in London he could often be found of a summer afternoon in the tavern at Lord's; he would travel hundreds of miles to cheer the Irish rugger team at international matches; and he played a vigorous game of tennis until he died. How good a games player he was I do not know but I am sure he played to win and, if it seemed called for, could be pretty unscrupulous. I saw him play rugger once, in a game between the first team of my old school and a scratch XV of Old Boys at the university got together by Reggie Smith, who had been two or three years my junior at school. Reggie, through whom I first really knew him, had persuaded Louis to play. He must have been the oldest player on the field by half a dozen years and, since he was always a drinker and a smoker, not in the absolute pink of condition. It didn't stop him playing with great dash.

MacNeice sums himself up both as man and poet for me in two sentences of his book *Modern Poetry*:

> My own prejudice is in favour of poets whose worlds are not too esoteric. I would have a poet able-bodied, fond of talking, a reader of the newspapers, capable of pity and laughter, informed in economics, appreciative of women, involved in personal relationships, susceptible to physical impressions.

Though at the time, he often seemed much less politically committed than other poets, Auden included, he remains for me *the* Thirties poet. He did not have to repudiate his early work; he underwent no conversions; there are no dramatic changes in the nature of his craft or in the preoccupations that inform it. There is no obvious development in his poetry. He reached maturity in his second volume, *Poems*, which contains work as fine as anything he ever wrote. What he did in the next thirty years was to go on writing poems that were no less fine. And the Thirties, I believe, was the right period for him to have emerged in, for, better than any one else's, it seems to me, his work embodies the decade's poetic ideals, ideals expressed a generation before by J. M. Synge in a passage Louis quotes in *Modern Poetry*:

> I have often thought that at the side of poetic diction, which everyone condemns, modern verse uses a great deal of poetic material, using poetic in the same special sense. The poetry of exaltation will always be the highest, but when men lose their poetic feeling for ordinary life, and cannot write poetry of ordinary things, their exalted poetry is likely to lose its strength of exaltation, in the way men cease to build beautiful churches when they have lost happiness in building shops. Many of the older poets, such as Villon and Herrick and Burns, used the whole of their personal life as their material, and the verses written in this way were read by strong men, and thieves, and deacons, not by little cliques alone.

But I run ahead of myself. As an undergraduate, I knew MacNeice only in his capacity of university lecturer, and, as a poet, it was Auden I knew first.

IV

After I graduated I set up shop as writer. In retrospect, I am astonished at my recklessness. But I knew no writers, and there was no-one to warn me of the hazardousness of the enterprise. It seemed the obvious, even the natural thing to do. In those days, there were virtually no jobs for arts graduates except in teaching, and teaching jobs were not easy to come by because the Depression had begun. And in retrospect I think I did not do so badly; I did not make a good living, which at that time I put at four pounds a week as a minimum, but I didn't starve. I was helped of course by having sympathetic parents; I was unable to help them financially as much as I ought to have done but at least I was not a burden on them. I don't think it could be done today, and for all it was hazardous enough in the nineteen-thirties, I do not now see what else I could have done. The freelance writer's life is not the happiest. From its nature, it is anxiety-ridden: there are always fears that one will not be able to sell one's wares and fears that one's flow of ideas may dry up. In the absence of regular working hours it breeds bad habits, indolence, procrastination, and when things are going unpropitiously, self-pity. It demands, in other words, considerable self-discipline. And yet, what were the alternatives? I have taken part in many discussions on how the writer, the young unestablished or unpopular writer who has no private means should support himself in order to be able to write. Common sense says he should have a job outside writing as a crutch. But what kind of job? It mustn't be an interesting job; if it is, it will deflect him from his 'real' work which the job is supposed to be a crutch for. If he teaches and is conscientious the preparation of lessons will gnaw into his free time, and he will find himself involved in the school's extra-curricular activities, play production, literary societies, musical societies, and coaching of games, foreign travel. If he takes a job in applied writing, such as advertising, he will find the work too close to his real work, too easy to become a substitute for it. He may prepare himself for a career in industry or business, hoping to write later when he has established himself. A few writers have done so: Henry Green told me that he wrote his novels during his lunch-hour at his engineering firm. But the world is full of would-be writers who have put off the moment of writing too long, for writing, the learning to write, is a matter of constant practice, constant exercise. Mr Eliot had a job in a bank, and we know how zealous his friends and admirers were to get him out of it. Everything, all experience, is grist to the writer's mill, but he must have time to be the miller. There is labouring, which makes few demands upon the labourer except physical fatigue, and that deadens the mind. Short of a private income, the young writer had better lived on national assistance until such time as he can support himself by writing.

Looking back on it, I am surprised by how well I did. I was lucky that Birmingham had two morning and two evening papers, one of which, the *Post*, was certainly very good. It offered splendid opportunities for the freelance. It was a literate paper. It had daily a woman's page which was quite unlike the ordinary woman's page. There were fashion articles and articles on cooking, of course, but there were three or four articles of a miscellaneous nature. I began to write sketches of children and their behaviour for the page. They were not, I think, bad: perceptive and imaginative, sketches as it were from a novelist's notebook. Writing them was a very good exercise for a young novelist, and I took the writing of them very seriously and made them as sharp, exact and unsentimental as I could. I found I could rely on the *Post's* publishing a couple of these sketches a month.

The *Post* also had a weekly book page which contained a literary causerie. I found the paper would take one from me about once a month; and the book page paid more than the woman's page. The leader page too had a daily column which, when it wasn't taken up by the dramatic critic's reflections of drama and the music critic's reflections on music, carried an essay by an outside contributor. I remember these as grave beyond me, but every so often one of mine was accepted, and the fee was no less than three guineas.

The other papers were more popular. I could usually place an article in one or other of them once a month. I remember I sold an article on Auden to the *Birmingham Gazette*. I think not to his pleasure: but the quotations, I think, were good enough. And then I was broadcasting my own children's stories on BBC Midland Region, and though I complained about the meagre money it paid – it was in fact about the same as the ordinary provincial newspapers – the stories I broadcast proved profitable later. My literary agent discovered I had written children's stories, and after the war I got them together and they were published in a book. It had no large sale, but royalties tripled the fee I had from the BBC.

There were other things too. I had no success with the national daily press but I did sell some stuff to *Radio Times*, which was then seriously interested in broadcasting as a new art form. I remember they published an article in which I 'proved' that Shakespeare was a model radio dramatist. And *Radio Times* paid five guineas for a fifteen-hundred word article; and as every writer knows, it is easier to write fifteen hundred words than eight hundred. Then there was an old-established monthly called *The Bookman*. I thought of it as a stuffy, belle-lettrist thing printed on glossy paper and dedicated to the Georgian poets, but then there was a change of editorship. The new editor was Hugh Ross Williamson, who was later an historical novelist. He came to *The Bookman* I think from the *Yorkshire Post*. He wrote what I think was the first book on T. S. Eliot, and that indicates the change in *The Bookman* under his editorship. It became an advocate of the modern. Admittedly, it did not survive long but it did so long enough for me to sell him an article on the literary associations of Birmingham. Emboldened by this, I asked him for reviewing and by return came a parcel containing three volumes of short stories, which I duly reviewed. I had two more reviewing assignments from it and then *The Bookman* went out of existence. But I shall always feel gratitude to Ross Williamson.

But mostly I remember my year or two as a freelance writer as miserable. I dreaded the postman's knock: it too often meant the returned manuscript in the self-addressed envelope. There were compensations. Sometimes the manuscripts weren't returned and sometimes there appeared what seemed compensations for rejections. I sent an article to *The New Statesman*. It came back, but with a letter from Kingsley Martin, saying he liked it but it wasn't what the paper was looking for; he suggested I send it to Gerald Barry at *The Weekend Review*. My spelling in the manuscript had been corrected, and I knew that if you are an editor you do not go to the trouble of correcting spelling unless you think there's a possibility that you may accept the article. I sent it to Barry, who went beyond the call of duty and wrote back that he liked it but it wasn't what *The Weekend Review* was looking for. The tone of the letter was such that again I was emboldened to ask him for reviewing. He answered by saying he already had too many reviewers but that he hoped to find me a book he could send me. Soon after which *The Weekend Review* suspended publication. But I remain grateful and hope I thanked Barry whom I knew quite well much later. He was a delightful and charming man, who put paid to his career in journalism by inventing the notion of the Festival of Britain when he was editor of the *News Chronicle*. It appealed to Sir Stafford Cripps, received official blessing, and Gerald was invited to direct it. It was a considerable event. Gerald had to resign from his paper to direct it, and when it was over he received his reward, a knighthood, which, as he explained ruefully to me, put him out of the running in Fleet Street for any editorial job. He did return for a time to the *News Chronicle* as literary editor, and I reviewed for him. But he never again found a job that engaged his full capacities. He applied for the Director-Generalship of the BBC. He would have made a splendid Director-General but he was not appointed.

My ambitions as a broadcaster went beyond reading my own children's stories at the microphone. I found no difficulty in writing them, but it was plain that at a guinea-and-a-half a time it was no way to become rich. I suggested I should write and broadcast a talk in the evening programme on new Midland authors. The suggestion was accepted, and I learned I would be paid four guineas. One of my authors was Auden, and I wrote to him care of Faber asking if he would see me. I sent him a copy of my script, and he replied that he would.

I had bought his first collection, *Poems*, published in a sugar-bag-blue paper cover at two shillings, as soon as it appeared. I had seen it reviewed in one of the weeklies, I think the *Spectator*, by, I think, Naomi Mitchison. It was a good review, and the quotations impelled me to buy the book. I had read no poetry like it before. It was reading Auden that finally cured me of trying to write poetry myself, for after reading him I found I could write nothing except pale carbon copies of his work. I could achieve his mannerisms but no more. That was common enough: he gave me, as he did so many young writers of the time, an entirely new vocabulary, new terms of reference, new ways of looking at the world. *Poems* changed the poetic landscape of England like an earthquake or volcanic eruption, and what was particularly exciting was that he was of my generation, four years older than I almost to the day. I do not think he was ever quite my favourite modern poet, but he was my great contemporary hero.

His letter explained that he was teaching at a prep. school near

Malvern. I went to see him. When I arrived and was shown into his room, he was writing; but to my surprise was writing standing up, in a manuscript book propped in front of him shoulder-high on a lectern. He approved of my choice of young Midland writers; besides him, they were Cecil Day Lewis, John Hampson and Henry Green. And he approved of what I had written on him and them. 'But,' he said pointing to some lines I had quoted from him, 'You can't use that. I've scrapped the poem.' It was a poem which appeared in the first edition of *Poems* only and has not, I think, been reprinted, beginning:

> Which of you waking early and watching daybreak
> Will not hasten in heart, handsome, aware of wonder
> At light unleashed, advancing, a leader of movement,
> Breaking like surf on turf on rod and roof,
> Or chasing shadow on downs like whippets racing,
> Then stilled against a stone, halting at eyelash barrier,
> Enforcing in face a profile, marks of misuse,
> Beating impatient and importunate on boudoir shutters
> Where the old life is not up yet, with rays
> Exploring through rotting floor a dismantled mill —
> The old life never to be born again?

I still like it as an example of Auden's early manner, though I suspect he thought it bore too plainly the imprint of Bridges' prosodic experiments in *The Testament of Beauty*. I substituted for it 'Doom is deeper and darker than any sea dingle'.

I think he was amused by me. I was very earnest. He asked the blunt, direct questions that only he could ask, and I stammered out my answers. I told him I was hoping to get reviewing from the weeklies and even as I did so I realised that that must be what he himself had tried to do, and here he was, the most famous poet at his age of the century probably, an assistant master at a prep. school, a fate that I was praying to avoid. What hope was there for me? I was very much in awe of him. He was as I said only four years older than I, and even at twenty-two that is not a large gap. And he looked younger than he was, still very much the Oxford undergraduate in dress, or even the public school prefect, with the tow-coloured hair above the putty-coloured face. And part of my awe was because of his youth and his achievement: he had already done so much that one spoke of him in the same breath as one spoke of Mr Eliot.

I told him of the novel I was writing, and he gave me his views on fiction. Unless it was Tolstoy, he said, he wanted it light. Though he could see he was a genius, he couldn't read William Faulkner. He praised Henry Green's *Living*, but his special enthusiasm was for two writers I had not heard of before, Christopher Isherwood and Edward Upward. We talked of poetry, I told him of my passion for Robert Graves and of how I had tried to write a book on the poetry of Ezra Pound and had found myself defeated. I was with him about two hours, I suppose. It was all curiously like a tutorial. When I left, he lent me *Ulysses* in the original edition, the first book of Pound's *Cantos*, Graves's new collection and the bound manuscript of Isherwood's *The Memorial*. It was a generous action, typical, I think, of Auden and his attitudes to life and people at this time.

I was never a friend of his but during the next three or four years I saw Auden many times. He was very much the great man who dropped in among us from time to time. He was a schoolmaster no longer but working with the Post Office Film Unit and often he was in Birmingham at his parents' home. He wrote in his 'Letter to Lord Byron',

> and on my heart I always have stamped on
> The view from Birmingham to Wolverhampton,

but I don't think he regarded himself as a Birmingham man. He was born at York and, as his life shows, he was at home anywhere, in Berlin, London, New York, Ischia, Austria, Oxford. He was remarkably self-contained, and though, as he said again, remembering his childhood, in the 'Letter to Lord Byron', 'I like to see the various types of boy', other people were necessary to him only in the way that fossils in rocks are to a geologist.

Auden owed much to his father, from whom a great deal of the furniture of his mind came. He was a doctor, Medical Officer for Special Schools in the City of Birmingham and Professor of Public Health in the university. At an early age he had come under the influence of Freud; he was also an archaeologist; and he had been president of the Classical Association. His varied interests filtered down to Wystan and informed his early poetry.

I have said that Auden was very much the great man among us. This may be misleading. It was we who saw him as the great man; he did not behave like one. He astonished us as much by his unconventionality as by his energy and we recognised him as a law to himself. I remember a trivial example, which certainly cut across the way we had been taught to behave. He was with us one evening in The Hope and Anchor, a pub opposite the now demolished Mason College, wolfing—it seems the appropriate word for the way in which he ate—a ham sandwich when the ham fell out on the sawdust-strewn floor; immediately, still eating, he dived under the table, retrieved the ham and crammed it into his mouth. A few days later, I reported the incident to John Hampson, for whom it was merely further evidence of the effect on them of the poor, inadequate food on which, he asserted, public school boys were fed. You could always tell a public-school boy, John maintained, by the ravenous way he wolfed his food. 'They are always hungry,' he said.

One of Auden's favourite tricks at this time, I recall, was to pretend, especially when travelling on the top of a bus, that he had a cleft palate; he conducted long and elaborate conversations in a very loud, painfully garbled voice oblivious of the compassionate stares of the other passengers. I have learned since that 'Struwwelpeter' was his favourite poetry as a child and I suspect that its influence was never far away from him throughout his life. Some of his sayings passed into our mythology. Once, after visiting a man whose wife we disliked because she was self-opinionated and given to rebuking in public her husband, who was a lecturer in the university, he dropped in on us in the Hope and Anchor. He was in a state of considerable excitement. 'He'll cut her hands off,' he told us. 'One day, he'll cut her hands off.'

When my first novel was due for publication my publisher suggested we should send Auden a copy, hoping of course that he would say something which could be quoted in advertisements. Auden wrote to me that he believed a novel should be a paradigm of the human situation, the statement of a universally applicable metaphor, and this he didn't find my novel to be. I didn't either, so I saw the point, but I was immensely pleased that Graham Greene was more charitable and let himself to quoted.

After he went to America, I did not see Auden again until 1964 in, of all places, Budapest. It was the venue of an international PEN conference, and on the aeroplane out David Carver, the secretary of PEN, told me that Wystan was 'batting for England'. How could he? I wanted to know; he was an American citizen. The explanation was simple: Stephen Spender, who was to have been in the English delegation, discovered he could not attend and prevailed on Auden, who happened to be in Berlin, to take his place. On the evening of the second day we were invited to a reception at the Ministry of Culture. I had been to such functions before and since I did not much care for apricot brandy it seemed better to go to the hotel bar first for a couple of gins. Who should come in a few minutes later but Auden, looking almost exactly the same as when I had last seen him more than a quarter of a century before? True, his face was the famous Auden face of the later years, wrinkled like an ancient Red Indian chief's, but one half of the front of his shirt was still hanging out of his trousers. I didn't know whether he would remember me, but he came straight over and said: 'I knew I'd find you here', adding that mine was the only name he recognised among the delegates. That seemed improbable. We talked. He commented on the recent race riots at Notting Hill and said how salutary they were; they might teach the English to have rather more sympathy with the Americans and their colour problems. He struck me as being much more critical of England and English attitudes than my American friends were.

We took a taxi to the Ministry. At the reception, he and Mary McCarthy fell into each other's arms. During the intervening years I heard his voice from time to time on the radio and thought he had acquired a perceptible American accent; now, when I heard him among native Americans, I heard the indisputable tenor bleat of the English upper class.

He addressed the conference next morning. His speech was by far the shortest and by far the best. It was greeted with some consternation, for he began: 'My name is W. H. Auden, and I am a member of the British delegation. But though I am British by birth, I am not British. I am an American.' The Germans clapped madly; the French and the francophones appeared not to know who he was. Later, we had a drink. He was driving back next morning to Kirchstetten and suggested I should go back with him and stay a few days. I couldn't. It was the last time I saw him.

My abiding memory of Auden and his behaviour is as he was on the occasion of John Hampson's wedding. I saw him as it were in full display; it was as though aspects of him that appear in the early poems and particularly in *The Orators* had taken dramatic form. This must have been in 1936. He was of course homosexual and at this time he did not bother to disguise it much, though in later life he was more discreet. He had married Erika, Thomas Mann's daughter, in order to provide her with a British passport. It somehow seemed typical of him that the woman he had done this service for should have been the daughter of the most illustrious of living novelists. He persuaded John, who was homosexual, that he should marry Erika Mann's friend Therese Giehse, an actress and a very fine one, later associated with Brecht and the Berliner Ensemble and at this time running an anti-Nazi cabaret in Zurich for which Auden wrote some satirical sketches. Hampson asked me what I thought of Wystan's suggestion. He was obviously wistfully attracted by its romantic appeal. I suppose I said all the conventional things; I advised caution; later, he might discover he wasn't homosexual, fall in love with a woman and want to marry in a real sense. Now I see my advice as comic: Hampson was ten years older than I and knew incomparably more of life. He listened to me and said: 'Wystan says, What are buggers for?' I knew I was defeated. Put in that form, Auden's appeal, I realised, was irresistible.

The marriage took place in the register office at Solihull, a posh suburb of Birmingham two stations down the line from where John lived. We were to meet, the bride and witnesses, under the clock at Snow Hill Station at nine in the morning. Reggie Smith and I were there first, and at nine precisely Auden and Louis MacNeice arrived with Therese, who was clutching an enormous bouquet, between them. She did not match my naive and young Anglo-Saxon expectation of what an actress should look like: in other words, I thought her disappointingly plain and dumpy. Auden was very much in charge of the party and very much in his prep. school or scoutmaster vein. At the ticket office he put down a five-pound note and bought the tickets. In the train he produced a ring from his waistcoat pocket, gave it to me, for I was to be best man, and admonished me not to lose it. He was very excited; one felt it was *his* day more than John's. In the train, except for shooting a few words of German at Therese, who spoke no English as the rest of us, apart from Wystan, spoke no German, he talked solely to MacNeice. At Solihull station John, also clutching an enormous bunch of flowers, was waiting for us. He was very tense and nervous; he was terrified he might be seen by friends of his employers, who knew nothing of the marriage. Auden took over completely. In a voice that had become high-pitched he demanded a taxi of astonished porters. He might have been enacting a parody of one of his own 'short-haired mad executives'. He was very conspiratorial. A taxi having been found, he disposed of us inside it. He was the supreme master of logistics. 'Solihull register office', he ordered, with the urgency and in the tone that characters in Edwardian spy-stories say: 'A sovereign, my man, if you can reach Victoria in time for the boat-train.' Anti-climax followed, for the register office proved to be not much more than a hundred yards from the station.

Auden leading, we climbed the stairs of the municipal building into the register office. Peremptorily, he demanded of the clerk: 'Is this where marriages take place?' It was. 'And which gentleman is the groom?' the clerk enquired mildly. Auden the circus-master produced John as from a hat. The clerk turned to John: 'And may I have the bride's full name, Mr Simpson?' Auden answered. 'And her father's profession or occupation, Mr Simpson?' 'Merchant,' answered Auden. 'And her place of birth, Mr Simpson?' 'Lübeck, Germany,' answered Auden. While we waited for the registrar to enter Auden plied the clerk with questions. 'Would you say this is a *popular* register office? What do you find the favourite month for weddings in Solihull? Why is that, do you think?' It was as though he was putting up a smoke-screen of verbiage; I suspect now that he was very nervous.

The registrar came in. Wystan arranged us for the ceremony. There was a row of three chairs on which John and Therese sat and Wystan next to Therese. He was, one understood, giving the bride away and he was also interpreter. As best man I stood behind John, flanked on either side by Reggie and Louis. I felt a mounting hysteria. What the registrar and his clerk made of it I cannot imagine. Reggie stuffed his handkerchief into his mouth to stop himself laughing out loud. Hastily, I looked at Louis. His face was rigid in apparent disapproval. He seemed, even ostentatiously, to be dissociating himself from the proceedings. I realised afterwards that this was not in fact so; over the years he and I had long arguments as to which of us the literary rights of John's wedding belonged to. I claimed them as a prose-writer and in the end he conceded them to me.

John said; 'I do' and Therese said 'Ja'. The registrar called on me to produce the ring, and Wystan swung round in his chair to stare at me in minatory sternness. Bride and groom signed their names, and we signed ours as witnesses. The clerk said to John: 'Shall I send the marriage lines to you at Four Ashes, Dorridge, Mr Simpson?' 'Yes, please,' said John. 'No, no, no,' said Wystan impatiently. 'They are to go to the bride at the Plough and Harrow Hotel, Hagley Road, Birmingham.'

Well, John and Therese were married in the eyes of Sir William Joynson-Hicks, the Home Secretary, if not in God's. Wystan chivvied us down the stairs. In the street he said: 'We all need a drink' and led the way to a large mock-Tudor pub on the other side of the High Street. We seated ourselves in an empty lounge. The barmaid came, and 'Large brandies all round' Wystan ordered. When she brought them, 'Is there a piano here?' he demanded. 'Yes, sir,' she said, 'but you can't play it.' This made Wystan very indignant. 'Who is to stop me?' he wanted to know. The girl answered: 'It's Mr . . . He's dead. He's in there.' She pointed to the billiard room. Led by Auden, we rose and went into the billiard room. There was a coffin on the billiard table. An occasion when Wystan was not allowed to play *Hymns Ancient and Modern*.

Back in the lounge, he ordered another round of double brandies. It was as though all the money in the world was his. Under his eagle eye we drank them down. 'We must go,' he commanded; 'we must catch the train.' He led us out of the pub into the street, striding ahead of us like intrepid Stanley in darkest Africa. Arm-in-arm, clutching their enormous bouquets, John and Therese followed. Louis, Reggie and myself brought up the rear. We were conscious that things like this did not take place in Solihull every day.

At the station, Wystan produced another five-pound note and bought first-class tickets. At Snow Hill we took a taxi to the Burlington Restaurant, where a table was waiting for us. Wystan was fairly dripping with money, and in a most lordly way, to my surprise, for he was reputed to be rather mean where money was concerned. But today it was plain that expense was no object, and under his encouragement we ate and drank lavishly. At two-thirty he got up and said: 'I must get back to work', and summoned the waiter. He took a wad of notes from his pocket. When he had paid the waiter he said philosophically: 'It's all on Thomas Mann.'

We went our different ways, Auden I assume to his curtained, artificially-lighted room in his parents' house in the Lordswood Road, Harbourne, Reggie to the University and I to my office. Louis took John and Therese to the Futurist Cinema in John Bright Street for their honeymoon. When the show was over, bride and groom walked back to Snow Hill, for John had to catch the 6.30 train. Just before it departed, Therese slipped away, to return as the train was beginning to pull out, with a bottle of Scotch, which she pushed into John's hands.

It proved to be a very happy marriage. Husband and wife saw each other only rarely and during the war years not at all, for Therese was in Switzerland. John was always very proud of her, and I think there was genuine communion between them.

I met Hampson the week after I met Auden. I had written to him care of the Hogarth Press asking if I could meet him and enclosing a copy of my radio script. I had read and greatly liked his two novels *Saturday Night at the Greyhound* and *O Providence* and my notions of him were derived solely from these novels. The Greyhound of the first was a pub in a North Derbyshire mining village and the young hero was the barman, who was the landlord's brother-in-law. I took the barman to be in some sense modelled on the author. The background, beyond Derbyshire, was Birmingham. At first sight, *O Providence* was disconcertingly different. It was an autobiographical novel of the youngest child of a wealthy Midland family that loses its money and slides disastrously down the social scale.

Some days later I had found an answer to my letter on writing paper that bore the legend Four Ashes, Dorridge, Warwickshire. John suggested I should come over one evening to dinner, proposed a date and a train from Snow Hill and said he would be on the platform at Knowle Station to meet me. When I descended from the train there were two people on the platform, a man who seemed very tiny and was walking up and down and, sitting on a bench, the ruins of a beautiful boy, a mongol rapidly running to fat. I was one of two dozen people who got out of the train, and the tiny man, who seemed tiny because he was an inch or so shorter than myself, made unerringly for me. His appearance was striking: he was plainly an unusual man. He had a large undershot jaw, deep lustrous brown eyes and brown hair that came down over his right temple like a lick of paint. We identified ourselves and he introduced me to the ruined boy on the bench. 'This is Ronald', he said, and Ronald made an uncouth noise and let me shake a limp hand. He was an imbecile; his beauty was larded in fat; his age I could not guess. Later, I learned he was slightly older than John, who was ten years older than I. John was his nurse, though he was called tutor.

We walked the mile or so to Four Ashes. Ronald shambling ahead, grunting from time to time. He could not speak, though he could imitate a cockerel, a cow and a dog and say 'bikyckle', accomplishments he was proud of and gave vent to on making new acquaintances. His mental age, I suppose, was that of a child before he can talk. A winding drive half a mile long brought us to Four Ashes. The façade was that of an Elizabethan cottage, which had been added to and enlarged. In front of it was a very small pond on which moorhens were nesting, and it was surrounded by a garden of several acres, with orchard and paddock.

I was presented to John's employers, the Wilsons, who were unaffected and charming too. They gave me sherry and discreetly withdrew; every so often Mr Wilson would pass the window trundling a wheelbarrow. Later, I was to learn that Mr Wilson ('Skipper') was managing director of a large firm of wholesale grocers. The Wilsons were wealthy Nonconformists, simple people but people of talent. One of 'Skipper's' brothers was a painter who taught at the

Birmingham School of Art; another was F. P. Wilson, the Shakespearean scholar and Merton Professor of English at Oxford. When they discovered that Ronald was mentally deficient the Wilsons had retired from Birmingham and bought Four Ashes, in the comparatively unspoiled Warwickshire countryside and within easy commuting distance of Birmingham. They had enlarged and modernised the cottage and bought more and more of the surrounding land; their lives revolved round it and Ronald. How they and John had come into contact with one another I never knew. When I met him he had been with them for about ten years and he seemed to me on that early summer evening in 1933 very much like an eldest son to them. *Saturday Night* was published in 1931. Until then they had known nothing of John's writing life and ambitions. And then, as it were overnight, they found themselves entertaining men like E. M. Forster and William Plomer at weekends.

I do not remember what we had for dinner that evening, though I am pretty sure we had asparagus from the garden. I remember the bowls of sweet peas reflected on the highly polished refectory table and I remember the horse-brasses on the beams. I don't think I had ever seen them before except on cart-horses.

After dinner, John took me to his room, which was bedroom and study combined. It was in the old part of the house, long and narrow with a very low ceiling and leaded windows. It struck me as being something of a shrine to himself. It was dominated by two paintings of him in which he looked very *farouche*. Above his bed was a framed cartoon from the *Daily Mail*, whose cartoonist had had a field day at a Heinemann cocktail party. Against a background of glass-juggling guests in evening clothes was John in a lounge suit, his face lit up with gay malice, talking to a lady who towered above him in a tuxedo and with an eyeglass clamped in her eye. This was Una, Lady Troubridge, Radclyffe Hall's friend. She had certainly been at the party, John told me, for he had seen her there, but they had not spoken to each other. The chest of drawers was lined with photographs and snapshots of John in a group with Virginia Woolf, with Forster, with members of Bloomsbury. One wall of the room was lined with books: John had the finest collection of twentieth-century novels I have ever seen. In two or three years' time the aspect of the room as John's shrine was to be still further emphasised by the presence, on a low table which became the room's focal point, of Gordon Herickx's bust of him.

I discovered more about John. *O Providence* was autobiographical: the little boy Justin was John. The Hampsons (Simpson in fact) had been lessees of the Theatre Royal, Birmingham, for the best part of a century and during the period of John's early life had dropped from middle-class affluence to something close to working-class poverty. Now they were moving up again. John's elder brother Jimmy Simpson was the famous racing motor-cyclist, a fact that had led to an amusing confusion. Jimmy's fame was featured in the publisher's publicity for John, and when *Saturday Night* was translated into French and published in Paris by NRF. John was described in the introduction, by the eminent critic Ramon Fernandez, as the illustrious rider in the British TT races and therefore a notable example of the man of action as novelist: he was compared with T. E. Lawrence.

John had suffered from the decline in the family fortunes. He had had little formal education and, insofar as he was educated, was entirely self-educated. There were some things he never mastered. Spelling was one, and his pronunciations tended towards eccentricity. I remember he prounced 'mature' as though it rhymed with 'nature'; he knew it didn't but preferred it that way. His punctuation was also eccentric, though in a curious way was right for him. It became an integral part of his style. Brought up in Leicester during the First World War, he had run away from home at sixteen and worked in hotels first as kitchen boy and later as a waiter. What led him into reading I do not know. For a time he made his living as a book thief. He told me the most profitable book to steal was Gray's *Anatomy*, which all medical students had to possess and was expensive. As a book thief, he had served a sentence in Wormwood Scrubs. I imagine it was after that that he came to Four Ashes, and its sequestered situation was part of its attraction for him. He was terribly frightened that his past might be uncovered, and this made him very suspicious of journalists and of publicity. This was one reason, I think, why he had suppressed for writing purposes the family surname of Simpson and adopted his second name of Hampson.

I have said that John seemed very much the eldest son to the Wilsons. They were grateful to him for what he had done for Ronald, who, on his worst days, John alone could control. His influence was everywhere in the house, which was a house full – every room was full – of novels. The sixpenny weeklies were everywhere. He had introduced the Wilsons to wines and food exotic to Birmingham. He had taught them, when celebration was called for or in times of undue depression, to open a bottle of champagne. And they had responded.

I would not have cared myself to spend my life as companion to an imbecile but I saw that in some respects John's life at Four Ashes was enviable. He lived in civilised comfort there and had distinguished friends in London. Which made me the more surprised when, in the week following our meeting, without warning he called for me at my home and invited me to spend the afternoon and evening with him, for it was his day off. It took me some time to realise that he knew almost no one in Birmingham, though it was his native city. He was lonely, he was also cock-a-hoop, for he had become successful very suddenly. Entirely unknown, he had been published by the Hogarth Press. According to Leonard Woolf's autobiography, *Saturday Night* was one of the most successful books the Press published. It had brought John into contact with Virginia and Leonard Woolf, both of whom he idolised, and had brought him the friendship of Forster, whom he adored. No wonder he had become arrogant, and the arrogance was intensified by the fact that he had no one with whom he could share his success. In a way, I now think, this sudden success wasn't good for him. It led him to equate Bloomsbury with the world and to overrate the nature of literary success. When after his second novel, the Woolfs stopped publishing him, he was thrown too much on his own resources. He was anything but a commercial writer; he never mastered the crafts of journalism and writing for radio. So I think he found everything after that first big success with *Saturday Night* an anti-climax. That early success also, I suspect, reinforced his own lack of self-criticism as a writer. It is a dangerous thing to *know* that one is right, and I am pretty sure that he died believing that justice had not been done to him. Which is perhaps only a way of saying that he was a very unworldly man.

That Thursday afternoon when he called for me was the beginning of the closest friendship of my life. It is impossible for me to overestimate what I owe to John, however critical of him I may have been later. Ever afterwards, when I was in Birmingham, my Thursdays were spent with John. That first Thursday set the pattern. I had no money, or not much more than half a crown, and I realised that that was immaterial. We went straight to the Birmingham Library, which was much like the London Library though smaller and half a century older. John took out all the books he was allowed. Then we went to Boot's Library, where he took out more books, novels mainly. Then we went to a café for tea and to a pub when pubs opened and at seven-thirty to the Burlington for dinner. He was not a food and wine snob but he took food and wine seriously. And on occasion we went to a theatre.

We talked of everything under the sun but mainly of writing and of the novel in particular. He was the first novelist I had met and certainly the first man who fell into Henry James's prescription of the novelist as he found him in Flaubert, who 'was born a novelist, grew up, lived, died a novelist, breathing, feeling, thinking, speaking, performing every action of his life only as that votary.' As I met more novelists, men and women of the calibre of Graham Greene and Elizabeth Bowen, I learnt that James's prescription was one which all good novelists fell into, as though without a passionate seriousness, a total dedication, the practice of the novelist's craft was impossible. It was from John that I first realised this, and it was all-important not only to me as an aspiring novelist but also as a corrective to my overweeningly literary education and literary view of life.

He introduced me to a new world. He could tell me, from first-hand knowledge, of Bloomsbury and not only of the great figures, but also of the comparatively minor ones like Ralph Partridge and John Morris and Leo Charlton. He could tell me the scandal and the gossip, in other words establish for me what Lionel Trilling called 'a culture's hum and buzz of implication'. He knew many of the younger writers of the time, Graham Greene, whom he had first met at a Heinemann party, and H. E. Bates and James Hanley and John Brophy.

He gave me much, and meeting me, I think, made Birmingham less bleak for him. I introduced him to my friends, to Auden and MacNeice and Professor Dodds and to Herickx and the Melvilles, and later to Birmingham journalists and to people in the BBC. Each of us as it were gave the other the freedom of himself, though I was obviously the principal gainer. I remember haring up to London with a letter of introduction from John to J. R. Ackerley, who had just been appointed Literary Editor of *The Listener*. Ackerley was a great charmer and a very handsome man, who received me in a most kindly manner. He invited me to look at the books and pick out one I'd like to review. It was the first Literary Editor's office I had been in, and I was shy and impressed, mainly conscious of my lack of qualifications for reviewing anything. I saw nothing on the shelves I could write a word on, yet as I looked it became more and more a point of honour not to depart without something. There was a book on the Jacobean dramatist John Ford, very much an academic thesis. Ackerley seemed surprised when I took it down but made no comment. My review of it duly appeared. I think it was adequate. I had been helped by the fact that there was no reference in the book to T. S. Eliot's essay on the dramatist.

For the next decade Ackerley sent me occasional books. I never knew him well, for I was inhibited by his good looks, among other things. He had written a fine play on the first world war called *Prisoners of War* and an extremely amusing travel book, *Hindoo Holiday*. As Literary Editor, he did as much as anyone for English poetry in the Thirties and Forties. He was also a notable eccentric. A story I treasure is of his being in Harrods one day standing behind an upper-class woman who was bullying the assistant. Everyone waiting was embarrassed and impatient, and after a time Joe could stand it no longer. He stepped forwards and said: 'Go away, you silly old woman. You smell.'

Ironically, his posthumous autobiography *My Father's Son* did him great harm. It is entirely frank and utterly fascinating but the work of a tortured man. The self-portrait Ackerley presents is distorted; the reader who knew him only through his book could only see him as a compulsively homosexual chaser of guardsmen and sailors, which, while no doubt true, was far from being the whole truth. Of his work as editor and writer nothing was said at all in the book. One might have expected the reviewers to correct the version he gave of himself. None did. Most of them were probably too young to have known him, but some should have known better, Auden, for instance, who reviewed the book in the *New York Review*. Beyond those I have already mentioned, I have my own reasons for being grateful to Ackerley. One night in 1943 I dreamed a poem; or rather I awoke from sleep with an image in my mind that I knew contained a poem. I worked the poem out and sent it to Henry Reed for his opinion. Some days later, I had a proof of the poem from *The Listener* with a note by Ackerley to the effect that Henry had sent the poem to him. He had improved it, he thought, but if I didn't agree he would have the piece set up as I'd written it. Ackerley's version was much superior to mine: it was the poem I had had in mind but was too incompetent technically to achieve.

It was John also who provided me with a letter of introduction to Graham Greene. He was editing a magazine called *Night and Day*, which was an attempt at a London version of the *New Yorker*. It was very lively: Evelyn Waugh reviewed new novels, Elizabeth Bowen was the dramatic critic, Graham himself covered new films. V. S. Pritchett's short stories appeared in it, and there were things that seemed somewhat odd. Louis MacNeice reported Rugby football, and also dog-racing; William Plomer was all-in wrestling correspondent. I set myself up as the soccer expert with an article on Aston Villa, tracing its origins to the bible class of Aston Villa Wesleyan Chapel,

Birmingham. *Night and Day* survived about a year and then it was shot down under Graham. As film critic, he was sued for libel by an American film company for something he had written about young Miss Shirley Temple. Graham was not in court, and the judge, I seem to remember, demanded, 'Where is this Mr Graham Greene?' He was in Mexico writing *The Lawless Roads* and gathering material for *The Power and the Glory*.

It was at Four Ashes that I first met Forster and William Plomer. Plomer, who in his last years seemed something of a Grand Old Man or a universal uncle and is now better known as a poet than a prose-writer, was then a chubby, dandyish, bland young man still not far removed in time from his experiences in South Africa. His urbanity was at odds with the ferocity of his writing. His early novels and short stories, *Turbott Wolfe*, *I Speak of Africa* and *A Child of Queen Victoria*, were wholly intransigent attacks on the Afrikaner ideology later expressed in the doctrine of apartheid. If, as I think, he never fulfilled his early promise, it was because he was a man who needed the stimulus of hatred, of hatred of cruelty and injustice and of those who perpetrated them. In England, he could not find it: he found instead the liberalism of E. M. Forster, who was a close friend, and Bloomsbury. But his early books seem to me seminal in South African writing, in which he is a father-figure. He was a most agreeable man and a great wit. I remember one wet Saturday night, when he was staying at Four Ashes, conducting him across Birmingham to see Gordon Herickx's sculpture. It was the first time he had been in Birmingham, and as we stood in the rain in New Street waiting for our bus, he marvelled at the size and bustle of the city. He recited the destinations as they were announced on the front of the buses. They seemed to fascinate him. A number 12A as it may have been came into view, and he declaimed the legend it bore: 'World's End Via Lakey Lane'. 'Pure Auden,' was his comment.

He was an intensely private person and almost impossible to reach because he lived outside Brighton and refused to be on the telephone. I saw him only rarely but once, on the occasion of the publication of his novel *Museum Piece*, broadcast a survey of his work. After this, for years I had a Christmas card from him, usually in the form of an Edwardian picture-postcard, of which he had a rich collection.

Forster I used to run into often when I lived in London before the war. He was living in Brunswick Square, and we used to meet on the last underground train to Russell Square station. We'd walk together as far as his flat. He'd sometimes ask me in for a nightcap. On one occasion, I remember, the telephone rang and he had to go into another room to answer it. He was away so long that I was able to read his copy of T. E. Lawrence's *The Mint*, which had just appeared in a private edition. Once he apologised for not being able to invite me in; he had Plomer staying with him, and Plomer was sick.

This must have been some time after I went to Abinger Hammer with John for the first performance of Forster's pageant *England's Green and Pleasant Land*. We were invited by Forster's mother to sherry. She had the reputation of being a battle-axe. So, I must admit, she struck me.

Forster was a great man who deliberately refused to be great. In appearance he was the least obvious great man one could meet. With his not-too-carefully trimmed moustache, steel-rimmed spectacles and shabby old raincoat, he appeared almost a parody of the affectionately regarded schoolmaster who will never become a housemaster because he cannot keep discipline. This, of course, was totally deceptive. In terms of influence upon the young in the Twenties and particularly the Thirties, he was the English counterpart of André Gide, a disruptive influence or, if you prefer it, a great liberator. He was the great exemplar of the Thirties virtues as they appear, for instance, in Auden's poetry and Isherwood's novels. He was completely without side of any kind: 'An "I" can never be a great man' was the first line of one of Stephen Spender's early poems: he might have had Forster, who was obviously not an 'I', in mind. I planned at one time, before I had published a novel or gone to live in London, to write a critical book on Forster, for then none existed. I felt I should acquaint him with my plans and ask him permission. He replied that Rose Macaulay was currently writing a book on him (it was not in fact very good) and he did not think the market would stand two books on him. I wrote a review later of *Two Cheers for Democracy* for an undergraduate magazine; it was full of forebodings of the coming war. Forster wrote to me about it, saying that though we were not immortal, we had to live as though we were. I think of him with affection. I remember running into him once in the spring of 1939 in Waterloo Place as I was coming out of the MGM offices. He stopped and chatted. I said I read for MGM. Whether one confession spurred on another I do not know, but he said: 'I'm walking across the Park to lunch with Willie Maugham. I do so whenever he's in London.' Then it was as though he were assailed by sudden doubt. He thought and then he said: 'I can't think why.'

I saw him only twice after the war and did not speak to him. He was already old, and I thought he would not remember me. The first time was at a lunch for John Lehmann after he had given up his publishing firm. It was in a private room at the Trocadero and it was organised by Henry Green, who told me he had done some research and discovered that this was the first time writers had banded together to honour an editor since Leigh Hunt had come out of prison for libelling the Prince Regent. We were in a room opposite one in which the members of an ironmongers' trade association were lunching, and ironmongers kept drifting into our luncheon as we did into theirs. I recall nothing of the lunch which cost 18/6, except that Forster was present and didn't speak, that T. S. Eliot did and made it seem that as poet, editor and publisher Lehmann was altogether his superior, and that towards the end of the meal Cyril Connolly complained loudly: 'We've had the sixpennyworth. When do the eighteen shillings' begin?'

Years after that I saw Forster for the last time, and it remains my strongest memory of him. It was in the lobby of the Old Bailey at the beginning of the *Lady Chatterley's Lover* case. I was one of the witnesses for the defence and so was Forster. We were not allowed in court till we had given evidence. Suddenly Forster appeared; he slipped into his place among us as it were silently and anonymously. He was wearing a cloth cap and his old raincoat. He sat down on a bench, pulled a Penguin from his pocket and began to read. We were all, I think, abashed by his presence. A legendary figure was among us. He was so famous, so old, – he was 79 and had travelled up from Cambridge that morning – and so utterly without pretensions. We didn't wish to crash in on his privacy, but it seems to me now that only one among us behaved with decent adequacy. Rupert Hart-Davis came into the lobby and sat down beside Forster, welcoming him.

He was one of the first witnesses to be called. The policeman at the door of the court bellowed 'Mr Foster'. He took his stand in the witness-box and made, one was told, a great impression on the jury, of whom it is possible that not all of its members had a clear idea who he was and quite likely that none had read his novels. He was treated with great deference by the court; there seems to have been a feeling that it was honoured by his presence. No doubt he spoke softly and without fuss as the great man in the shabby raincoat who refused to be a great man giving his testimony to a greater novelist. He disappeared from the court as suddenly and swiftly as he had appeared.

He stood for liberal values and the holiness of the heart's affections. Among younger writers, his influence – it was of attitude not of technique — was enormous. Outside literary circles he was always being confused with C. S. Forester, an honourable writer but not as good as Forster. A story is told of the BBC announcer who introduced him once at the microphone and after the broadcast produced one of the Hornblower books for his signature.

Sometime in 1934 John and I were often joined in our Thursday meetings at the pub in Martineau Street which we visited every week by two other young writers, Peter Chamberlain and Leslie Halward, who were both some four or five years younger than John and some four or five years older than I. The man who brought us together was E. J. O'Brien, who edited an annual volume called *The Best Short Stories of 19—* and was the chairman of the editorial board of a newly founded little magazine called *English Story* for which we all wrote. Finding the four of us from Birmingham in his magazine, Edward had invented something he called the Birmingham Group and he added to our number by including in it two young men from Derbyshire, Walter Brierley and Hedley Carter.

Chamberlain came of a wealthy Birmingham family of bedstead manufacturers. He had been to school at Clifton and on our first meeting seemed to me very much the public school man, by which I mean that I found him arrogant. He was a large man, tall and broad, who looked as though he would have become fat and flabby in later years. I did not think we could have very much in common, he was so obviously a man of a quite different world. He knew London at least as well as he did Birmingham and he had his own circle there. He knew writers: he had met Anthony Powell and told me of the cocktail party Powell had given for the people he had, unknown to them, put in his novels. Peter's literary heroes were the Americans, Hemingway and Fitzgerald especially, and it was from him that I first heard of John O'Hara. He lent me *Appointment in Samarra* and *The Doctor's Son*. He was, I thought, a bit smug. He had written a very short, astonishingly fresh story called *What the Sweet Hell*. It was published in the *New Statesman*, and on the Monday after publication a postcard arrived there saying the story was the most original thing the writer of the postcard had read for several years. The writer of the postcard was I. A. Richards. I think now that Peter had good reason to be smug.

I remember too, that when his first novel, *Sing Holiday*, was accepted by Chatto and Windus he said, with what seemed to me maddening complacency, 'Well, you can't do better than the best, can you?'

He suffered from narcolepsy. In the simplest terms he could not control his sleep. I was with him in Regent Street one evening when he went to sleep walking and walked into a lamp standard. That woke him up. We went into the Café Royal. He put his arms on the table and his head on them and slept. It was my task to persuade the waiter that he wasn't drunk and hadn't passed out but that sleep was simply not in his control.

Before I met him he had been a racing motor cyclist. His condition had forced him to give that up. His ambition, if there was a war, was to join the Army as a motor cycling instructor, which carried with it the rank of sergeant, and remarkably enough, when war broke out he did exactly that. His disease was unspotted at the medical examination, and he successfully hid it throughout the war.

Leslie Halward was a complete contrast to Peter. He was pure Brummie, speaking no other tongue than the Birmingham accent, the product of working-class Birmingham, in a district of which his father had kept a pork butcher's shop. Leslie as a boy had worked as a pork butcher, had then served an apprenticeship as a toolmaker and, when the depression ended his engineering, had become a plasterer on building sites. At first glance, he struck you as sullen, from a combination, I think, of his accent, the seemingly unhealthy urban pallor of his skin, and a broken nose he had acquired as an amateur boxer. I am pretty certain that his first impulse was to react against the rest of us. He had had very little education and had remained thoroughly working-class as if he gloried in being so, though, I suspect, as much out of fear of the ways of life outside the working class. Somehow — and this seems to me verging on the miraculous — he had discovered the stories of Chekhov, and Lawrence apart, his stories of working-class life collected in the two volumes *To Tea on Sunday* and *Arch Anderson*, seem to me without rival in British English. For a few years in the Thirties, he was naturally and properly much admired. He was thought of, of course, as a proletarian writer, but I am sure that meant nothing to him. He was as unpolitical a man as I have ever met, as much likely, I think, to vote Conservative as Labour.

Within his limits he was a wholly admirable writer, but his limits were very narrow, and lack of education seems to have prevented him from broadening them. For two or three years, with a sympathetic publisher and two or three editors behind him, he rode the crest of the wave. He got married and went to live in a farm labourer's cottage in Worcestershire which he called O Providence after John's novel, partly as an expression of gratitude to John and partly because the finding of the cottage did appear providential to him. We rejoiced in his good fortune, hoping he would discover a new vein of life to write about. Sanguine, I saw him rivalling Bates and Manhood as a writer of stories of the countryside. Nothing like this happened. At the end of the Thirties he was making much of his living, which cannot have been a great one, reading for MGM. The war came, literary fashions changed, working-class writing seemed at an end, magazines featuring short stories disappeared. Leslie joined the RAF as an aircraftman. An aircraftman he remained. He might have done for other ranks what Bates, as Flying Officer X, did for bomber crews and fighter pilots; but he was never given the chance. The working-class stories that he continued to write seemed increasingly like carbon copies of his Thirties stories. He was, I think, the victim of his own lack of education and adaptability, and of the lack of imagination of bodies like the BBC that failed to exploit his talents.

His tragedy, if that is the word (and what he achieved in the end must have seemed to him far short of his expectations) was not dissimilar from John's. It was to John that I owe my introduction to what is called the literary world. I owe him much more besides. He was a generous man and as honest as he was generous; and everything he knew he had learned himself. He owed nothing to schools or universities. Some of his weaknesses as a novelist may be due to that, but it also gave him strength. After the first two, which had been published by the time I met him, I read the manuscripts of his novels as he wrote them, in brown ink. He is the only man I ever knew who used brown ink. Where he got it from I never learnt; I have never seen the stuff on sale; but he must have had gallons of it. What strikes me now is how short the span of his effective career was. Though he went on writing until well on into the Fifties, the best of his work was written in the Thirties, and it all had its genesis in his experience of life gained before he went to Four Ashes. His best novels are *Saturday Night at the Greyhound*, *O Providence*, *Family Curse* and, perhaps, *Care of Grand Hotel*. Despite the difference in their setting, all bear Hampson's thumbprint. In almost all of them there appears the figure of a young man, often a youngest son, who is or sees himself to be in permanent estrangement from society because he is homosexual. He is wiser, more clearsighted, more disinterested, than the other characters; he sees through them and foresees the consequences of their behaviour. He is both agent and chorus. There is obviously room for sentimentality here, yet that is the last quality one finds in these novels. They have a remarkable objectivity and both in texture and in attitude they seem to me very Anglo-Saxon.

With the war and my marriage and the appearance of a family, John and I inevitably moved away from each other, but every year he and Ronald came to spend a week with us in Romney Marsh and, later, in Devon. Ronald enjoyed small children and was quite happy to stand at an upper window all day watching passing cars. And John did, I am glad to say have one experience in his life which he saw as a great adventure. After the war, with the help of a small inheritance and, I believe, a loan from Forster, he went to India for six months. It was the eve of independence, he found India congenial and as a protégé of Forster's he was made much of. He was invited to a cocktail party at the Viceroy's in New Delhi and discovered that Lady Mountbatten, the Vicereine, whom thereafter he adored, had read his novels.

In the first half of 1956 I was in America. It was not until I returned that I discovered John was dead.

V

In the autumn of 1934 my circumstances suddenly changed. I had a telegram from Joe, my old head master, asking me if I would deputise for a few days for a master who was ill. I did so, and the few days stretched to two terms. I cannot say I enjoyed my new role. Most of the time I was very inefficient, for I was not trained, I was ill-prepared and remained so because of the circumstances: I was living from one day to the next. But there were compensations, of which the greatest by far was the monthly cheque. I could now pay my whack when out with John, and even on occasion entertain him. Above all, I could save, and this was important because I had been offered a post of visiting lecturer in the summer session of 1935 at the University of Iowa. I would not have to ask my parents to lend me the money for the passage.

I was to teach courses in the English social and political novel and twentieth-century British drama, and most of my leisure-time was spent in reading and preparing my lectures. I sailed at the end of May, my choice of line and route being dictated by the fact that Canadian Pacific were offering cut rates across the Atlantic since it was the King's jubilee. So my port of entry was Montreal. I recall little of the crossing. I was not seasick, and since most of the other third-class passengers were, I was inordinately proud of this. I played long sessions of draughts and ping-pong with a young farm labourer from Ulster who was going to Canada to settle and marry a girl he'd never seen, something he seemed to accept as in the nature of things. I beat him at draughts and he beat me at ping-pong; but occasionally I took advantage of the ship's rolling and won at ping-pong. But it was not a ploy I could indulge often, for he became very upset and then I had to let him win at draughts.

We sailed up the St Lawrence and I was much impressed by the wildness and barrenness of the Gaspé Peninsula, though the Quebec countryside with its struggling, mean-looking villages with tin churches with aluminium-painted spires seemed drab and poverty-stricken. At Quebec, United States immigration officers came on board to examine the credentials of passengers bound for the Republic. I greatly puzzled the officer who questioned me. I explained the purpose of my visit, produced the letters I had had from the University and proved that I had on my person the ten dollars without which entrance to the United States was illegal. He was still obviously uneasy at accepting me; I imagine he thought me too young to be a college professor. What, he demanded, was my status in a British university? The question appalled me: mother wit saved me. I answered truthfully: 'I am an elector in the constituency of the Combined English Universities.' It must have sounded like the equivalent of being an elector of the Holy Roman Empire. He stamped my passport.

At Montreal, I waited an hour or two at the railway station for the train to Chicago. I was bemused by the language those about me were speaking and by the references to Tirana, which I knew to be the capital of Albania. At last it dawned on me that Tirana was Canadian for Toronto and that the language that mystified me was French Canadian. It was dusk when the train drew out, and all I remember of Montreal outside the station is a tiny, electrically lit street fair with a merry-go-round. For me, Montreal is a toy city.

Next morning, staring out of the window, I was excited by everything I saw. The flat countryside seemed endless, raw and new, the surface scarcely more than scratched and almost deserted, the farms, each with water-tower and silo, seemingly miles apart from one another. Every so often, we passed a dirt road, and all the time on the front of the enormous locomotive that pulled the train through this empty land the bell tolled. I was at once excited and solemn: I was achieving an ambition, to visit the United States. I was actually in them! Most men of my generation are supposed to have been in love with an idea of the Soviet Union: I was in love with an idea of the United States, and for me the romantic names, the Great Good Places, were Kansas City and Omaha, Nebraska.

At Chicago, I got a cab and asked the cabbie to take me to a good cheap hotel. He drove me to a place not far from the Loop called the Midland Club, which was pleasant and quiet and quite unlike my idea of a hotel, for there was no dining room nor bar. When I enquired about a meal, a coloured waiter brought me in a dish of steak and

French fries and a bottle of beer from a restaurant near. Having eaten it, I walked out in order to find the Hotel Sherman, where next morning I was to catch the bus to Iowa City. And next morning, I went with my tin trunk and typewriter in a cab to the Sherman, where a man coming out of the hotel sized me up as English and insisted on waiting with me till the bus came. He told the driver to be sure and take good care of me.

The friendliness and kindness of people I had so far encountered impressed me, as did the absence of class-distinctions, though this was also disconcerting me. When I read it a year later, I could see myself in the account Thackeray gives of his feelings when, on his first American visit, the hotel porter in his presence told a bell hop to 'take this man's baggage to his room'. He was first taken aback and then wryly amused: he had expected to be referred to as 'this gentleman'.

The journey to Iowa City took about eight hours. I noticed in a working-class district in, I think, Cicero that the New Deal Café was shut, 'gone out of business', and wondered whether this was symbolic. In the country, I was struck by the quietness and leisureliness of the small towns we went through: they seemed summed up in the old men standing outside the general store or the hotel. Their trousers hung from braces of a kind I knew could only be galluses and their shoes were buried, in retrospect at least, in a froth of peanut shells. We crossed the Mississippi at Rock Island. The river was a mile wide, which astonished me. At last we reached Iowa City. I engaged a cab-driver to take me to a rooming-house, which he did. He pushed away the tip I offered him and said surlily, 'I get my wages'. From this I drew conclusions which were false.

Next day, I took over the room that had been reserved for me at a university hall of residence, I remember nothing of the hall now except that it seemed enormous – it housed a thousand men – and chillingly impersonal. I cannot recall having a meal there, though I must have done. I have a memory of suffering so much from the heat of the Middle West in summer, which I was quite unprepared for, that in evenings I was driven to go down to the soda fountain at least once an hour in search of cold drinks. None of them, cola, root beer, fizzy pops, had the least effect on my thirst; plain lime juice and iced water alone would quench it.

The Volstead Act had been repealed two or three years, but the United States was still very much under the shadow of Prohibition, or at any rate Iowa was, as I was constantly discovering. Thus on my first evening I went into a restaurant for a meal and ordered a bottle of beer with my meal. The waiter was immediately suspicious; he may have found my accent anything but reassuring. 'You ain't going to spike it, are you?' I assured him I wasn't. I didn't even understand what he was implying but I guessed from his manner that it was reprehensible.

A day or two later, I was invited out by a banker, a millionaire. How it came about I have forgotten, but he must have been a good banker, for his bank was one of the very few that were not bankrupted after the Wall Street crash of 1929. We met in the foyer of the Hotel Roosevelt and he ushered me to his car, which was enormous and driven by a Negro in livery. We drove to a spot that seemed remote from anywhere, and the chauffeur set up a cocktail cabinet by the side of the car while my host and I sat on the running board and drank the highballs the chauffeur offered us. I was thankful we were remote from anywhere, for even I knew that in Iowa it was illegal to drink anywhere but in the privacy of one's home. Of our conversation I remember only one thing. He assured me the President was in the pay of Stalin. I thought it improbable but I didn't say so.

Though bootleggers were still about – they supplied rotgut to students, Negroes and poor whites – the only legal source of drink was the state liquor store. You paid a dollar for a licence and were given a little book like a miniature passport in which all your purchases were logged. In it, I entered my name, address and date of birth and then found my race was requested. I asked the clerk what I should put. He said authoritatively: 'C for Caucasian'. I had not met the term before.

I had almost no contact with the thousand young men I lived among: I felt isolated and imprisoned by my Englishness. My friends were instructors and graduate students of about my own age. The hall of residence was about a fifteen minute walk from the building in which I lectured, on the opposite bank of the Iowa River. I found I could shave a minute off the time it took me to get to class by climbing into my lecture-room through the window. This was important; I had to be punctual because my lectures were broadcast. There was a microphone on my desk and an engineer in attendance.

On the second day a man came into my class whom I had not seen before and sat down in the front row under my nose. He was a few years older than I and formally dressed; he wore a tie and a jacket. He took no notes but stared at me almost truculently through horn-rimmed spectacles for all the fifty minutes. I was very scared. From his dress and behaviour, I decided he must be a functionary of the university sent to check and report on my competence. The lecture over, I retired in haste to my office. There was a knock on the door and the man entered. He introduced himself and apologised for not having been present at the first lecture. He told me how much he had enjoyed and profited from today's. He could not have been more charming; I was utterly disarmed. He was an assistant professor at a college in Kentucky and an American of a sort I had not met before; he was very formal, his politeness was elaborate and he spoke very slowly. When he left he urged me to be his guest after the session ended at his in-laws in Kansas City.

The invitation, so sudden, so unexpected, so different from anything I had ever met in my life before, bowled me over. I accepted gratefully. Ross and I were on terms of friendship immediately. A short man, disproportionately broad and with bow legs, he had ridden horses since childhood and worked for a time as a cowboy. He was a Texan, though he had been born in Oklahoma when it was still a territory. His father had been a judge there and administered justice with a revolver on the bench in front of him. Ross was a Harvard man and an officer in the U.S. Cavalry Reserve.

Some of us held a party every Friday night in a fraternity house, empty for the vacation, which a friend occupied as caretaker. At the first of these, I stumbled across Ross sitting on the floor alone in a corner and quietly weeping. I was very concerned and implored him to tell me what was wrong. Between sobs, he stammered out: 'If my dear old grandmammy hadn't sold the land which Dallas, Texas, now stands on, I'd be the richest man in the whole goddam world.' Thereafter, there came a point, I found, at every party Ross attended when he sat down by himself in a corner and wept over his grandmammy's short-sightedness.

It was a great season for parties. On Saturday nights, I used to go to an enormous one, also held in a vacation-empty fraternity house, by Vardis Fisher, who was a novelist well-known at the time. What Fisher was doing in Iowa City I never knew, for his teaching days – he had been on the English staff of New York University and of the University of Utah – were over. But among some of the graduate assistants he had the status of a guru. Some fifteen years older than I, he had been born in the Rocky Mountains of Mormon farming stock and had remained a Mormon, the first I ever knew, until his university days, I suspect until his days in graduate school at the University of Chicago. When I knew him, he was in full reaction against Mormon mores, for in a space of four or five years he had evolved through five centuries of European thought to become the confident herald of a glorious dawn when superstition should be no more and all men totally free, like Vardis himself. He was writing an autobiographical tetralogy, all the titles coming from a famous passage in Meredith. They were *In Tragic Life*, *Passions Spin the Plot*, *We are Betrayed* and *No Villain Need Be*. They were powerful works – 'confessional' would be the word today – but I did not greatly care for them. Their naturalism seemed old-fashioned, and I felt that Fisher resorted to psychoanalysis and behaviourism alike at his own convenience to explain his hero's character.

I did not know him well. I remember he talked to me once of the unreality of the world given to him as an ardent literary youth by English poetry, a world dominated by the strains of the nightingale, a bird unknown in America. The standards imposed on him by his teachers, he thought, had been false and alien. He developed this in an anecdote he told me later of his first trip to Europe as a graduate student. All his life, he had read about Scotch whisky, which, as a Mormon in Utah and Prohibition America, he had never seen, much less smelled or tasted. When his liner berthed at Liverpool he set about remedying this. He made a beeline for the Adelphi Hotel and bought a bottle of Scotch. 'How,' I asked, 'did you find it?' The answer was short: 'It's got nothing on Idaho corn-liquor.'

Fisher died in 1968. After that first visit to America, I don't think I ever heard him referred to or saw his name in print until I came across an article on him in *Novelists and Prose Writers*, the appropriate volume in the recently published Anglo-American compilation *Great Writers of the English Language*. He seems to have written twenty-eight novels, some on the early days of Mormonism. I suspect he was never fashionable in New York or Boston or, for that matter, anywhere east of Chicago. I do not regard this as in any way damaging, though it took me many years to realise that the poetry and fiction of regional America can be significantly different both in form and assumption from what rules in New York. And I suspect I might today be more sympathetic towards Fisher's point of view than I was forty-five years ago, though I have no means of knowing whether he held to it until the end of his life. I imagine he was never well known in England and perhaps published there only intermittently.

So I discovered the pleasures and tribulations of the summer session, a peculiarly American institution. It is a time when past deficiencies can be made up and progress towards greater achievement registered. And though it is a period of concentrated work, there is always something of a holiday atmosphere since it takes place in vacation and since many of the teachers and staff alike have come to the campus from places comparatively remote and therefore are conscious of the freedom and anonymity that being in a novel atmosphere confers. Life at summer session has, in fact, something in common with that on an ocean liner: anything may happen; anyone may be met; the unexpected is the rule. The mood prevailing is quite distinct from that of the university in its regular terms. Everything is speeded up and is at once more tense and more relaxed.

And I, I can only think now, was especially privileged. I was standing on the threshold of a career, but the career was not sharply defined; I was not committed to the academic life; and the very fact that I was in a country not my own gave everything I did a feeling of irresponsibility that was delightful. I was living as it were out of time. I knew it would soon be over, but while it lasted I could enjoy the frivolity known only by the uncommitted. In addition, I was being paid real money, no less than $800, for doing what I greatly enjoyed doing and found I could do rather well. A friend reported that Vardis Fisher said I was like a kid let loose in a candy store. I did not much relish the remark, but it was apt enough. I was living not only in greater space but in greater spaciousness than any I had known in England. Here, I felt, the possibilities life offered were endless.

I was enchanted by the exotic in my surroundings. The sudden, early descent of night never failed to delight me, I could not tire of hearing the night-long multitudinous chirping of the cicadas or weary of the lightning-bugs that zigzagged on all sides. There was even pleasure in knowing that the foul stink drifting across the fields was that of a skunk that had been disturbed. When I was told that the columns supporting the pediment of Old Capital, the administrative centre of the university, which had been the state legislature in the days when Iowa City was the capital of the state, were hollow and in ante-bellum years had been the hiding places of young runaway slaves going north to Canada, I was thrilled; I was in the presence of history.

Other things were surprising, even shocking. I met anti-Semitism for the first time. I don't suppose I had known more than two dozen Jews in my life and I wasn't prepared for the strength of feelings against them. I realised that the common hostility to New York and Wall Street as a symbol of the economic Establishment was part of it. On campus, Jews, I learnt, were not admitted to fraternities, the Greek-letter societies, and their own fraternity house was talked about almost in whispers, as though it were a witches' coven.

I was surprised by the power of football in the university, partly because, unlike at home, it seemed to be played by none but specialists, and to be an accredited footballer seemed like belonging to a professional caste, like being an enlisted soldier. Colleagues warned me never to give a footballer a low grade or get on the wrong side of the football coach. That, I was assured, was academic suicide. I was surprised, too, by the pasts of so many of the people I came in contact with. Ross, as I have said, had been a cowboy and had driven long-distance oil-tankers as well. Professor Edwin Ford Piper, the kindly old gentleman who taught creative writing, was known as 'the cowboy poet', for he too had been a cowboy. There was the assistant professor fired for moral delinquency just before I arrived who said philosophically: 'I sold ice-boxes before I was a college professor and made more money. Guess I'll go back to selling ice-boxes.' There was the Professor of Psychiatry, the only Jew I knew on campus, whose wife was a great friend of mine. He had been born in Bessarabia when it was part of Romania. After graduating in medicine in Vienna, where he had studied under Freud, he had migrated to the States. Meeting him for the first time, you could have been pardoned for thinking you were meeting someone out of a Ring Lardner short story or who had at least been born in the Bronx. One could never have deduced from the way he spoke the English language his passion for the Greek tragic poets and Dostoevsky or his love of Browning's poetry. He was the exact opposite of what he seemed to be.

By comparison with the United States, England, I realised, was an intensely sheltered society, difficult not to see as in some sense fuddy-duddy. To be in the United States was liberating in the most intoxicating way, and this despite the fact that the economic state of the country was about as bad as it could be and that there were not even such cushions against adversity as Britain provided. No one, it seemed to me, despaired, certainly no one in my circles. We speculated about the possibility of Right-Wing dictators seizing power; there was talk of a mythical Man on the White Horse and of a very real Catholic priest in Detroit named Father Caughlin; but by and large the mood on campus, as it came through to me, was optimistic, the reverse of what it was in Britain. This was reflected in what happened about me. In these weeks I heard at university public lectures, held after nightfall in the open air, Harry Hopkins, who was Roosevelt's aide, Rexworth Tugwell, who was one of the original Brains Trust, and Robert Hutchins, the young President who was doing exciting things at Chicago University. One had the illusion that one was living in a current of events that were electrifying, and it wasn't all illusion. One day walking across campus, I ran into an acquaintance with whom I occasionally visited a saloon in Iowa City. He was an avant-garde dramatist who taught in the Speech Department; his plays seemed to me very silly. He surprised me by shaking my hand and wishing me goodbye: he was off next day to Washington to join the Federal Theater Project.

The difference between the two countries, as I see now, was the difference between Baldwin and Chamberlain on the one hand and F. D. R. on the other. They were heightened times, despite the Depression, even because of it. Wordsworth's lines,

> Bliss was it in that dawn to be alive,
> And to be young was very heaven,

were current, and it did not seem silly to apply them to the times we ourselves were living in.

The Summer Session ended, overnight the campus was deserted and Iowa City became a small town again. There were, I suppose, five or six weeks to go before the Fall semester began, and I stayed on for I hoped I might get a permanent appointment. A friend lent me his apartment and, a contented hermit, I began to write the novel that after many revisions was published four years later as my first. I wrote in the evenings, beginning at about half-past five, with a glass of scotch or bourbon beside my typewriter. I would telephone the University Drug Store for sandwiches, which I ate as I wrote. Outside the circle of light thrown upon my work by the desk-lamp, all was dark; the lightning bugs banged against the window I wrote beside and enormous flying things hummed drunkenly round and round the lamp. I wrote for five or six hours, sometimes to the accompaniment of the dance music of Guy Lombardo and his Royal Canadians broadcasting from an hotel in Montreal. The first draft of the novel was almost complete by the time the vacation ended.

But before I began to write I spent a week in Kansas City with Ross at his in-laws. They lived in what I thought must be the millionaire quarter. In my memory, gargantuan Anne Hathaway cottages stand cheek by jowl with sham Alhambras, though I have to admit that when I was next in Kansas City, which was more than thirty years later, I could find no trace of them.

Kansas City was perhaps eighty years old and owed its importance to the fact that it was a railhead from which steers, driven by cowboys over the plains of Texas, could be shipped to Chicago. According to Ross, until very recently it had been a gangster-controlled city. Johnny Lazia, the ruling mobster, was found dead early one morning, 'filled so full of lead', Ross said, 'it wasn't even funny'. Who shot Johnny was never discovered, but next week the wages of the police force were being paid by an immigrant from Yorkshire named Tom Pendergast. Pendergast, who later controlled the Democratic Party in the state, was Harry Truman's political sponsor.

This lawlessness, I thought, explained the armoury Ross's father-in-law maintained. It was housed in a cupboard by the front door, and was opened up for my inspection by Dr Brooks himself. I was much impressed, even awed, for I had never before seen rifles and revolvers kept in a private house for what you might call business purposes. Dr Brooks told me he slept at night with a loaded revolver under his pillow, a story his antecedents made the more startling, for he was a former President of the University of Missouri and had once been a professor of Latin at Harvard.

Term began, and the job I was hoping for did not materialise. I was offered a graduate assistantship. As I know better now than I did at the time, it was a generous offer, for it was a time of intense academic unemployment and I was not even an American citizen. Cavalierly, I turned it down, for it would have meant working for a Ph.D. degree and taking more examinations. I was unwilling to be *in statu pupillaris* again and teaching, even university teaching, seemed a second-best. So I took a Greyhound bus for Chicago, where I spent a few days before going on to New York.

Chicago was no longer in its great period, but I was bowled over by the beauty of the skyscrapers seen from the lake front and by the Art Exposition, where I thought I saw, laid out in all its prodigality, the plunder of the Old World. There were more El Grecos than in the Prado, and I found the display of French Impressionists astonishing. Rome in its imperial days must have been something like this, I thought.

On my first night in Chicago, Joe Louis fought Max Baer for the heavyweight championship of the world and beat him. The Blacks rioted in triumph, though I knew nothing of this until I read about it next morning in the *Tribune*. I made contact with a friend of my father's and Uncle Ted's who had migrated after the war. I found meeting him curiously touching, for after fifteen years he still spoke with a Birmingham accent and seemed to me more foreign than the people he lived among, a revenant from the English nineteenth century.

My bus journey from Chicago to New York took twenty-nine hours, not including the night I spent at the University of Notre

Dame, South Bend, Indiana, where I was entertained by priests who were friends of Edward O'Brien. And the trip cost, I recall, thirteen dollars. On the bus, I reflected I was approaching New York in the traditional American way: from the West. Absurdly, this pleased me. It still does.

I had reserved a room at the Algonquin. I cannot think why; I knew nothing of its literary associations and, if I had thought a moment, would have realised it was much too expensive for the likes of me. Its location was very convenient, but I made no use of what it had to offer. I have no memory of having even a single meal there and I wasn't in the famous cocktail lounge for another thirty years. John Hampson had given me letters of introduction to two men he knew in New York, the poet Horace Gregory and Robert O. Ballou, who was a publisher. I spent a weekend with Gregory and his wife at their home in Bronxville, the seat of Sarah Lawrence College, where Gregory taught. He had spent the year before in England on a Guggenheim fellowship and told me he had sat with Mr Eliot on Sloane Square tube station waiting for the last train. They had dined together, were not quite sober and Mr Eliot passed the time waiting in goddamming the bloody British.

Ballou I remember as a lined, anxious-looking, youngish man who had been forced out of his publishing business by the Depression. He published Steinbeck, who pays tribute to him in his collected letters, before he was famous, and Henry Roth's *Call It Sleep*, which in 1935 was almost unknown, for Ballou had gone out of business just after publishing it. He had sent a copy to Hampson, who lent it to me. It went unpublished in England and in America was damned by the conservative critics as too proletarian and by the left-wing critics as not proletarian enough. It is easy to see now that it is not in any real sense a proletarian novel. The setting is life in Brooklyn among poor Jewish immigrants who have fled the pogroms in Russia, and the action is concentrated on the small-boy hero, who lives in a state of aspiration approaching ecstasy, a state that seems to illustrate the striking image Leslie Fiedler brilliantly rescued from Doughty's *Arabia Deserta*: 'The Semites are like to a man sitting in a cloaca to the eyes and whose brow touches heaven.' The novel seemed to have totally disappeared, and towards the end of the Fifties I happened to mention it to Victor Weybright, of the New American Library, who told me it had recently been re-discovered and republished. He sent me a copy of the new edition. I wrote an article on it for the *London Magazine*, with the result that a London publisher brought it out, almost thirty years after its initial publication.

Ballou was very kind to me. He read my first novel, said he'd publish it if he were still in the business and passed it on to an agent who, I cannot help thinking, was more worldly-wise; having read it, she told me I was a very young man. I decided to put it aside and forget it. Most of the people I came to know in New York I met through Ballou. The first thing he did was to ask how I could afford to live at the Algonquin, and on his recommendation I moved into the Breslin, on the corner of Broadway and 29th, where I got a room for a dollar a night. It was in the heart of the garment district, most of the guests seemed to be permanent and as far as I could see were unemployed. We were all comfortably miserable together, and I have pleasant memories of the Breslin and the bartender, Al, a man of vast cynicism who until the Depression had had his own business in the rag trade.

I went with Ballou and a number of his friends one evening to Harlem. In those days, Harlem was not a place you went to at your peril, though if I had wandered in it alone I don't imagine I'd have found it very rewarding. We were there for a specific purpose: to visit Father Divine's 'Heaven' on 125th Street. I, certainly, was uncomfortable, for I thought our visit might be construed as slumming and we should not be welcome, which was quite untrue. The slogan 'Black is beautiful' had yet to be coined and the notion of Black Power did not exist. Negroes were still trying to straighten out their crinkly hair, and the great ambition of many was still to 'pass'. Father Divine's movement was one of the first to preach the dignity of colour and in its way it challenged current assumptions of the automatic superiority of the white man. I doubt whether Father Divine himself ever claimed in so many words that he was God, and indeed he did not have to, for his disciples did it for him. Nor, I think, did he repudiate the miracles he was alleged to have performed, as, for instance, that it was because the *New York Times* had attacked him and his movement editorially that its proprietor Adolph Ochs had dropped down dead almost immediately after.

Among other things, the movement was a way by which Blacks coped with the Depression. It offered Negroes an alternative to the New Deal, and from the point of view of authority Divine could not have seemed other than in conscious competition with the President. His disciples proclaimed their faith, and their allegiance to him, by taking new names, such as Praise the Lord, and when they renounced their old ones in effect they renounced their civic identities and the right to vote. They would not answer to their old names, and their new ones were not recognised by the electoral register. They had opted out of American society. Nor can it have been by accident that Divine maintained an estate, to which the faithful flocked, on the bank of the Hudson immediately opposite and in full view of Hyde Park, President Roosevelt's family home.

The 'Heaven' at 125th Street, very near the railroad station, was only one of several in Harlem; a free meal was combined with a religious service. I remember 'Heaven' as much like the assembly hall of the elementary school of my childhood. Service, both religious and culinary, seemed continuous. We were shown to vacant places at the table that ran the length of the hall, but we explained we hadn't come to eat and stood with the rest of the congregation, if that is the word, between the table and the wall. So far as I could see, we were the only whites present. No one showed any hostility to us or, indeed, took much notice of us. Father Divine, with his wife Mother Mary, looked down on us from a dais.

It looked a very acceptable meal, lamb chops and greens followed by ice cream. Everything was all very informal. Those who were not eating were calling out things like 'Peace, Lord, it's wonderful', 'Father Divine is God' and 'Praise the Lord' or executing dance-steps to a three-piece combo playing what I suppose were hymns in jazz. As it played, the fervour mounted. It was an orderly fervour. 'Peace, Lord, it's wonderful!' resounded round the hall; more and more people improvised their own dances. For the first and only time in my life, I saw dancing come into being spontaneously, as a natural mode of worship.

Meanwhile, Father Divine and Mother Mary looked down on the angels, as his followers were called, and I looked at Father Divine. In my memory, he is a stockily built, light-coloured Negro (though not as light as Mother Mary, who I thought could have 'passed') with a close little beard; reminiscent, indeed, of the conventional representations of Lenin. He is dressed in a light grey flannel suit and wears a red tie. He was not what I imagined an evangelist to be, not a showman, and when he rose to address us he did so in conversational tones and indulged in no rhetorical outbursts. He gave us good advice, of a common-sense, self-evident kind, telling us to work hard, be sober and be kind to one another. It was unsensational and undramatic – and then, without warning, he and Mother Mary were coming down from the dais, and we were swept aside by the congregation rushing forward to see them leave 'Heaven', pushed aside unceremoniously and without malice. We followed and saw them climb into a waiting Rolls and be driven away.

Of Father Divine's provenance and subsequent history I know nothing. By now, I can only suppose, he is in heaven.

Edward O'Brien arrived in New York. He gave me dinner with Martha Foley and Whit Burnett, the editors of *Story*, at an Italian restaurant off Fifth Avenue, at about 48th Street. He took me with him to cocktail parties and he was instrumental in my becoming a guest-member of the Harvard Club, which was very useful since one didn't pay on the spot for what one ate and drank but was billed a month later. Though I didn't want to leave, I realised that my time in America was rapidly running out. I had been unable to get work, apart from a reviewing assignment Malcolm Cowley gave me at the *New Republic*; I reviewed an anthology of college verse which was distinguished because it contained Elizabeth Bishop's 'Newfoundland'. She was, I think, still at Vassar, and of course I had not heard of her. It has always been something I was proud of, that I was among the first to salute her. I didn't meet her for another thirty years. I wrote my review with great satisfaction but not, I am afraid, with much profit. *The New Republic*, I seem to recall, paid me at the rate of two cents a word, and in any case I did not get their cheque till I was back in England.

It was half-way through October, the evenings were becoming chilly, and I had no greatcoat. I walked on the ventilation grills in order to be warmed by the hot air rising from the subway tracks below. I realised one day that I no longer had enough money to pay for a third-class passage on a conventional liner. Friends advised me to get work under the Federal Writers Relief Project. But not being an American citizen, I could see no way in which the United States owed me a living. I was worried, too, about what was happening in Europe. Mussolini had just invaded Ethiopia, and the Romanian who ran the cigar-store at the Breslin told me England should declare war on Italy. I remembered that one of the party with whom I had been to Harlem was a journalist on a travel magazine. I invited her to dinner and learned that you could travel by freighter for five dollars or one pound a day, and she promised to find out about current freighter sailings to Europe for me. It came out in the course of conversation that she came from Oxford, Mississipi. Did she, I asked with great excitement, know William Faulkner? She was surprised. 'William Faulkner?' she asked, 'the Town Drunk?'

She telephoned me next day to tell me there was a freighter on which I could get a berth sailing to Le Havre in a few days' time. The day was the day I was to have lunch with Edward O'Brien, his other guest being Hemingway. I went to the shipping company's office downtown and booked my passage; the season was over, and I discovered I would be the only passenger. As we sailed out of Hoboken, on the New Jersey side of the Hudson, I bitterly regretted having to miss lunching with Hemingway. My admiration for him now is qualified, and I cannot help thinking I wouldn't have liked him much or he me.

The ship I sailed on was a vessel of 5,000 tons carrying a cargo of shellac, among other things. By comparison with what it would have been like in steerage in a passenger liner, my accomodation was luxurious. I had a large cabin to myself, with the words 'Certified to accommodate one US master' painted over the door. I was left alone or taken for granted and spent the voyage reading Proust. I messed with the officers, who, it seemed to me, had a sort of innocence that would not have allowed them to survive long on land. My notions of sailors and the merchant navy were derived from Joseph Conrad, and it was quickly plain to me that life in the American merchant navy was like nothing in Conrad. I met the captain at breakfast the first morning out. He was a friendly Finn named Johan Johansson, and though I suppose among his officers he was *primus inter pares*, they did not seem to hold him in any great respect. He sat at the head of the table and waved aside cereals, waffles and syrup, ham and eggs and coffee, and told the steward all he wanted at mealtimes this voyage was a glass of orange juice. The effect of the announcement was stunning. 'You sick'nin' for sumtin', or sumtin', Skipper?' the second officer asked. The captain explained himself in an engagingly simple way. This last shore leave, at his wife's behest, he had read a book on dieting and decided to try the prescribed regimen himself. Solicitude changed to derision and expostulation. If he wanted to go on a diet he should wait till he was back on shore; a sailor's meals were part of his wages. It came of listening to women! He merely smiled beatifically. He attended at meals assiduously, thrice daily running the gauntlet of the officers' ribbing; they competed in recalling memorable meals they had eaten and describing in detail others they hoped one day to eat. We salivated with relish and Captain Johansson sat there sipping his orange juice and smiling his beatific smile, which was at once childlike and saintly.

Of that first breakfast, too, I remember the chief engineer. He came in after everyone else and sat down in the chair the Skipper had just vacated. He was a very tall, cadaverous man who looked strikingly like Neville Chamberlain. He did not say a word and ate everything put in front of him. When he got up to go, he said philosophically and to no one in particular: 'Ah well, they say it's not the length, it's the way you swing it.' One evening, he invited me to drink beer with him in his cabin. It was fitted out as a photographer's dark room. In his lugubrious way, he was proud of it and of the photographs he had taken. They appeared to me very good, and he seemed pleased to hear my praise. Not that things had turned out as he hoped. It had all begun some years before when he saw a photograph in the *Christian Science Monitor* of a three-masted barque on fire. 'They pay dollars for pictures like that,' he said, and it dawned on him that by not having a camera he had been missing out on good money for years. 'So I got me a camera,' he said. He hadn't seen a fire at sea or anything notable, but, as he said, 'It takes your mind off things.'

He subscribed to all the photographic magazines and kept a bicycle in Le Havre, for he had joined the local photographic society.

The ship's officers were united in thinking a sailor's life a mug's game. They all seemed by origin to be country boys from inland states who had been betrayed, I surmise, by boyish romanticism. Now, their dreams seemed to centre on a single ambition: to retire to a small farm in Ohio or Illinois.

The crossing took two weeks. When we were still four or five days out from New York the captain said he'd like my advice. I was flattered, until I realised he had already consulted everybody else on board. His problem was this, and it made him very anxious. Since leaving Hoboken, he had not had a single bowel-motion; should he take Epsom salts? I disavowed specialist knowledge but told him that since for more than a week he had had only a few glasses of orange juice, I did not think he could expect anything memorable in the way of bowel-motions and said I thought dosing himself with Epsom salts would be unwise. He took Epsom salts all the same, and that night we ran into a gale. He was violently seasick and had to keep to his bunk till we were in port.

From Le Havre I made my way to Dieppe and the Channel ferry. At Newhaven a customs officer wanted to know whether I was bringing any dirty French books into the country. I offered him Scott-Moncrieff's Proust. I was acutely aware, all the same, that I had confiscable material in my baggage, for I had a copy of the recently published American edition of *Ulysses*, which was still banned in England, that Peter Chamberlain had commissioned me to buy for him. It lay among my shirts and socks in a book-jacket of *Son of the Morning: A Life of Nietzsche* by Edward J. O'Brien.

Nietzsche attracted no attenion. Two other books did, *America Faces the Barricades* by John Spivak, which was a present for a friend, and a new anthology, *Proletarian Literature in the United States*, which I had bought for myself out of sheer interest. These were borne away to a room behind the trestle tables, from which two gentlemen in bowler hats and civilian clothes presently emerged. They held the books in their hands. They were very polite. Why did I have *these* books, *these* in particular? Was I aware who Spivak was? All I knew of him was what it said on the blurb. The two men smiled at me pityingly. He was, they said, a notorious agitator. They wrote down my answers in a black notebook. I assured them that I had no interest in the English publication of the books. The following week, of course, *Proletarian Literature in the United States* appeared in London, without any help from me, published by Lawrence and Wishart. The books were returned to me, and I found the boat-train had been held back for me. From that time on, the customs officer's remark in *Vile Bodies* has had a special savour: 'Very hot against literature the Home Secretary is.'

I got into Birmingham just after nine that evening. I'd worked it out that when I'd paid off the taxi-driver I'd have five shillings. I was helping the cabman strap my trunk on to his luggage rack when a man who had been a student with me and whom I had not seen since university days, came over and said, 'Where have you come from?' 'America,' I replied. He gave me a long look and said: 'You bloody liar.'

VI

I took it for granted that, back home, I should take up my life as freelance journalist again and so I did, but in a way I had not expected. Herbert S. Cater, for whom I had bought Spivak's *America Faces the Barricades*, suggested I should join him in a sort of partnership. He would provide me with a room in his office, a typewriter and all necessary equipment, a telephone, the use of his quite sizeable library of reference books, his store of press-cuttings and his professional advice, and I would write articles that he would market. We would take a fifty-fifty split of everything sold and he would guarantee me a minimum of £3 a week. I accepted like a shot, without attempting to determine which of us had the better of the bargain, if bargain it was. What interested me was the assured £3 a week. I'm pretty sure Kay did not lose by the deal, even if he did not gain as much as he might reasonably have expected, for I could have applied myself much harder than I did without turning myself into a human battery-hen. I was not interested in money beyond my immediate needs, and the journalism I was practising, which I found only briefly and sporadically amusing, I saw essentially as a crutch to enable me to write my novel. I don't, in fact, think Kay ever seriously expected to reap profit from me. I was, indeed, only the first of three or four young men he helped in this way. He was, I think, a man of great generous impulses who could yield to them only if he persuaded himself they might be a source of profit for him. So, later, he insisted on paying for the typing of my novel in return for the manuscript, which, conceivably, might one day be valuable.

I had met him when I was an undergraduate through a young man I knew who was a reporter on one of the local papers. He was a dozen or so years older than I, had served through the war in the trenches and in 1928 or 1929 had written a war novel that was never published. I liked him enormously, for he was stimulating and rose to ideas like a fish to a fly. He reminded me in some ways of Bennett, both the Bennett who preached the acceptance of life as something to be made the best of and the Bennett who wrote those maddening little primers *Mental Efficiency* and *Self and Self-Management*. He saw himself as a hard-headed man of business, and in some ways, I think, me as a good man who had fallen among aesthetes and intellectuals, much as Lenin saw Shaw as a good man fallen among Fabians. At the same time, I think I represented a path he himself might have taken had it not been for the war, a path he still had a hankering after.

To me, he looked anything but a journalist. His Devon origins showed in his speech, and his heavy build and ruddy cheeks suggested a farmer, though this is immediately contradicted by my abiding memory of him. He is at his typewriter and has just rushed into the office to meet a deadline so imminent that he has had time to do no more than unbutton his raincoat and push his trilby hat to the back of his head. It is obvious that he will be rushing off to another assignment as soon as this is finished. But the ash on the cigarette stuck to his lower lip is over an inch long, and he has, in fact, been at the typewriter all morning. His appearance belies him. He is essentially a daily newspaperman, for whom the passing moment is everything and willing self-deception part of his stock-in-trade.

He had served his apprenticeship on the weekly newspaper in Devon edited by the father of W. N. P. Barbellion, the author of *The Journal of a Disappointed Man*, whom he had known and, I think, been influenced by. He had come to Birmingham after the war and joined one of the local papers. He had lost his job in a re-organisation and rationalisation of one of the groups. Immediately, he had set up his own news agency, to which he brought a ferocious energy and an uncanny nose for a news-story. By the time I joined him, he occupied one floor in an old office-building round the corner from the Law Courts and employed seven or eight young reporters.

I was with Kay for the best part of two years, until my novel found a publisher and I followed it to London. I enjoyed my association with him and the daily discussions we had on almost every subject under the sun. Journalistically, our ideal was very much the *Daily Express* of the day as represented by Tom Driberg's William Hickey page. I produced a seemingly endless supply of Driberg-like gossip paragraphs for the Birmingham papers. But the appeal of journalism as an end in itself was wearing very thin. Sometime in the first half of 1937, A. J. Cummings, the star writer of the *News Chronicle*, decided to write a series of articles on what the provinces were thinking. Kay represented the paper in Birmingham and had to arrange Cummings's interviews there. These were to be with representative business men, representative trade unionists, representatives of university opinion, and so on. Kay said to me: 'You can be the educated young.'

The evening came when I was to be interviewed. In the lounge of the Midland Hotel, I made myself known to Cummings, who sat me down, pressed the bell for the waiter and ordered drinks for us. I sat back and waited to be interviewed. He talked about himself. He had recently interviewed Stalin and was full of it. He poured scorn on H. G. Wells's interview with Stalin. He said: 'The difference between H. G. Wells and me is that H. G. sits on his arse all day.' I wondered, as I still do, at his nerve in seriously comparing himself with Wells. He went on to tell me how, before he was President, Roosevelt had entertained him on his yacht and how he, Cummings, had outlined to Roosevelt the principles of the New Deal. All this with great solemnity. In the two hours I was with him, he did not ask me anything. Later, he told us, through the *News Chronicle*, what the educated young were thinking. From all of which I learned one thing, which the experiences of later life have reinforced: that it is the besetting sin of successful journalists to confuse themselves with their by-lines.

I resumed my Thursday-evening meetings with Hampson and on a Saturday morning very soon after I joined Kay ran into MacNeice in a bookshop. I did not know whether he would remember me, but he came over and asked me about America. We chatted for a few minutes and then, abruptly, he switched off, as it were, turned on his heel and walked out of the shop. I was struck with consternation: unwittingly, I must have offended him. I had encountered what I later found was MacNeice's common way with people he did not know well. I need not have worried, for I found myself again in his company within a matter of days. He had become very friendly with Reggie Smith, who was still a student at the university. How Reggie appeared to him at this time comes out very vividly in his long autobiographical fragment written in 1940, *The Strings are False*.

I had run into Louis at a time when, as he says, he 'began to go out a great deal and discovered Birmingham'. Until then his life in Birmingham had been spent in a cocoon of early-married domesticity. Now, his first wife, whom I never met, had suddenly left him for an American. One effect of this on Louis seems to have been to bring him to life in a way he had not known before. This sense of a new life all about him can be felt strongly in the verse he was writing at this time and which he gathered together in *Poems*, published in 1935, the collection which made his reputation. It can be felt, for example, in the poem 'Birmingham', which showed me a city whose existence I had not suspected, a city enormously exotic and glamorous, though I could see that the exoticism and the glamour were truly properties of scenes and places I had known all my life.

Birmingham was not the only industrial city Louis had known. He had known Belfast from his childhood, and in my view Belfast was and is uglier and grimmer. I suspect that his attitude towards Belfast was more ambivalent, for it was at once home to him and alien. He thought of himself as an Irishman rather than an Ulsterman. Though his father was a bishop of the Church of Ireland, he came from the west and both he and Louis were opposed to the Ulster ascendancy, to Lord Craigavon, Stormont and the Orange order, to all those things symbolised by Protestant Belfast. By contrast, Birmingham presented no threats. In appearance and attitudes, Louis was both an aristocrat and a peasant, as no Englishman can be, and in social attitudes he was the most democratic of men. He became friends with the workmen who from time to time did jobs at his flat. There was a young electrician, I remember, with whom he often went drinking; the man was an ardent pigeon-fancier, and this, no doubt, was part of the attraction, for Louis loved all skills and specialised knowledge. He often wore on his face the expression I associate with him many years later; with him as one would see him standing at the bar of the George in Great Portland Street, a rendezvous of BBC men and radio-actors; standing there one of a group but in it rather than of it, his mouth lifted in a half-smile, half-snarl, of incredulous delight at the company with whom he was finding himself. He was always somewhat detached from the company he was with, an outsider, a chiel among them taking notes. I think this stemmed from his being an Irishman who after infancy had spent his life among the English, with whom he could never wholly identify himself, though he was anything but a narrow nationalist, except possibly when drunk.

Now, his marriage broken up, he discovered Birmingham. He was still living where he had always lived in the city, in the flat above the coach-house at Highfield, Philip Sargant Florence's house. I recall, the first time I was in his flat, being surprised and I fancy a little shocked by the way in which the furniture, chairs, tables, wardrobes, had been painted in patterns and curlicues of bright pinks and greens and blues. I suppose I found it too frivolous for my taste; one felt in the world of Russian ballet. I was more at home with his books, which impressed me enormously. There seemed to be all the Greek, Latin and English poets, all the literary critics, a formidable array of the works of philosophy, psychology, anthropology and sociology I. A. Richards was editing for Kegan Paul, besides a fascinating assortment of novels and miscellaneous books. And the like of his collection of gramophone records I had not seen. Doubtless there was classical music in it, but what excited me were the early jazz, the Irish jigs and the music hall songs. One in particular caught my fancy. It ran something like: 'Here we are at duh palais de dance To trip duh light fantastic. Say what comes here? A classy dame Chewing a hunk o' pulastic. Say she look duh goods to me', and so on in demotic American. It was sung, I think, by Eileen Stanley. I was having, it seems to me, a glimpse of the Twenties, of the first decade of the Sitwells and the world encapsulated in *Decline and Fall* and *Vile Bodies*.

That evening, too, I must have met Betsy for the first time. Betsy was a very handsome Borzoi bitch and one of the hazards of visiting Louis. She had the habit of poking her long snout into the private parts of his guests, behaviour which seemed to amuse him rather than not. I had the feeling that he saw one's reaction to Betsy as a test one passed or did not pass. They made a splendid couple when they were out together and I can only suppose she was an aspect of his vanity. He assured me she was very stupid. In his poems she is compared to a film star.

Louis was one of the most silent of men. He very rarely talked about poetry, his own or other men's, unless it was to elicit information, as once in London when writing *Autumn Journal* he telephoned me for the names of the constituencies of the Birmingham Labour members, information which in the event he did not use. He confined his comments on other writers and other art forms to curt expressions of approval or its opposite. He was a man with whom one could sit for hours in companionable silence interrupted from time to time by a 'What's old So-and-So up to now?' to which the answer was generally 'Oh, the usual' or 'Much the same'. He was very fond of the prefix 'old'. Auden was always 'old Wystan' and Spender 'old Stephen'. The word seemed to comprise both affection and appreciation of a rare phenomenon.

In the autumn of 1936 Louis was appointed lecturer in classics in Bedford College, London, and his Birmingham period ended with a spectacular party which began at about nine of a Saturday evening and for some of us, Louis included, did not end until more than twenty-four hours later. My memories of the party are appropriately hazy.

Professor and Mrs Dodds were there at the beginning and so was Auden, with whom Louis had recently visited Iceland. They did not stay long. Those who came from London included Spender, Rupert Doone, the director of the Group Theatre, which had recently staged Auden's and Isherwood's *The Dog Beneath the Skin* and was soon to do Louis's translation of the *Agamemnon* of Aeschylus, and the painter Robert Medley. I remember Doone, at one point during the night, sitting cross-legged on the floor and reiterating with great impressiveness, 'The theatre is like a basket of eggs: you take some out and you put some in.' I remember someone, for reasons best known to himself, throwing a glass of brandy on to the fire and a jet of flame shooting out and scorching the backside of the person standing in front of it, who I have always believed was Henry Reed. And I remember, as we woke up at first light from our impromptu beds on couches and blankets strewn on the floor, seeing Gordon Herickx standing at the window and surveying the grounds of Highfield, which must have been two or three acres in extent, and saying meditatively to himself: 'So this is how the poor live!'

Herickx must have a paragraph to himself. Sculpture was his passion and his vocation. He was tall, blond, ruddy and almost totally hairless. His output was small, for sculpture is the most expensive of pursuits for a working-class man. The cost of stone is prohibitive, as is the cost of transporting work for exhibition; and he was married, with two or three small children. He was, besides, interested in many things, in films especially. He read widely and discussed what interested him with wit and zest. He had an engaging gay seriousness and he seemed always to be seeing himself from a slight, half-comic angle. I remember him saying earnestly to me once, in his perceptible Birmingham accent, of Wyndham Lewis: 'You know, kid, I *like* Lewis. I always think he's read the same sixpenny books as I have.' Auden and MacNeice admired his sculpture and tried, in vain, to interest their wealthy friends in it. He did some beautiful work based on the structure of flowers; there was a piece called 'Chestnut Bud' and another called 'Cyclamen', and before them he had done a stylised figure, which I saw only in photographs, called 'Unemployed Man'; it was shown in the Soviet Union, whence he never recovered it. And he did a remarkable portrait head of John Hampson. He had one London show, soon after the war. He was vastly excited, for he had waited for it for years. We wanted to give a party for him after the private view, but he could not be induced to stay the night in London and insisted on getting into his car and driving straight back to Birmingham. He died in his sleep that night. In his lifetime, he was practically unknown, and I suppose he is entirely so today. I hope the Birmingham Art Gallery at least has some of his work.

Early on the Sunday morning after Louis' party, I remember that Rupert Doone and Medley went into Selly Oak village in search of eggs for breakfast, after which they and the other guests from London left. A day or two later, Louis left too. I followed him two or three months later. But not before I had gone to London one Sunday to see the Group Theatre production of his play *Out of the Picture*. I am afraid it was not a good play. I think he would have preferred success in the theatre to almost anything, and he wrote three or four plays, only one of which achieved professional production, in Dublin after his death. The theatre of the Thirties and Forties was not interested in the kind of thing he had to offer. He needed something less naturalistically-dominated than existed then, and by the Fifties, by which time the theatre had taken a different path, his passion for the drama had been at least partly satisfied by the demands made upon him by the radio play.

I did, in fact, before leaving for London, take a small part in one of Louis' plays, *Station Bell*, which Reggie Smith produced for the University Dramatic society. As I remember it, it was very funny. At the time, I believe Louis had hopes of its being put on at the Old Vic. It was never published and had disappeared from the MacNeice canon until I mentioned it in an article in the *New Statesman*, after which E. R. Dodds traced the typescript of it to the library of the University of Texas.

Which reminds me that I took part in what I think was the first public reading of *The Ascent of F6*, at one of the University English Club's fortnightly meetings. Auden took charge, distributed the scripts and alloted the parts. We read at sight. I remember how astonished and impressed we were when, the reading ended, Auden went round the tiny audience of perhaps forty undergraduates literally with a hat, saying that the labourer was worthy of his hire and that nothing should ever be given free. It is conceivable he pocketed fifteen shillings.

Suddenly my novel, *Innocence is Drowned*, found a publisher. I never doubted it would, but for a year it had been floating round London in a progress slow, stately and tortuous. It had been rejected by nine publishers, six of whom had returned it with letters saying that in less depressed times they would have accepted it and two of whom sent copies of their readers' reports, which were glowing, and invited me to meet them to discuss my future plans. But it seemed to have taken each of them at least six weeks to have it read and to make up his mind about it, and here was the tenth, Michael Joseph, accepting it after having it only ten days. He stated his terms: he would pay £25 in advance of royalties. I didn't quibble but accepted by return of post, told Kay I was leaving him, and set about making plans to go to London. But the plans had all been made. I even had a pretty good idea where I would live, in the beginning anyway. Weekly, there appeared a 'small' in the *Daily Telegraph's* column of furnished flats to let beginning 'A Hundred Little Homes', announcing completely equipped furnished rooms to let for fifteen shillings a week. They sounded grisly enough, but I doubted whether anything cheaper could be had, and besides, they were in Regent Square, which my *A to Z* showed was in Bloomsbury, half a mile from Euston Station.

I wrote to Edward O'Brien and by return heard from him that he'd just been appointed story editor of Metro-Goldwyn-Mayer British Studios and could let me have reading. Within ten days of Joseph's accepting my novel, I was installed in Regent Square, which like much of Bloomsbury seemed Bloomsbury only by courtesy, though local folklore claimed Aldous Huxley had once lived in it, and just off it, I found, was the street where, on Tuesday afternoons turn-and-turn-about with Festing Jones, Samuel Butler visited his French prostitute.

The room I had was small and crowded, understandably so, for it contained a sink and a gas cooker behind a screen and a settee which you converted into a double bed. Before a month was out, I had transferred myself to another much larger room on the other side of the square, for which I paid nineteen shillings.

Having taken the room, the first thing I did was to go to Henrietta Street, Covent Garden, to meet Michael Joseph in his office. He was in his first season as a publisher, but I had known his name for several years as that of the author of *Journalism for Profit* and *Short-Story-Writing for Profit*, books I tended to look down my nose at. He was a man with a clipped military moustache – after the first war he had been demobilised as the youngest captain in the British Army – and a flattened nose that had been broken in a boxing match. He spoke with military briskness. He told me precisely how many copies my novel would sell: 420. In fact, it sold one less. I enquired what the prospects were of reading for publishers. That was no way to get rich, he said, but, if I liked, he'd let me have a manuscript from time to time. Indeed, he did so and after the war invited me to be his literary adviser, which I was for more than ten years. He told me who had read my novel for him: Derek Verschoyle, the literary editor of the *Spectator*. Unscrupulously, I called on him next and asked for reviewing. I went away with the latest Thurber, and thereafter Verschoyle sent me books on occasion.

Later in the week, O'Brien took me to lunch at the Café Royal, and I became reader for MGM and thereby what was almost the lowest form of literary life in London, though I am sure that O'Brien, who was a kindly man, saw his position as giving him an opportunity to help young writers. He told me how the job of story editor had come his way. There had been a highly successful play on Broadway called *Boy Meets Girl*, in which one of the characters, a highbrow short-story writer, declares that if he doesn't get into the next edition of O'Brien's annual anthology he'll give up art and go to Hollywood as a scriptwriter. 'Who's this guy O'Brien?' asked the MGM scouts at the first night, and the same question was repeated in the higher circles of Culver City. And one day O'Brien looked out of his cottage window near Oxford to find the lane outside blocked by an enormous limousine. It was MGM come to offer him a job, and he suddenly found himself earning £5,000 a year. It was ironical that his all-consuming zeal for the short story as an art form should have been thus rewarded. It forced him into a continual compromise with commercialism. I remember he spoke of Maugham with distaste, almost even of moral disapproval, as of one who had knowingly perverted his talent. But it was an attitude less and less easily held. I went into the MGM office one afternoon and asked to see him. I was given the routine answer: Mr O'Brien would be free in five minutes; would I take a seat? I did so, and immediately some one else came in, asked for Edward and was straight away ushered into the presence. The fleshy beak of the newcomer was unmistakable, and I reconciled myself to wait. Forty minutes later, the man was ceremoniously conducted through the reception room by Edward himself. He beckoned me into his office. 'You know who that was?' he asked in a respectful voice. 'Hugh Walpole, wasn't it?' I answered. Edward nodded and said, very seriously: 'He asked who you were.' I had, I was given to understand, been blessed from afar. I wondered why Edward should have been so impressed by Walpole and why he should expect me to be, until I realised that Walpole was one of MGM's most illustrious assets. Had he not, in addition to his reputation as a bestselling novelist, even appeared in *David Copperfield*? His name on the pay-roll signified the approval of Film by Literature.

I found that the living one could earn by reading for MGM was a modest one. The normal payment for a report was half a guinea; for something special, what was called a treatment, a synopsis of two or three thousand words, one got a guinea-and-a-half. With luck, one might get half a dozen normal jobs a week. From all sources, MGM, the publishers I occasionally read for and the papers where, even more occasionally, I reviewed, I managed to earn something like three pounds ten a week. And it soon came home to me that at least one very famous publisher paid even less than MGM for reading; as little as seven-and-six. Even so, London seemed full of readers for MGM, at one time as many as sixty. Some of them have since become well-known. For a short time H. E. Bates read for MGM, though I cannot believe that even in 1938 it was necessary for him to do so, since he was the most famous of the younger short-story writers. He made the pardonable error of assuming that the books that came to one to read were one's perks, like review copies, and having read them, he promptly sold them; but in fact they were on loan from the Times Book Club.

A carrot was dangled before our noses: if we were outstandingly good we stood a chance of being sent to a mythical place in California called 'The Coast' to be trained as script-writers. Only one of us, I think, was ever sent to 'The Coast', and for almost fifty years I believed my own moment of triumph was similarly unique. Late one evening, Edward telephoned me to ask if I could read immediately and report on an anonymous script by a young English novelist who was under contract to MGM. I said I could, and within half an hour the script was delivered to me by taxi. I took my report into the office at ten o'clock next morning. Don, Edward's young American assistant, was waiting for me. 'Say,' he asked me with some excitement, 'what's it like, Walter?' Flippantly, I said: 'It'll knock 'em cold in the stalls'. Don smiled painfully at my irreverence. The greatest moment of his life had been when he saw Garbo in the flesh, at 'The Coast', of course. But he was a very nice young man, who never rebuked us for our frivolity towards the good, the true and the beautiful. He had a master's degree in film art from UCLA and believed implicitly that what was good for MGM was good for the USA.

The title of the script was 'The Boy from Barnardo's'. A boy who was a muff at the Orphanage makes good in the Boer War. He was played, I believed, by Freddie Bartholomew. I boasted of being the only reader for MGM British Studios who had ever had a film made from something he had recommended. The film, I further believed, was a tremendous box-office success, nothing short of a 'Wow'. Alas, in his memoirs, Anthony Powell, who wrote the script, says it was never produced.

Not, in any case, that I'd have seen it. It was assumed we saw all new MGM productions as a matter of course, but we were given no viewing privileges, and since the cheapest seats at the main MGM house were three shillings and sixpence, a third of the reading fee, it was easier not to see them. Most of us were pretty contemptuous of the work we were doing, partly because no one liked to be the sort of wage-slave we were and partly because of the mumbo-jumbo that surrounded what we were doing. It was as though we held very humble positions in the civil service of the Kingdom of Heaven. We had to provide six carbon copies of every report, our typewriters were rarely adequate to do this, and so we were constantly being rebuked for the illegibility of the bottom copies. At the same time, there were slave-girls in the typing pool making further copies of our reports. Once at 'The Coast', it seemed, every report was card-indexed under as many headings as were relevant. One might be, say, fire at sea. A producer planning a film in which a fire at sea occurred would have all the reports under the heading taken out of the library and gone through.

The sheets of paper on which we made our reports had a space at the top right-hand corner for the names of the stars and feature-players we thought the film, if made, would be suitable for. At regular intervals, we were given up-to-date lists of the stars and feature-players under contract. Then at the top of the sheet was a narrow space headed 'Story Line'. Beneath this a much larger space, to take perhaps three hundred words of single-space typescript, labelled 'Synopsis'. Then followed a section to take perhaps three lines of type with the heading 'Comments'.

We were certainly cavalier enough in our attitude towards 'The Coast' and Culver City, and it may be thought MGM was a long-suffering organisation. All the same, I cannot persuade my heart to bleed for the company, for I cannot believe it need have been so mean and niggling. From time to time, we were presented with samples of reports made at 'The Coast', to be taken as models. They seemed incredibly naive and solemn, representative of America at its most gullible and provincial. Apart from 'The Boy from Barnardo's', which was a special case, of the five hundred or so books and scripts I potted, I remember only two. One was an immensely long and eminently scholarly life of Pitt the Elder by the military historian Brian Tunstall, which took me three days to read and synopsise and at half a guinea was therefore financially a dead loss; the other was Beckett's first novel *Murphy*, on which the only comment possible to write seemed something like: 'This is a highly original and appallingly funny novel which would be entirely useless for Hollywood.' For the most part, what I used to read were whodunits, sentimental romances and undistinguished thrillers.

But O'Brien, who doubtless had his own problems with MGM was kind, kept open house for readers every Saturday evening, invited me to dinner whenever he had guests he thought might be useful to me and lunched me regularly at the Café Royal.

It was in the autumn of 1937, too, that I met Graham Greene at the office in William IV Street, near the Strand, of the new magazine he was editing, *Night and Day*. We talked of Hampson, whom he admired, as a positively good man, and who had given me a letter of introduction to him, and he commissioned the article I proposed to him. He was not yet famous, was still merely 'promising', but I read everything he had written. It was not that I was unreservedly enthusiastic about his novels. All the same, of my near-contemporaries he excited me more than anyone except Auden, and though they weren't comparable, I see now that they had more in common than I realised. They shared an obsession with frontiers, spies and betrayals, and though I do not think either influenced the other, there is sometimes a similarity of phrase that is astonishing. The image, 'kept tears like dirty postcards in a drawer', which is from Auden's sonnet on Housman, would not surprise us if we met it in Greene.

With both of them, whether in the flesh or on the page, I knew I was in the presence of powerful idiosyncracy. Meeting Greene for the first time, with his account in *Journey without Maps* of his march through Africa vivid in my mind, I remember thinking: how could this man have made such an expedition? He was very tall and thin; one felt a gust of wind would blow him over. His face was lined, as though he were under strain or perhaps in some pain, and his smile seemed somehow reluctant, as though he were using facial muscles not much exercised. His voice, which was lightish tenor, was not so much high-pitched as curiously strangled. I recall telephoning him once at *Night and Day*. I began by asking how he was, not expecting any considered answer. In the working-class environment I grew up in it was merely good manners to preface a meeting with a ritual 'How are you?' It normally evoked the answer 'Very well, thank you', or at worst, 'Not too bad'. Graham replied, 'Mediocre', or it may have been 'Middling'. I was momentarily taken aback: it seemed to demand a new response. Later, I realised it was a tiny instance of a quality Greene shared with Auden. Most people, it seemed to me, lived habitually by assumptions they did not question and they were startled when they appeared to be challenged. But Greene and Auden were not like that. They lived not by commonly shared assumptions but by their own autonomous reactions. They did not live by fictions, they saw for themselves, they walked alone, with their own gait. This gave authority to everything they wrote, to their most trivial, unconsidered utterances, and to everything they did. I remember how Greene, whom I think of always as wearing an anonymous raincoat, embodied the notion of someone walking ahead, as I had imagined him doing in Sierra Leone and Liberia.

He represented the most formidable challenge to the values I had inherited and, I believed, made my own. I recall something he said to me apropos of nothing a few years later. We had lunched together at Rules and in the cloakroom he suddenly said how much he wished he lived in a seedy South American republic where everyone took bribes and frequented brothels. I was shocked and even now I cannot conceive of a greater start to anyone brought up in the English Nonconformist tradition. And I don't believe he was talking, as they say, for effect.

He was an enigma to me. He was quite unlike other Roman Catholics I had met; neither bog-Irish nor reach-me-down Chester-Belloc. Catholics themselves seemed to share my puzzlement, try as they might to dismiss the source of it as the notorious eccentricity of the convert. At times, I thought Greene's Catholicism was the furthest extreme of Nonconformity. Beyond this, it was Greene who first made me realise, through *Brighton Rock* and *The Power and the Glory*, that in the last analysis all opinion and perhaps all action comes down to the clash between Nietzschean values and Dostoevsky's, as dramatised in *Crime and Punishment*.

Soon after I met him in the *Night and Day* office Greene invited me to a cocktail party at his house on Clapham Common North Side. I went with Hampson and of the party itself all I now remember is meeting Pamela Hansford Johnson, who has been a friend ever since. A year or two younger than I, she had recently published her first novel, *This Bed Thy Centre* and was reviewing new fiction for the *Liverpool Post*.

Some weeks later, I was invited to dinner at Clapham Common. I was the only guest, and before dinner I went with Graham and a large jug to a nearby pub. While we were waiting for the jug to be filled he told me that he proposed to write four novels a year. 'If Edgar Wallace could do it,' he said, 'why shouldn't I?' It was at this time that I learnt he was a great inventor of practical jokes. One he recounted was confirmed in an unsolicited story I heard from a man whom I met during the war and had been a participant. As an undergraduate, Graham had written to the master in charge of lectures at Highgate School. He purported to be an Army officer and an African explorer, gave a list of his books, and offered to give a lantern lecture. The offer was warmly accepted and on the appointed day Graham turned up at Highgate hiding behind a false moustache, wearing riding breeches and carrying a box of slides bought for the occasion as a job lot in the Charing Cross Road. He was introduced to his audience as the author of many books with which they were no doubt familiar, and Greene began to improvise. It was pretty soon obvious that Highgate School was being hoaxed, but, having put himself in a false position, the master in charge could not easily extricate himself. Curious to see what it would be, Graham called for his first slide. It was put in upside down, a picture of Brighton Pier.

Other practical jokes he dreamed of I remember from another dinner at Clapham Common on a Sunday evening during the Munich fortnight in September 1938. When I arrived, Mrs Greene was at the convent school seeing her two small children being fitted with gas masks. Both Graham and I took it for granted that war was imminent, and there seemed nothing else worth talking about. Did I, Graham asked, think he could support a wife and two children on thirty shillings a week? I didn't. He was trying to imagine what would happen to him. Perhaps, he said, he would end up like Maugham in the first war and find himself a secret agent rowing to a rendezvous on Lake Geneva. On the whole, he thought he'd probably join the Royal Air Force Regiment, which had recently come into being. Why the Royal Air Force Regiment? I asked. Because, more than any part of the Army, they would be where the action was.

I had recently taken part in a 'Chamberlain Must Go' march. 'If they really wanted to get rid of Chamberlain,' Graham said, 'I could do it for them tomorrow.' How? I asked. There was any number of ways, he said, and proceeded to tell me two. You had visiting cards printed bearing the names of various members of the Cabinet. You then made a selection of pornographic books up into parcels and despatched them to Mrs Chamberlain, Lady Simon, Lady Inskip and the rest as from Sam Hoare, Leslie Hore-Belisha and Kingsley Wood. A cross-traffic of such parcels, Graham asserted, would cause the government to cave in in a matter of days.

Or there was that actor who was giving such a brilliant impersonation of Chamberlain in the current show at the left-wing Unity Theatre. Surely he could be used. You got hold of half a dozen out-of-work actors who could also make up as Neville, found out the date of the next Tory meeting he was addressing in Birmingham Town Hall, lined up your Chamberlains on the day in question, and an hour before the meeting began you wired the organisers as from Chamberlain: 'Delayed stop Shall arrive Birmingham thirty minutes late stop Do not hold back start of meeting.' By that time, the first ersatz Chamberlain is already on the train, and you send off the others at half-hourly intervals. Thirty minutes or so after sending the first telegram, you despatch a second: 'Urgent stop Have reason to believe Chamberlain due to arrive Town Hall now not genuine stop Arrest.' Chamberlain arrives with three or four other Chamberlains angrily denouncing one another as imposters, and in the confusion is promptly arrested and clapped in handcuffs.

There was a day in August, 1945, when we had lunch at Rules. I had not realised when we were making the arrangements that we should be meeting on the day the result of the General Election, polling day for which in Britain had been a fortnight before, would be announced. I came up from Birmingham, getting into Paddington an hour or so before I was due at Maiden Lane. From the placards of the lunchtime editions of the evening papers, it was obvious there was going to be a landslide victory for Labour. At Rules, I waited for Graham, who, his wartime job in West Africa ended, was back as literary editor of the *Spectator*. He joined me at our table and almost straightaway, his eye catching the banner-headline of someone's *Standard*, said 'Damn!' I was amused by the tone of irritated frustration. 'Don't you approve, Graham?' I asked. He answered that he didn't care one way or the other, he hadn't bothered to vote. He'd assumed the Tories would get back and had planned to make a telephone call at three o'clock. 'There won't be any point in doing so now'.

Greene, I think, by temperament hated anyone who was his boss, and his boss at this time was Wilson Harris, who besides being editor of the *Spectator* was an independent member of parliament supporting the Churchill government. Greene always spoke of him with dislike, as of someone especially sanctimonious and mealy-mouthed, and took much pleasure in persecuting him. Thus when Frank Harris, who was best known as a pornographer and whose antecedents were mysterious, died, Graham sent a paragraph pseudonymously and on Authors' Club writing paper to the Londoner's Diary of the *Evening Standard* to the effect that it was not generally known that the late Frank Harris, author of *My Life and Loves*, was the cousin of Mr Wilson Harris, MP, editor of the *Spectator*. It was, alas, not used.

On this occasion, he had planned to telephone the Reform Club, where Harris lunched daily with his cronies, announce that he was speaking from the Cabinet Office, and request the telephone operator to inform Mr Wilson Harris immediately that he was to call at 10 Downing Street at 3.30.

In such practical jokes, executed or not, one gets a glimpse, it seems to me, into the mind of the man who wrote the novels, the 'entertainments' particularly, though the difference between them and the novels proper is a hairsbreadth only and the element of the practical joke is as evident in a late novel like *The Comedians* as in *Gun for Sale*.

These practical jokes, I think, come into the category of what Swift, and Thackeray after him, called 'bagatelles', things of trifling importance which are valuable because specifics against boredom. Vive la bagatelle! He seemed to suffer from boredom or the fear of boredom to an almost Baudelairean degree. The first time I had dinner with him at Clapham Common he suggested that one night we ought to explore the nightlife of Peckham, of all places, which, he had been assured by a police superintendent, was unrivalled in London. Twenty years later, I had occasion to interview him in the Overseas Service of the BBC. He had come up from Brighton, where he was staying, for the recording. When it was over, the producer led us to the Duty Room for drinks. When we were invited to have a second, 'I'd love to,' he said, 'but why should I sponge on the BBC? I've got plenty of drink of my own in Albany. Why don't we go there?' And there he piloted the producer and myself. I assumed he'd be moving on to a dinner date, as I was. I noticed that in his chambers he had a collection of miniature whisky bottles like that described in one of the novels. The producer left, but Greene urged me to stay for another drink, and it suddenly struck me, though I found it mystifying, for he was almost the most famous novelist in the English-speaking world, that he was at a loose end and lonely. I was dining with John Raymond, and I suggested to Graham that he should join us, which he did. After dinner, he suggested I should go back to Brighton and spend a few days with him. I couldn't. We were in the last few days before a general election, and next day I had to settle down to report for the *Statesman* the television coverage it was receiving. Ever since, I have regretted not having gone back to Brighton with him, or, for that matter, explored the nightlife of Peckham with him, though I suspect it was the exact truth he was telling when Malcolm Muggeridge told me: 'Where Graham is, sin stops.'

During my first months and years in London, I was constantly running into him. He seemed part of the London scene, like Eliot and Forster. He was there, in the streets and in the underground trains and above all he was a denizen of Bloomsbury. Certainly no writer has caught its seedy underbelly so exactly, and I remember one day following the peregrinations of the hero of *The Confidential Agent* round Guilford Street and the purlieus of Russell Square tube station which, together with the shabby little hotels of Bernard Street and Cartwright Gardens, become under his spell romantic places in which the exotic and the grotty are one.

It was about this time, in 1939, that I ran into him one lunchtime in Guilford Street. I was disconcerted by the encounter because I sensed that he was. We crossed the road to the pub on the corner of Milman Street, which was destroyed by a bomb a year or two later. I asked him what he was doing in that part of the world at that part of the day. He said he had taken a room in Mecklenburgh Square, where he was keeping office hours. He had taken it in order to have a place where he could write in peace, away from the telephone. The address and the telephone number he was keeping secret; apart from himself, only his wife knew them.

I acquired a local social life. Two friends of university days lived within two hundred yards. One, a dentist, introduced me to the novelist R. G. Goodyear. A few years older than I, he had already published two novels. We became close friends, and he too started to read for MGM. I found myself meeting more and more young writers and painters struggling to wrest a living from a not over-sympathetic world. As I look back on it, we lived for several days in each month largely on half-crowns borrowed from one another.

Once or twice a month, I looked in at Charles Lahr's Blue Moon bookshop in Red Lion Street, where an amusing half-hour was more or less guaranteed, since it was a resort of rebels and eccentrics as well as writers. A frequent visitor was the Count Potocki de Montalk, who claimed to be King of Poland but, according to gossip, was a New Zealander. He had long hair down his back and wore medieval robes of scarlet and an apparently heavy chain of what I cannot believe was gold. He referred casually to 'my cousin the Count of Paris' and honoured me once by accepting a pint of Guinness in a neighbouring pub. He was one of the most familiar of Soho characters and published a volume of verse which was adjudged pornographic and was prosecuted.

At the opposite end to the Count was a man whose name I have forgotten but who I have always thought of as the Socialist Party of Great Britain. He had written many books, expositions of Marxism, exposures of capitalism and the armaments industry, denunciations of Stalin and the Comintern. He cannot have earned much money from them, nor from the weekly meetings he addressed in Hyde Park and Lincoln's Inn Fields, but he must have been famous, at least to ardent readers of the small ads at the back of the *New Statesman*, where his meetings were advertised. He was always cheerful and, as is the way with the professionally discontented – Kingsley Martin was similar – the worse the news, the more cheerful, the more optimistic he was; as though the tyrannies of Stalin, the advent of Hitler, were merely so many stations to the Promised Land, which was inevitable and ineluctable.

Lahr himself had been a rebel and was now an eccentric. He had fled from Germany as an Anarchist in the early years of the century. He used to tell a story of how he had stood in the crowd in the Strand to watch the Kaiser pass by on a state visit, how he had lifted his hand to scratch the back of his head and been immediately jumped on by four Special Branch men. At that time, he worked as a baker's roundsman in Bloomsbury and pushed his cart of loaves along the street with a plain clothesman walking beside him on the pavement.

Now, Charles satisfied his revolutionary impulses by assembling, with the aid of scissors and paste, mock-ups of *Daily Mail* placards bearing messages monstrously subversive, blasphemous or obscene. The latest examples of this art form, of which he was a master, were always on show in his shop. In its idiosyncratic way, it was a good bookshop. The stock was selected according to Lahr's own taste, a clue to which you could get from the stories he published in limited editions from time to time, stories by T. F. Powys, Rhys Davies, Liam O'Flaherty, James Hanley, Hampson and Bates among others. All these could be seen on occasion in the shop, which, it sometimes seemed to me, existed as a place for the exchange of literary news and gossip of a not quite orthodox kind. Books were bought and sold, it is true, in an as it were absent-minded way. With his little black beard, open-necked shirt and sandals, Lahr was a picturesque figure who could be seen cycling at any hour of the day in London in pursuit of books or a particular book. Stories by Rhys Davies and Bates contain memorable pictures of him.

Very soon after I came to London I became a member, almost certainly through E. R. Dodds, of FIL., Writers for Intellectual Liberty. After the war, I was told that it was a Communist 'front' organisation, which did not horrify me since it in no way invalidates the good it did, particularly in bringing refugees from Nazi Germany to Britain, looking after them, finding them work and so on. More narrowly, it was a place where I could meet other writers and discuss subjects that absorbed me. The meetings were sometimes silly, as one dominated by a discussion as to who among us were the more authentically working-class. I like to think I took no part in it, though I remember being surprised by the relish and ease with which Wykehamists and old Etonians established their membership of the proletariat. But it was at these meetings that I first met Rose Macaulay, a most gallant woman, and the Indian novelist Mulk Raj Anand. Most important of all, it was there I first met V. S. Pritchett.

I knew his name as that of a reviewer but had become conscious of him a few years earlier when a boy I had been at school with and who also had ambitions to write, suddenly appeared more or less out of the blue and asked me to read a manuscript. He had the habit of disappearing for months at a time and he explained that he was just back from Spain, where he had been living rough. It was the account of his experiences he wanted me to look at. It was by far the best thing of his that I'd read, Spain fairly leapt off the page before your eyes, and I wrote to him enthusiastically. He replied with disarming modesty, saying he thought I exaggerated the merit of the manuscript. A day or two later, in the Birmingham Public Library I found myself looking through travel books. I took a book down and discovered I had read whole sections of it before, very recently and in typescript. My friend's account of his experiences was a transcript of the early chapters of Pritchett's first book *Marching Spain*. I felt an awful fool, and not even the thought that at least I had recognised the real thing comforted me.

Pritchett talked on Dickens in a lecture series we had arranged. He captivated me; I had not thought that lectures could be as exciting as the printed page, and Pritchett's was. My surprise was probably natural enough: he was not then known as a broadcaster nor had he written any of his critical essays. His lecture on Dickens came to me, as it were, as a new publication. The quotations were brilliant, and when he read from Pecksniff or Miss Havisham he seemed to become the characters themselves. He showed me a new Dickens, immeasurably richer than the one I had known before. We left together after the meeting, for we found our ways lay in the same general direction, though after a time I was diverted from mine by the pleasure of his company. He was ten years older than I, and since he had already published three or four books and reviewed in the *Spectator, Statesman* and *London Mercury* I thought him an established and successful writer. I have no clear memory of what we talked about but he seemed to see himself as in some sense self-made, for he was not a university man. About that, he seemed a little self-conscious. After leaving Alleyn's School, he had gone into the leather trade, the background of some of his best early work, taken a job in Paris and walked across Spain and then through the Appalachians. In North Carolina or it may have been West Virginia, he had stumbled across a village of hill-billies, all of them half-wits and all named Pritchett. But that was a story he told me many years later.

While not in an ordinary sense a mimic, he had a wonderful ability to evoke rapidly in speech the manner and mannerisms of others. Thus, I remember, though I did not hear it from him till years later, the story of an encounter on the one occasion with both Wells and Yeats, whom he had met when as a young man he had worked as a correspondent in Ireland for the *Christian Science Monitor*. As a relatively new member, he had gone into his club early one lunchtime, found the dining room still almost empty and sat down alone half-way along a long table. Then Wells, whom he knew slightly, came in and joined him. They had just begun to eat when Yeats appeared, hovered in the doorway and peered round him myopically. Recognising Pritchett, he came and took the place beside him, so that V. S. was now sandwiched between the two great men. Wells craned round and said: 'Yeats? It is Yeats, ain't it? I ain't seen you since that weekend at Lady Warwick's in 1913.'

Wells's high-pitched slightly Cockney voice was admirably suggested, as was Yeats's sonorous gravity. 'It was indeed a long time ago, Wells,' he concurred. Wells was now in spate. 'D'you remember that beautiful girl who was there that weekend at Lady Warwick's, Lady —, wasn't her name?'

'She was indeed strikingly beautiful,' said Yeats.

'Well, Yeats, you should see her now. I ran into her yesterday. 'Orrible, Yeats, 'Orrible.' He drew his hand down his left arm and clutched it to his side, so indicating paralysis, and twisted his mouth askew. 'Orrible, Yeats,' he said again, with relish. Yeats was on his way to the south of France, where he died soon after.

A day or two after my first meeting him, Pritchett wrote me a letter and enclosed an introduction to Raymond Mortimer, who was literary editor of the *New Statesman* and who, he thought, would give me reviewing. I don't think I saw Pritchett after that until 1946, but it was the first of many kindnesses to me and the beginning of an association I find splendidly memorable.

I was not, Pritchett wrote, to be frightened of Raymond. But I was; as I knew him through the *Statesman*, he was the ultimate arbiter of taste, and when I presented my letter to him in the office next door to Lincoln's Inn I was defeated by his manner. I had not met his Bloomsbury variety of High Camp before and had no way of knowing it masked a genuine benevolence. He invited me to choose a book from the shelves to write a 'shorter notice' on. There seemed nothing I felt competent to write up, but I dared not depart without taking something, so I took away a very long and learned book on the origins of the American War of Independence. It has always seemed to me one of the defects of the brief review is that its brevity makes it comparatively easy for a reviewer to conceal his ignorance and also injects into the piece a phoney authority.

Later, I learnt that Pritchett's letter on my behalf to Mortimer had been prompted by Margaret Gardiner, the secretary of FIL., who had become a friend of mine. Margaret knew everybody, it seemed to me. She had climbed the Matterhorn with I. A. Richards; she had known Auden and Isherwood in their Berlin days; she had even, as a very young woman, met D. H. Lawrence and, later, she wrote an engaging account of their solitary meeting in *Horizon*, as thirty years on she wrote a valuable account in the *New Review* of her friendship with Auden. She was the daughter of the famous Egyptologist Sir Alan Gardiner and had a house a stone's throw from the Heath in Georgian Hampstead in which for the first time I saw paintings by Ben Nicholson and sculpture by Barbara Hepworth. Merely by knowing Margaret, my world became bigger.

I was seeing MacNeice at least as often as I'd seen him in Birmingham. Very soon after my arrival in London, he asked me if I'd talk about the contemporary novel to the literary society of Bedford College. What I said I have forgotten, though I remember I was stern towards Mrs Woolf; it must have been a mishmash of orthodox left-wing Thirties stuff. Louis was in the chair. My talk ended, I sat down and waited for questions. Louis was having none of that; without waiting, he led me out of the room. Outside, he asked: 'Have you got that thirty bob you owe me?' That I owed him thirty shillings was a fiction he clung to for several years. I hadn't, and he said philosophically: 'Oh well, we'll have to try the girls.' We went into a common room. 'Could anyone lend me ten shillings?' he asked, and immediately a dozen hands were rummaging in a dozen handbags. We went into Charlotte Street for dinner at Bertorelli's and later that evening, I recall, he gave me a set of the proofs of *The Earth Compels*.

One day, we met in the Café Royal for lunch but, first, walked round the perimeter of the brasserie to see if there was anyone we knew. 'Look,' said Louis, indicating a slight, curly-haired, youthful man at a table by himself, 'there's Ben Britten. Let's join him.' To me, Britten was the faintest of names. Louis knew him slightly because he was a friend of Auden's but only slightly. I remember we talked money. Was it easy, Louis wanted to know, to earn a living as a composer? Easier than for a poet? How much did Britten make a year? Britten, who could not have been more than twenty-five, said that he earned £15 a week writing music for films and that he lived in a converted windmill in East Anglia. £15 a week! It completely altered our notion of the earning capacity of composers, and we were very envious.

About this time, Reggie Smith turned up for a day. He was teaching in an elementary school in the Black Country and he had come up to be interviewed for a job with the British Council. He had dressed for the part, and this new presentation of himself took me by surprise. I do not think I had seen him in a suit before or often wearing a tie, and here he was, all six-feet two or three, looking impressive indeed. The suit, he explained, belonged to John Waterhouse. It fitted him pretty well, but still, he felt, judged as an ensemble, something was lacking. I agreed, went round to my dentist-friend's in Gray's Inn Road and came back with a rolled umbrella and an Anthony Eden hat. The hat was too small, but since he proposed in any case to carry it, that did not matter. Off he went to Hanover Square, to be interviewed by the Council's founder and director-general, Lord Lloyd, who asked him, among other things, whether he considered his French good enough to allow him to take a duchess in to dinner. Reggie thought it was; without any knowledge at all, I would have doubted that, purely, as I see now, as a matter of principle.

Until that time, I had, I suppose, regarded Reggie as in some sense a protégé of mine. I was suddenly made to realise that it was true no longer, even if it had ever been. He was a man very much in his own right, who went his own way, didn't give a damn for anybody and was governed only by his principles and affections. He completely transcended his background, and Lord Lloyd, not at all abashed by his political views, offered him a teaching post, and before the year was out he was no longer in the Black Country but in Bucharest.

Louis telephoned me one Sunday morning to say he was marching that afternoon in a demonstration demanding arms for Spain. Would I join him? I hesitated; I was not a great one for marching in demonstrations and neither, I felt pretty sure, was Louis. It would be quite all right, he said; we'd walk at the back of the procession so that we could easily slip away if we became bored. Just before half-past two, I was in Malet Street, outside the Senate House, waiting for him. The demonstrators were assembling in the courtyard: I was not a member of the university and decided it wasn't for me to go through the wrought-iron gates to join them. Through the gates, I could see J. B. S. Haldane, that incomparable populariser of science, wandering about, clutching to himself what seemed like an enormous scroll. The procession had formed and was about to move. A taxi drew up, and Louis stepped out of it. I joined him. Haldane was coming through the gates, and we walked towards him. Unfurling his scroll, which was a banner slung on two poles, he thrust one of the poles into Louis's hand, the other into mine.

We grimaced at each other: we were at the head of the procession, carrying an enormous banner. Almost at the head, anyway, for Haldane, who seemed as big as two ordinary men put together, marched two yards in front of us, his moustache like a roll of thunder, to borrow an image from Herbert Read's poem on Nietzsche. He carried a walking stick as thick as a young tree, ready, I am sure, to cudgel anyone who tried to stop our progress. No one did, and we marched through Bedford Square, swung into Tottenham Court Road and proceeded down Charing Cross Road, through Trafalgar Square and thence to Whitehall, bawling or murmuring as we went the slogans of the day, 'Arms for Spain!' 'They Shall Not Pass!' and, most popular, 'Chamberlain Must Go!' At the top of Downing Street, we shambled to a halt, and there was much toing-and-froing by stewards and policemen preparatory, I assume, to the departure of a deputation to No. 10 led by ferocious Jack Haldane. But now I am guessing, for we saw and took our chance. A taxi was passing, Louis turned round and thrust his pole into the arms of the man behind him and I did likewise. We jumped into the cab and went back to Louis's flat, which looked on to Primrose Hill.

The things one remembers are almost always the unusual ones, simply because they stand out from the course of one's existence, and the number of days that are memorable must in the nature of things be relatively few. Generally, life, as we say, merely 'goes on'. So the great, overwhelming fact for me at this time was reading bad thrillers and whodunits for Metro-Goldwyn-Mayer and waiting from day to day for the monthly cheque. On a certain date, one assumed, the cheque would arrive, and one worked out one's monthly budget with reference to this date, though one learned quickly enough that it seldom arrived exactly when one expected it. One was in a state of constant waiting, which brought in its train a series of petty though none the less real anxieties, not decreased by there being at least six deliveries of letters a day in central London. More than once, I endured the irony of having the monthly cheque arrive by the Saturday lunchtime delivery, by which time the banks were closed for the weekend. In my experience, publicans and small shopkeepers were extremely unwilling to cash cheques and generally refused utterly to do so.

Sometimes, it seemed one would never escape from this carking, niggling anxiety about money, never reach that regular £5 a week which had now come to represent security and freedom from financial worry; though, according to my dentist friend, who was employed by London Transport, it was when you earned £500 a year that worries really began. You found that, perforce, you had to live up to your income. You had to have suits to wear, accommodation you could invite people into and, after a certain age, a car. And, on £500 a year, he told me, the income tax was astronomic, crippling. I didn't believe him and I still think that on the whole the rich are not as poor as the poor.

What was wonderful was the sense of exhilaration you felt when you had an unexpected windfall. An editor, perhaps, had suddenly commissioned an article or one accepted months before at last been published. The very unexpectedness turned it into a bonus, and though earnings were relatively small, so too was the cost of living. I remember that in 1938 or 1939 a new restaurant opened on the site of Stulik's famous Eiffel Tower in Percy Street. Stulik's had been a great rendezvous of the Vorticists; it is the setting of paintings by Lewis and William Roberts and, fifteen years later, turns up in Huxley's *Point Counterpoint*. I never knew Stulik's but I was eating in its successor soon after it opened. It was Greek, good and cheap. What was called a 'business man's lunch' was served for one shilling and sixpence, and for ten shillings you could get a very decent dinner with a bottle of Greek wine for your girl and yourself.

So, reading for MGM, reporting on occasional manuscripts for publishers, reviewing from time to time, I passed my days celebrating when it seemed called for at the White Tower or the Café Royal or Chez Victor, in Wardour Street. The thread running through my days and giving them purpose was the novel I was writing. My first, *Innocence Is Drowned*, was published in 1938. Yeats, in a gracious and charming letter, had given me his permission to quote as an epigraph the lines, from *Second Coming*, in which my title appeared. It was published with a narrow wrapper round the jacket bearing Graham Greene's commendation, won a rave-review from Brian Howard in the *New Statesman*, more sober but still heartening notices from Forrest Reid in the *Spectator* and W. W. Gibson in the *Manchester Guardian*, and sold as Michael Joseph had predicted. My second novel, *Blind Man's Ditch*, I finished at midsummer 1938 and Joseph accepted it immediately. And over all, of course, hung the cloud of apprehension Spender summed up in the lines:

> Who live under the shadow of war,
> What can we do that matters?

What I did sounds lame enough. I took part in a campaign to make Churchill Prime Minister, which involved sending postcards to the Foreign Secretary Lord Halifax demanding an immediate military alliance with the Soviet Union. One Friday evening in September, I attended a meeting of the Churchill for PM campaign in the Friends Hall, Euston Road. It was to have been the climax of the campaign and proved to be the anti-climax. Bob Boothby, who I think was the chairman of the campaign, made a brilliant speech, and there were speeches too from Captain Vivian Adams, who was a 'rogue' Tory MP and Eleanor Rathbone. The hall was half-empty: Chamberlain had arrived back from Munich earlier in the day, brandishing a piece of paper and quoting from *Henry IV*. What, indeed, could we do that mattered?

Next morning, MacNeice telephoned me to say that, since there'd be war by Monday and petrol, even if obtainable at all, would be rationed, he'd just sold his car for £14. Would I join him for lunch at the Café Royal? I think both of us assumed it was the last good meal we'd have and we did ourselves proud. Then, floating on brandy and cigar-fumes, we took a taxi to the Tottenham Court Road, where a cinema was showing one of our favourite Westerns. Until checking dates, it was my cherished conviction that it was John Ford's *Stagecoach*, which I have seen many times. Unfortunately, it had not been made by this time.

When we came out of the cinema it was dusk and raining, and we took another taxi back to Regent Street, where we sat on the terrace at Oddenino's drinking and sneering at the passers-by, who were getting very wet. Then we returned to the Café Royal, where we did ourselves proud again. By the end of the evening, there was nothing much left of Louis's £14, and I hadn't much more than half a crown of the thirty shillings I had had that morning. But we had a satisfactory feeling of having gone down with all guns blazing.

War did not begin on Monday, Louis settled down to write *Autumn Journal* and, for me, life went on as before, though in an increasingly diminuendo way. 1938 became 1939, which I remember mainly as a period of waiting, as though life and significance were in suspense. For the first time for several years, I had no novel on hand; I was feeling towards a new approach to fiction. In the spring, Reggie Smith came back for two or three weeks bringing with him a party of Romanian students for a quick look at Britain. I helped to arrange the programme for the party. We got E. M. Forster to meet them and talk to them. Many of them, as I have realised only recently, were Jews consciously looking for somewhere they could escape to when the inevitable happened.

As a result of all this, I came to know people at the Romanian Legation. One of them, who had a doctorate from Birmingham, took me up and lunched and dined my friends and me. It seems improbable that his name was Decibel, though that is how I remember it. Reggie and his party went back to Romania and their place was taken by a group of Romanian schoolchildren roughly the equivalent of Sixth Formers. Unthinkingly, I accepted an invitation to a cocktail party at the Legation to meet them, and it was not until the day itself that I realised I did not have the right clothes. All I had were flannel trousers and sports jacket, none of them exactly impeccable. To go seemed impossible. Half an hour after the time the party began, Decibel telephoned. He was very stern. 'Where are you?' he demanded. 'Why are you not here?' I tried to explain. He cut me short. 'Get in a taxi right away,' he ordered. 'I have someone waiting to see you.'

At first sight, the party was just as I'd imagined, full of young men from the Foreign Office and the British Council in well-pressed dark suits and starched linen collars. I felt very shabby, but Decibel pounced on me and presented me to the Minister, who was cordial. Then I was pushed through a group of almost obnoxiously well-dressed young men who were gathered round an old lady with a large hat and a walking stick sitting on a small sofa. 'Madama . . .', Decibel said, 'let me present to you Mr Walter Allen, the young English novelist.' The old lady purred, patted the seat of the sofa beside her and made shooing noises in dismissal of the young men grouped around her. I sat down and found myself floundering in a very curious conversation. She bade me tell her about our young English poets and I said things about Auden and MacNeice. What she made of them I have no idea, but she seemed well satisfied and said she loved our English poetry. Then she told me a story. As a little girl of five or six, she had stayed with her parents at a hotel in Switzerland, where she had become great friends with a man who had a heavy moustache and who seemed positively to horde keys. He appeared to do nothing else, and she assumed he was a functionary of the hotel, the man whose job was to look after keys. She did not know his name and it was not until years later that she discovered he was Nietzsche, mad.

I have never dared check on the probability of the story. And I no longer remember the old lady's name, though I learnt all about her from Decibel. She had been a famous beauty and the mistress of the old king, Carol's father. The first thing Carol did on coming to the throne was to send the old lady into permanent exile, but since she happened to be the finest living Romanian poet as well as the late king's mistress she was appointed permanent delegate of Romania to the International Labour Office.

Forebodings of war pressed on us ever more urgently as refugees from Hitler became increasingly common. I had long conversations with one I met at Margaret Gardiner's, Elias Canetti, who was unknown in England and who fascinated me with his vigour and energy. Within a few weeks of his arrival in England, by concentrated reading in the British Museum he seemed to have mastered the whole of English literature. He had, I recall, an especial enthusiasm for Ben Jonson's plays.

I saw MacNeice often. Finding ourselves one evening at a loose end near Russell Square, he said, 'Old Stephen lives somewhere near here. Let's dig him out.' We went down Bernard Street to Spender's flat in Lansdowne Terrace. He was scarcely warmly welcoming. We could come in, he said, but we had to be quiet. Suitably abashed, we entered, sat down and saw why. Cecil Day Lewis was sitting at a desk beside the first Mrs Spender, who was I think a student at London University, coaching her in Latin.

In June or July, Reggie came back on leave from Bucharest, knowing he would be summoned back instantly the moment war was imminent. I introduced him to Olivia Manning, whose novels I much admired. She too read for MGM, and since we were comparatively near neighbours we often met to commiserate over common grievances. She had a wit that was devastating and was as formidable a young woman as any in London. I brought her and Reggie together simply because they were my friends and I thought each would find the other amusing.

MacNeice has an account of their wedding, in August 1939, in *The Strings Are False*. He reports that Stevie Smith, Ernst Stahl and I were present, besides himself. Stevie, who was also formidable and a close friend of Olivia's, I certainly remember but not Stahl, though I saw a fair amount of him with Louis at this time. A South African of great charm, he had been a lecturer in German at Birmingham though I had not known him then, and was to become Professor of German at Oxford. Nor do I remember the sojourn in the bar of the Ritz before going on to the register office that Louis mentions, with our drinking mint juleps and seeing Jim Mollison 'silent and sullen in a corner'. Since Louis was writing only a year or so after the event he is more likely to be right than I. What I recall is the ceremony itself and the happenings immediately after. It took place at the register office in I think Bloomsbury Square. When the registrar, who was a lady, invited the best man to produce the ring, Reggie came in with: 'Is the ring obligatory?' The registrar, taken aback, said: 'Well, not obligatory precisely but certainly customary.' 'In that case,' Reggie said, 'we'll dispense with it.'

From Bloomsbury Square we went to Wardour Street, for lunch at Chez Victor. We ate in the upper room and were looked at askance by the waiters, for it was well after two when we arrived and the restaurant was empty long before we had finished our meal. Then, as I remember, we sang, though what we sang I have long forgotten. Before the week was out, Reggie and Olivia were on the train crossing Europe to Bucharest, and before the end of the year Louis was crossing the Atlantic on his way to Cornell University.

A few evenings later, I was invited to a dinner party at Margaret Gardiner's. Rose Macaulay was there, and of the other guests I remember a refugee Czech cartoonist and a Russian who was said to be very high up in official circles in Moscow. None of us left until the late news. After the first item, the radio was switched off. We were gloomily silent, for there seemed nothing to say, until the Russian, as if he suddenly felt his knowledge of English was perhaps not good enough to permit him to understand, asked: 'What did the man say?' Someone told him that Stalin had signed a pact with Hitler.

The party broke up immediately after and Rose Macaulay drove me back to Regent Square. I think neither of us spoke a word, but when I got out of the car Rose said: 'Good night, Mr Allen, and may God help us all.'

I did not want to go in and turned and walked to Bernard Street to get next morning's *Daily Worker*, which was sold outside the underground station. A few passengers from the last train were still trickling out and the vendor, a pleasant young man with a public school accent, was still on duty. When he saw me he said as usual: 'Tomorrow's *Worker*, comrade?' I handed him my penny and took the paper. From the front-page headline, it was plain the *Worker* knew nothing. 'Heard the news?' I asked unkindly. 'What news, comrade?' he said. I told him. He was silent for a few moments and then he said, very fiercely: 'I'll never believe it; never.' But I didn't see him selling the *Worker* outside Russell Square underground station again.

The day before war was declared I spent some hours filling sandbags in Brunswick Square and the evening with a friend with whom I talked well into the night. It was as though we were afraid to sleep lest we missed something. Ostensibly, we were trying to decide what next we should do, for we had suddenly realised that we were privileged and could still, though it wouldn't continue more than a week or two, to some extent dispose of our destinies, since university graduates could still be directly commissioned into the Army on the recommendation of their university. Should we, we debated, avail ourselves of the privilege? My friend, who was a lawyer I had come to know through FIL., decided he would go down to Brasenose first thing Monday morning and get college backing. His decision cleared my mind wonderfully. 'Damn it,' I said, 'I'll take my chance. I'll write another novel first, and then they can do what they like with me.'

Next day, having heard Chamberlain's broadcast and the air-raid warning that followed, I settled down to plan my new novel. It was the poorest I have written, partly because it was written in a hurry almost as an exercise in will-power, partly and more importantly because, as I realised when I read it in print, it was written to formula. But I was pleased enough with the progress I had made that afternoon and at about half past six went for a stroll or perhaps to visit a local café. At the corner of Hunter Street and Tavistock Street, a soldier was hanging about in a shop doorway, as though at a loose end or waiting for a girl. That was unremarkable enough, for there was a barracks just round the corner. I crossed the road and the soldier stepped out of the doorway and said, with a smile of knowing mischief, 'Hallo'. I was nonplussed; I knew the smile, but did not think I knew anyone in the Army, and in any case the private soldier's uniform reduced all who wore it to cyphers. When it dawned on me who it was I could not hide my astonishment and said: 'Good Lord, how long have *you* been in the Army?' 'Oh, I've been in the Territorials for over a year.' It was Goronwy Rees, assistant editor of the *Spectator* and Fellow of All Souls, whom I knew from FIL. I had not imagined him in the context of the Army.

The war was soon being called the phoney war. The period of waiting, of hopelessness and expectancy, went on. Nothing dramatic happened. All the same, there were changes. Michael Joseph went back to the Army. He was, I suppose, forty or so, in Army terms an old man, and he was doubtless called Dad. I saw him two or three days before he went back. He was looking forward to it. He gave me some advice. 'Don't,' he said, 'if you can possibly help it, find yourself in the PBI.' His war, I'm afraid, was disappointing. In the first war, he had been in machine guns and he was sent off to supervise machine-gun training, only to find the weapon had changed almost out of recognition. His health was not good, and before the war was half through he was invalided out. My agent David Higham, who had been a major in the early Twenties, also went back, and though he ended as a lieutenant-colonel, according to himself he did not find the war years much more satisfying personally than Michael did.

What I was immediately aware of was that the sources of my income were drying up. Publishers, editors, film producers were drawing back from enterprises and fresh commitments. In a way, even the Armed Services were doing so. You couldn't walk into a recruiting office and join up; you were told to wait until your age-group was called. And when, after two or three months, air raids had not begun and showed no signs of beginning, you were no longer wanted in the Civil Defence services; Henry Green has a revealing account in *Caught* of how paid personnel in the fire service and ARP were popularly regarded at this time.

A month or so after war broke out, my second novel, *Blind Man's Ditch*, was published. For what it was worth, it was 'recommended' by the Book Society. It was a great advance on my first, and in the New Year of 1941 all copies were destroyed in the air raid which wiped out the publishers' warehouses. Almost the only satisfaction I had from its publication was the ironic one of reading a glowing review of it in, of all places, the *British Weekly*, which was to Methodism what the *Church Times* is to Anglicanism. For my Uncle George, it carried an authority second only to the epistles of St. Paul.

The flow of reading from MGM dwindled from month to month, and I found I had little to do except write my novel. Things were very tight, though I had eased them a little by moving into an unfurnished flat near Belsize Park which I shared with my lawyer friend. My fortunes sank to their nadir at Christmas, 1939. I had planned to go back to Birmingham and was counting on a cheque arriving from MGM to enable me to make the journey. It had not come by the morning of Christmas Eve, and I did not have enough money for my fare to Birmingham. But I had a telephone still and I began the weary business of telephoning friends whom I hoped might lend me a pound or two. The first I called was a reporter on a Fleet Street news agency. When he heard my voice he said: 'I was just going to ring you and tell you my news. I got the sack yesterday.' His wife was expecting a baby. All I could do was commiserate and ring off. There was no reply from Margaret Gardiner's number, and I realised that people who were going away for Christmas had already done so. I saw that I'd probably not be able to go to Birmingham but I still had to get hold of a pound or two to tide me over the three or four days that must pass now before my cheque came from MGM.

I telephoned Robert Goodyear, who would also be waiting for a cheque but would, I knew, lend me ten shillings if he had it. He was going home to Luton, was catching the next train and had just enough money for a single fare. At this I gave up. In its way, my plight was suddenly funny, and I became philosophical and perhaps a little hysterical. If I went along to the workhouse, would they let me in? With my Christmas dinner perhaps they'd give me a pint of beer and an ounce of shag. Could Robert recommend a good local spike? How long we went on like this I do not know, but we were suddenly interrupted by a voice, female, precise, unmistakably foreign. She begged our pardons, but our lines must be crossed. She was trying to get a number on the Primrose exchange and kept getting our conversation, which, we must pardon her, she could not help overhearing. Would I telephone her in about ten minutes, perhaps? She gave me her number and rang off.

I was considerably embarrassed. Should I, I asked Robert, take her at her word? 'Of course,' said Robert. I did so and half an hour later was walking over to Swiss Cottage. I spent what money I had in buying flowers for her. I had no clue at all as to who she might be. The address she gave me proved to be a doctor's house, and she was his housekeeper. She showed me into the kitchen. In a chair against the wall sat a nervously-smiling middle-aged man with a wispy moustache. He said very little, for he obviously could speak very little English. He was, she explained, her fiancé, a Czech lawyer. Over coffee we made strained conversation. She lent me ten pounds against a post-dated cheque. That was the only time I saw her, for embarrassed pride prevented me from getting in touch with her. I regret this, for I shall always be grateful to her. But there are situations which an Anglo-Saxon upbringing does not teach you to cope with.

In the New Year John Hampson's elder sister Mona invited me to stay with her for a few weeks. Her husband, who was an automobile engineer, was in the Army, and Mona was living alone in a small country house on the Derbyshire side of Staffordshire. She was a forthright, formidable, entertaining woman, at once disconcertingly like and disconcertingly unlike John. I enjoyed my stay with her and when I left her after six weeks my novel was finished.

Michael Joseph's gave me the advance on royalties due on publication, but I realised one night that I was in an impossible position. I was walking back after midnight from a party of Decibel's in Chelsea. It was very cold and snowing. Chelsea is ill-served by tube-trains, buses seemed to have disappeared, and I could not afford a taxi. As I trudged towards Belsize Park my spirits sank lower and lower. Somehow I had to exist until July at least, which I had worked out was the earliest I could expect to be called up. After that, I would be all right, for His Majesty would feed and clothe me and give me pocket money. But I had to survive until then, for four months, and I did not see how I could.

I struggled on from one day to another, and days turned into weeks. Action, though seemingly peripheral, had begun. Narvik fell, and Chamberlain with it. The war in France opened up, and, incredibly quickly it seemed, Boulogne fell. The war was now quite uncomfortably close. The day the news broke, I remember, there was an FIL. meeting in the upper room of a restaurant in Great Russell Street. I went along. Attendance was meagre, for the topic announced for the evening had become inconceivably academic. The speaker, who was Tom Wintringham, offered to talk on something else, on how he saw the war developing now. That was, indeed, the only thing in the minds of any of us. Wintringham was one of the romantic figures of the Thirties. From the upper middle-class, in my memory he is tall, ruddy, mostly bald, and with a blond moustache. He had fought with the International Brigade and within a few weeks of the time I write about was teaching guerilla warfare at Osterley. How seriously he himself took his discourse I have no means of knowing; I suspect he was temporarily intoxicated by the visions his romantic imagination conjured up. For the best part of an hour he raised the war to the level of a heroic boy's book, and though what he said may not survive scrutiny now, I must admit I was greatly heartened, which was what mattered. The prospect as he unfolded it had the simplicity and bold relief of an early Soviet film. The Germans would land; the royal family and the government would flee to Canada, to conduct a war from there; but virtually the workers would be left to fight alone. There would be Quislings from the middle classes, but it would become truly a *people's* war, and he painted a splendid picture of the boiler-makers of the Tyne improvising armoured trains which would travel ceaselessly up and down the railway systems of Britain firing shells at the enemy. Of the end there was, of course, no question. Working-class solidarity, improvisation and reservoirs of technical skill and invention would prevail.

Next evening or the evening after that, something happened that seemed like a small miracle. The fog was as dense as I have ever known it, when my bell was rung. It was my brother Frank, I had no idea he was in London, and he must almost literally have felt his way to my flat from Belsize Park tube station. Did I want a job? he asked me. He had recently been appointed chief chemist and metallurgist at a new light-alloys foundry in the West Country for the production of aircraft parts. He described the job, which seemed within my competence. It fell into a category recognised by the Ministry of Labour and National Service as 'technical assistant (information)' and the wage would be four pounds a week. If it interested me, I could start any time I liked. If it interested me indeed! I started on the following Monday.

VII

What immediately appealed to me in my new job was the fact that I was earning £4 a week. The job itself I thought of as simply a stopgap which would see me through in something like comfort until I found myself in one of the services. It took me some time fully to realise that the job put me automatically in a reserved occupation and that I couldn't join up even if I wanted to, at least not without what was tantamount to a special dispensation.

I found my first few days at the factory, which was on the Cotswolds side of Bristol, exciting; the work was new to me and so were the people, and I particularly liked the foundry and the men who worked in it. Then, quite suddenly, I had the strangest sense of *déjà vu*. I knew as a positive fact that, though I had been brought up among legends and stories of factories, I had never worked in one or for that matter been inside a foundry. Then it dawned on me: I was living within the scenes of my own novels. This I found disconcerting and uncomfortable, even though it made me realise how accurately I had rendered the imagined scenes of factory life in my novels. It made me realise, too, how much one unconsciously absorbs of the life that lies just beyond the perimeter of one's own experience. I might not be able to trace my forbears more than two or three generations back, but all of them and all the people round them had either worked in or been intimately connected with factories. In a sense, a factory was my second home; I was, indeed, coming home.

For all that, I felt very much a fish out of water, for life was lived by values utterly different from those I was used to. A small instance. Because it was the one nearest to the laboratory where I had my room, I used the lavatory just off the foundry. Within a week, it was politely intimated to me, not by a foundryman, that I shouldn't use the foundrymen's lavatory: they would think I was spying on them, had been planted by the management; I was Staff, a white-collar worker, and the likes of me were expected to use the toilets – and the word was horribly appropriate – at the front of the factory, where the administrative offices were.

My old way of life went on in an attenuated form. I don't think I had been in my job much more than a week when I had a telegram from MacNeice saying he'd be in Bristol next day and would I meet him at Broadcasting House, Whiteladies Road? This completely surprised me, for I thought Louis was still in the United States. I got time off and went into Bristol to see him. He told me he had intended to return and join the Navy but that he'd been struck down with peritonitis while still at Cornell and on his recovery had been recruited into the British Embassy at Washington. Then someone told him that John Hampson had been conscripted and was in the Army. 'When I heard they'd called up old Hampson,' Louis said, 'I knew I had to come back.' He was found medically unfit for military service and had joined the Features Department of the BBC.

He had come to Bristol to recruit me for a team of writers for a series of programmes called 'The Stones Cry Out' or, unofficially, 'Shrieking Stones'. Sometime later, I realised that my taking a job in Bristol had coincided with the beginning of a new stage in the war. 'Shrieking Stones' were programmes, broadcast only in the World Service, about famous or historic buildings destroyed in the Nazi bombing raids which were just beginning. I was deputed to write on the historic buildings of Bristol as they were destroyed one by one. In the course of the next year or so, I suppose I must have written some half a dozen scripts. For me, they were a new introduction to broadcasting, and I discovered they were also a way of getting back to London for a day or two. The BBC would pay my fare, and I found one could always get a bed as a fire-watcher at Bedford College, which was the wartime headquarters of the BBC Features, and not only get a bed but two shillings and sixpence for one's breakfast. There came the day, though, and sooner than one had thought possible, when the programmes had to be dropped. They were essentially propaganda, and as soon as the RAF and the American Air Force were bombing famous and historic buildings in Germany, their propaganda value was nil.

But this is looking ahead. At the beginning of September, I had a letter from the novelist L. H. Myers inviting me to spend a weekend with him at his temporary home at Marlow. I had been in correspondence with him since May, when his novel *The Pool of Vishnu* was published. He had sent me a copy at Margaret Gardiner's instigation.

I had greatly admired it and had written and told him so. In normal times, I doubt whether I would ever have met him, for he lived and moved in circles utterly remote from mine. I had read nothing of his before *The Pool of Vishnu* and all I knew of him was that he was the son of F. W. H. Myers, the late-Victorian philosopher, minor poet and pioneer in psychical research. I was to learn something of his life from conversations with him and from the fragment of an abortive autobiography he lent me. He had been at Eton and Cambridge and had lived, except for a year or two as a temporary civil servant in the first war, a life of what according to himself was idleness. He had travelled in America, where he had met the lady whom he married; she was the daughter of a railroad millionaire. As a young man, he had been a balloonist and a racing motorist at Brooklands. He had lived in that corner of the great world, as it is called, where society and the arts come together. He told me he dined with Churchill once a year. He had been a protégé of Lady Ottoline Morrell at Garsington and his friends were people like the Sitwells, Aldous Huxley and Oswald Mosley. But the war did strange things to people: many, confusedly and irrationally, thought themselves to blame for it and to many more, perhaps, the very fact of its happening pointed to a defect in themselves. It is not by accident that war is a great time for religious revival. Leo Myers, as I was to learn a few years later from L. P. Hartley, it caused to write to all his friends telling them that, though he loved them dearly and wished them well, he did not wish to see them ever again.

With the outbreak of war, then, Myers broke with his class in a way that was fairly decisive. He called himself a Communist, though I doubt whether he was ever a member of the Party or a Marxist in any strict sense. He seemed to me much more an anarchist of the Shelleyan kind. It was an article of faith with him that men were naturally good, and so he believed in the perfectibility of man, whom he saw as everywhere fettered in Blake's 'mind-forged manacles'. The churches and conventional religion were hateful to him; he believed they came between man and God and sundered man from man because they destroyed the sense of community that was natural to man. Myers knew this intuitively.

Myers was the only man I have ever met who claimed to have a mystical experience. It seems characteristic of him that it should have occurred in an expensive hotel in Chicago. He wrote a novel, *Strange Glory*, about it or something like it. The man to whom it happens, characteristically has made and lost four fortunes before becoming a hermit; he sums up the revelation as follows:

> 'For the first time in my life I saw Man through the eyes of God. I saw the exquisite beauty that springs – and can only spring – from the relation between creature and Creator. To Man is given the privilege of worship – that I have known and felt for a long time. But tonight I saw Man as he stands in the vision of compassionate God. Raised very little above the beasts of the field, feeble in mind, sickly in body, oppressed by circumstances; blackly and inescapably overshadowed by old age, disease and death, Man yet *struggles hard*. Consider the standards which he sets himself – his ideals of courage, of generosity, of endurance! Consider not only Man's disinterested devotion to truth, but his passion for nobility, his restless search after greatness! Consider that unconquerable fastidiousness which forces him to toil, always to toil, in order to bring the poor fleshbound, witless creature that he is a little nearer to what he wishes to be.'

I imagine the war was tolerable to Myers only if it could be seen as in some sense Armageddon, the final battle which would end in the destruction of the established order, the death of the old gang. And I think he felt the need for disciples or at least the need to be assured that someone, somewhere, was reading him with sympathy. *The Pool of Vishnu* seemed to me a work of great wisdom, and I wrote him a long, enthusiastic letter along with copies of my own two novels. *The Pool of Vishnu* is the final novel in a sequence called *The Near and the Far*, which, taken altogether, is a remarkable work, a *tour-de-force*, for the action is set in the India of the sixteenth century, the India of Akbar. In fact, Ceylon was the nearest Myers himself ever got to India, but his interest was in India only as the place that by historical accident became the meeting place of Christianity, Hinduism, Buddhism and Islam, and as the scene of ossified civilisations and vigorous new life existing side by side. In that India of Akbar, Myers found in microcosm all the illusions that according to the passage from Sir Francis Bacon which stands as the epigraph to the work 'intercept and corrupt the light of nature' and beset the human mind. We are shown the young Prince Jali being subjected to the influence in turn of all possible illusions, embodied sometimes in characters and sometimes in the organisation of society itself. These illusions are revealed to Jali in their true shape and colours by the Guru, who functions as a sort of psychoanalyst on the grand scale and is the spokesman of Myers's beliefs ('You see, for one thing,' the Guru said,

'I believe in the essential goodness of human nature.').

The Near and the Far still seems to me an absorbing novel of ideas. The ideas are of the utmost importance and admirably expressed, but one cannot overcome the feeling that they were there before the characters, that the characters, indeed, scarcely have life apart from the ideas they express; and though Myers wrote excellently in a conventional sense, his language is never quite adequate to the beauty and profundity of the thought he wishes to convey. Everything is a little too faint. This is especially true of *The Pool of Vishnu*. There, as he says in his preface: 'I have made little attempt to conceal my preoccupations' – or, one might add, their immediate sources. One of these, which I failed to recognise at the time, was an intense revulsion against Bloomsbury and all its works and values. His intuitions were his own, but he seemed constantly to be seeking authority for them and to find it he was prepared to ransack philosophy, psychology and anthropology. These appear too nakedly, so that one too often finds oneself translating, as it were, character and discourse back to the original Martin Buber, Freud or Jung.

What I didn't fully appreciate when I first met Myers was how impatient he had become of art. He saw it merely as another of the illusions that 'intercept and corrupt the light of nature.' I was bewildered by his seemingly capricious aesthetic judgements. It was natural enough that his taste in poetry should be rooted in the nineteenth century but it was disturbing to find that the only living poet who seemed to mean anything to him was Herbert Read. I found it difficult not to think that might be connected with the fact that Read was an anarchist. I was unprepared for, indeed astonished and dismayed, by the vehemence and virulence with which he attacked Eliot that first evening I first met him, though he seemed to be on lunching terms with him. Ten years or so before, Eliot had described himself as Catholic in religion, royalist in politics and classicist in literature, and it was Eliot's recent essay, 'The Idea of a Christian Society', that especially aroused Leo's anger. He found the opinions it expressed damnable. For my part, while I had no sympathy with Eliot's religious and political ideas, it was much more important that he was the revolutionary poet he was, and Leo's illiberalism made me anything but easy.

Of the living writers the one he was most enthusiastic about was Simenon, who he said was as good as Balzac. He approved of Orwell, for reasons that were obvious. He praised Henry Green's *Party Going*, which he took to be a satire on the idle rich. He liked C. P. Snow's

Strangers and Brothers, the first and at that time only volume of the sequence of the same name, which had been published, for he found the character of George Passant sympathetic. As I look through the letters I had from him, my relations with Myers seem summed up by the last, written only a few days before he killed himself in 1944. In it, he rebuked me sternly for having written a critical essay on Graham Greene which had appeared in *Penguin New Writing*. I had praised him. Myers reminded me that Graham was a Roman Catholic, which was tantamount to saying that nothing good could be said of him.

He had made his reply to the doctrine of Original Sin in the Guru's answer to Mobarek in *The Pool of Vishnu*:

> 'No!' returned the Guru in a voice that had become stern, 'There is no greatness at your end of the road – only despair. Spirit, which must stream through the individual man, if he is to preserve a sane and living soul, must stream through society as well. Every civilisation, every culture, that has ever existed, has owed its life to this. When the stream tarries the body politic stiffens into a prison-house; forms and institutions become manacles, and the State turns into a monstrous slave-driver. Demoniac forces have taken control. With the leaders there is only a semblance of leadership. The leaders will tell you that they are acting under divine inspiration, or that they are obeying inexorable laws; and always they will dangle before the multitude the vulgar emblems of an impossible glory. But there is death in their hearts. Your priests, too, will pretend to enclose the Spirit in the Churches. But those churches will be empty. Spirit is waiting in the market-place – waiting for the re-awakened re-awakening man!'

That, though *The Pool of Vishnu* is set in the India of the sixteenth century, is how Leo Myers saw the western world in 1940. Society had become so static, so evil, that a clean break with the past had become essential. Again, one quotes the Guru:

> 'The human spirit seems to me to be dragged in two opposite directions. The drag of the Past is always towards repetition, stagnation, and peace – peace of fidelity to tradition, obedience to authority, peace which is really decay. The drag towards anxiety and effort – the effort of constantly rejecting the letter of the law and reasserting the spirit. This involves a constant dying, accompanied by a constant re-birth. It is necessary to have faith – faith in the future.'

In conversation, Myers equated this view with Freud's idea of the struggle between Eros and the death-wish.

Such was the vision I found so moving and so attractive as I worked in my office off the laboratory, above the foundry. I suppose a belief in Leo's utopian ideas had become a necessary compensation for the all-too-aggressively-workaday world I had suddenly found myself immersed in. One Friday evening in early autumn I made the journey from Bristol to Marlow, whither Myers had retired with his invalid wife from their house in Charles Street, Mayfair. It was a beautiful September evening. The other traveller in my compartment had a copy of the *Listener*, which I borrowed from her, for my third novel had just been published and I was watching for reviews. I was delighted to find Edwin Muir reviewed it in that issue. It was not what is called a rave notice but it told me something about the novel and therefore about myself that I hadn't known before. Percipience of this kind is the rarest quality in a review. Muir was by far the best reviewer of new fiction to have written in my time. As a poet, critic and autobiographer, he was a man of great distinction and he died insufficiently recognised. It is a disgrace to British universities that he was never honoured with a Chair. He had no degree, for he left school at fourteen and made his own way in the world. With his wife, it was he who introduced Franz Kafka, whom they translated, to the Anglo-Saxon world. Ten years or more after this review appeared, when I was visiting the British Council in Edinburgh, he invited me over to Newbattle Abbey to talk to his students there. I stayed the night, and we talked for a long time. I have forgotten the details of our conversation, but what remains with me is the impression the beauty of his character made upon me.

I got to Tilecotes, Myers's house, at about half past seven, with no idea of the appearance of the man I was to meet. He proved to be a tall, spare, slightly stooping man with a clipped grey moustache and a bald scalp set in white hair: if one had met him in Cheltenham or Bath he might have seemed a retired Army officer of scholarly tastes. He smiled rarely and was a trifle testy in manner and speech. I was not conscious of any attempt on his part to get to 'know' me; we had been writing to each other weekly for five or six months and he seemed to take me for granted as an old friend who shared his opinions. I was taken aback by the vehemence with which he attacked those he saw as enemies. One was made to realise that those who were not with him he thought of decidedly as against him, which seemed to account for everyone he knew of his own class. I was shocked by the hostility with which he spoke of his father.

We dined alone. What we ate I do not remember but I know it was a very good dinner, with very good wine. There was no sign of war and wartime shortages. I was something of a prig and was not prepared for his eager appreciation of food and drink, a gusto which seemed to contradict both his ascetic appearance and his high thinking. I was amused when, after dinner on this or a later occasion, sitting on a sofa, he produced a small flask of brandy from behind a cushion and poured a drink from it for himself but not for me. This sudden and unconcealed manifestation of greed I found attractive rather than not. It tied in with the horror with which he spoke of the destruction in an air raid of a whisky train near Paddington. I did not know then that he was a director of one of the best and most expensive French restaurants in London.

I found that he had given up writing fiction. He wanted now to write a book in which all the conclusions he had reached about the nature of man and society should be set down unambiguously. At first, he thought he would show he had reached them from the experiences of his life, which meant that he must write an autobiography. He found this did not work; besides, he wanted the book to have as wide a public as possible, for his audience was 're-awakened re-awakening man' and he envisaged writing something like a Penguin 'special'. It was to be an anatomy of existing society, against which he would set the ideal of community. Its title would be *On Living Together*. He had begun it and had drawn on all his wide reading in psychoanalysis and anthropology as well as his own experience of life. But he could not finish it, and the reason, I think, was plain. He knew nothing about ordinary life, life as lived by people who have to work for their living. He had no acquaintance at all with ordinary men and women except as servants or stockbrokers or solicitors or except in the very brief encounters he might have had with fellow drinkers in the saloon bar of the pub where he drank two half-pints of beer each morning, a newly-acquired wartime habit. Even then, he was a poor mixer, a retiring man without small talk of any kind. All this he knew. It seemed that the whole nature of his being and experience made him the last man in the world capable of addressing and appealing to the vast audience he had in mind.

That, I discovered, was where I came in. He suggested that I should collaborate with him. I was from the working class, I worked in a factory, I was in touch with ordinary people; I could, as it were, provide the homely illustrations for his thesis. I found the idea enormously attractive to contemplate, and it was seductive because flattering. It was also wildly impossible. There was a war on, and collaborating in a book which had a professedly revolutionary purpose was scarcely likely to be construed as work furthering the conduct of the war. I think Leo himself realised this almost as soon as I did. Besides, I knew secretly that it was only my present situation that made the proposition so attractive. I knew that if I were free I should be doing other things that attracted me more. I knew that, compared with Leo, I was frivolous. The book, its conception, the driving force behind it, as well as its intellectual content, were all Leo's. The more I thought about it the more it seemed to me that my role in any collaboration with Leo would be to stand on the sidelines and applaud, and I realised that in so close a relationship we would very soon quarrel: what Leo really wanted was a disciple, and though hero-worship came naturally to me, the role of disciple was one I was incapable of sustaining for long.

Nevertheless, we wrote to each other regularly for the next three and a half years and I spent several weekends at Tilecotes. As he wrote it, he sent me *On Living Together* for criticism. I found it vastly exciting, but as I have said, it was never finished. For one thing, the semi-scientific, impersonal approach to his theme bored him: he was not an artist for nothing. And by 1944 I think he was no longer wholly confident that the revolution would come in his time or even that the future belonged to 're-awakened re-awakening man'. I suspect, too, that as the Allied air strength increased and there was still no opening of a second front, the course of the war was a source of constant disillusion to him. His letters became gloomier and gloomier. In one of the last I received, he complained that he was unable to sleep for brooding on the social solecisms he had committed as a young man. It saddened me that such a man should be persecuted in his old age by memories of the minor mistakes of his long-past self: I did not know then that the past and its trivialities haunt one all one's life.

Round about Easter, 1944, a few weeks before the Allies landed in Normandy, he took an extra dose of sleeping tablets and did not wake again.

I went to the West Country with the intention, of course, of writing in what free time I had, and I had in mind a rudimentary idea at least for a new novel. But I found writing very difficult. I could go through the motions but nothing I wrote satisfied me. This was partly because I was finding it difficult to settle down in what for me was an alien atmosphere and partly because I was no longer satisfied with the kind of novel I had written in the past. Anything that did not deal, at least by implication, with the war and the struggle seemed to me irrelevant.

There were increasing demands, too, made on my time, some of which were my own making, rationalisations to excuse my failure to write. The air raids on Bristol began. I was a little way out, in the foothills of the Cotswolds, in what was assumed to be and in fact was a safe area. My reaction to the raids was to move into central Bristol, into a bed-sitting room just off the top of Park Street, where Clifton begins. It was thought very silly of me, reckless or Quixotic. It was none of these. I had a place of my own again and once again in my free time could live my life to my own dictation. In a small way, I began to find myself one of a community, and I discovered that the sense of comradeship that common, ever-present danger induces is real and enhancing. As we went further into autumn, raids increased in frequency. One evening, I remember, coming home from work and within sight of the house where I lived, I was caught, as many thousands of others were, by a solitary Nazi plane — it was just before dusk — which flew over the city on a strafing mission. I don't think anyone was hit, but the machine gun bullets whanged against houses and pitted walls very convincingly. I had the distinct feeling that someone was firing at me personally, with malice aforethought.

Night after night, I found myself spending some hours in the air raid shelter. It was very boring and curiously humiliating: one craved for action. Nothing fell near us but there was considerable damage done within a quarter of a mile on either side. One evening I did what I should have done before, went round to the nearest air raid wardens' post and signed on as a warden. Since, besides the raids aimed specifically at Bristol, the city had an alert, often lasting through the night, and generally a bomb or two as well, whenever there were raids on the Midlands, South Wales and the North West, in the next two years I put in a fair amount of service. I also enlarged my cicle of acquaintants and made some good friends, people of a kind I would not have met in my ordinary life.

All this made it increasingly difficult to concentrate on a novel. Writing BBC propaganda scripts was easy enough. The fact of war changed the nature of everything, made everything provisional. There was no time to stand back, and dispassionateness was out of the question. One wanted, I thought, a new form of notation, a way of setting down the findings of one's immediate experience, different from that offered by the novel. I was haunted by the temporary nature of things.

This brought me back, after getting on for ten years, to poetry. I had realised that the poet's way of writing, which is essentially different from the prose-writer's, was not mine, but I evolved a theory that there was a special place for poetry written by novelists and that such poetry possessed its own virtues. I don't take the theory seriously now, but it gave me valuable support when I needed it. I found evidence for it in the poetry of Hardy, Edward Thomas and Lawrence and, to a less degree, in William Plomer's. This venture into verse did not last more than a couple of years but, in terms of publication at least, was relatively successful, for some poems written at this time appeared in *Life and Letters*, the *Listener* and *Penguin New Writing*.

The first of these, in fact, was the only one with a subject from the immediate present. I was much moved to learn of the death in action of John Mair, who was shot down while piloting his bomber back to base after a raid on Germany, moved because of its sheer incongruity. He was by no means a friend, indeed a remote acquaintance. I do not remember meeting him more than once and even then did not greatly care for him. His cleverness was immediately apparent. He was, one felt, a young man innocently on the make, intent on conquering by his talents, of which he was well aware. The son of G. H. Mair, who had been a well-known *Manchester Guardian* writer and Maire O'Neill, the famous Abbey Theatre actress, he was a year or two younger than I. In some sense, I suppose, I had thought of him as a rival. He had reviewed novels – one of mine once and not very favourably – for the *New Statesman* and published a novel. He was a quite considerable wit and, I thought, a poseur. Whatever one meant by 'literary man', it seemed to me, it certainly took in John Mair, and I saw him as in a recognisable tradition of Engish writers which included, conspicuously, Oscar Wilde and Cyril Connolly and perhaps Saki.

It seemed inconceivable that such a man could have perished in the cockpit of a flaming bomber as it plunged into the North Sea. His death obsessed me as I patrolled my alloted area of Clifton during the blitz on Bristol and as, next evening, from the top of Brandon Hill, I watched the German bombers swooping to attack Bath a dozen miles away. As I watched, I was thinking of John and also appreciating the elegant geometry of the searchlights as they swung across the sky in pursuit of German planes. In the days that followed I wrote my poem, and Mair's death, the destruction, as it appeared, of Bath and impressions of dockers and their families in a shelter near Bristol Cathedral all came into it. A month or two later, it appeared in *Life and Letters*. I cannot pretend it is a very good poem. The 'poetic' patches are embarrassing and the best lines, I am now conscious though I wasn't when I wrote it, are imitations and in one or two instances plagiarisms of Auden and Alun Lewis, whose *Raiders' Dawn* I was reading at the time. But it is partly redeemed, I hope, by an honest documentary, reportorial quality.

And something else happened at this time that cut across the writing of novels. I became a critic. John Lehmann, whom I had known in London, invited me to contribute to a regular feature in *Penguin New Writing* called 'Books and War', which I wrote in rotation with Stephen Spender. My first article was on Flaubert and *L'Éducation sentimentale*, and I also wrote what I believe were the first critical appreciations of Graham Greene, Henry Green and V. S. Pritchett. These appearances in *Penguin New Writing* were altogether more important than I realised at the time, since, for better or worse, they determined my way of life after the war, which was to be that of critic and literary historian rather than that of the novelist I had set out to be. It was on the strength of these articles that I received my first regular reviewing assignment when C. V. Wedgwood invited me to review novels for *Time & Tide*. Certainly, as I still discover, *Penguin New Writing*, which was *the* literary magazine of the war years, brought me a far wider public and a greater degree of fame than ever my novels had done.

The appearance of my article on Henry Green led to my meeting the author, who had been one of the young Midland writers I had talked about on BBC Midland Region in 1933, an occasion seminal for me since it proved to be my introduction to the world of letters. Then, I talked about *Living*, his second novel, which was published in 1929. I regarded it with dazzled admiration. Among other things, it seemed a rough equivalent in fiction to Auden's poetry. I knew nothing about Green at the time and assumed, on the strength of the novel's setting and subject-matter, that he came from the working class and had left-wing sympathies. *Living* seemed to me the conspicuous and most brilliantly successful English example of what we called the proletarian novel. I was, of course, dead wrong.

Living is set in Bordesley, the ancient heart of Birmingham and throughout its history an exclusively working-class district. The characters of the novel for the most part are moulders and labourers working in a local foundry. The theme was one that was to become familiar, the displacement of labour following reorganisation and rationalisation, which is linked with a young girl's infatuation with a young man who, scared of her overwhelming desire for marriage and children, finally and comically deserts her. The story is told mainly in very short episodes rather in the manner of a film, the author cutting from character to character, from scene to contrasted scene, taking in workers, members of management and the managing director and his family. The besetting sin of novels of industrial working-class life has always been an overemphatic naturalism, with a consequent impression of human submergence in bleakness and greyness. This is not so of *Living*. The title itself is defiant, and Green captures as never before or since what can only be called the poetry of working-class life.

That for me was the great enchanting quality of the novel. It showed me the Birmingham I knew caught from a totally unexpected angle, so that the rendering of what seem almost archetypical Birmingham scenes such as the football league match at St Andrews, the Whitsun bank-holiday outing to the Lickey Hills, the flocks of racing pigeons for ever circling over the drab streets, remain extremely fresh and vivid, as though seen and set down for the first time. 'New things,' as Johnson said of Pope's poetry, 'are made familiar, and familiar things are made new.' I found the prose in which all this is expressed utterly fascinating; bare, repetitive, angular, at first sight deliberately clumsy; the articles, 'the' and 'a' almost entirely suppressed, as are the relative pronouns. It was an unparalleled medium for transmitting the blackness and din of the foundry but it was also capable of expressing the genuinely lyrical, as in the episode in which the young Welshman, who has become a father a few hours earlier, sings in Welsh against the foundry's clamour. It seemed to me a prose based upon the patterns of Anglo-Saxon prose, and when I knew more about Green and learnt that he had read English at Oxford I assumed he had been influenced by it. Whether he was I do not know, for, foolishly, I never asked him.

After *Living*, I read his first novel, *Blindness*. I did not like it nearly so well. It was much more conventional, there were no experiments with prose. The action is set in a public school called Note, which I realised was Eton. Later, I saw that the name-change and the form of the new name were typical of Green's sense of humour. What I did not know was that Green had written the novel while still at Eton. If I had known that, I would, I hope, have seen it very differently, as an exercise in the imagination remarkable in one so young, for the subject is precisely blindness; an Eton boy is blinded by a stone flung at him and has to come to terms with his new condition.

We had to wait for Green's third novel, *Party Going*, until 1939. By then, I had learned more about him from Hampson. Far from being working-class he had aristocratic connections and his father was managing director of a foundry in Birmingham similar to that described in *Living*. Green had himself worked there on the shop-floor after coming down from Oxford. I knew too that Green was a pseudonym and that his real name was Yorke, Henry Vincent Yorke.

Hampson and I disagreed over *Party Going*. We both found it disconcerting, and John, who admired enormously both of the earlier books, disapproved of it entirely. I was enchanted by it and rejoiced when John confessed to me that Morgan Forster thought well of it. What was disconcerting was the utter difference in subject and setting from *Living*. In *Party Going*, we are in a world akin to that of Evelyn Waugh, whom Henry knew and, I gathered from his conversation, did not much like, though it is only fair to say that Waugh, on the evidence of Sykes's biography, admired Green above all other living English novelists. A party of 'bright young people' are going to France as the guests of an absurdly rich young man; they meet at Victoria, fog holds up their train, and they are marooned in the upper rooms of the station hotel while hordes of fog-bound commuters indulge in community-singing on the platforms below and threaten as their numbers increase to burst into and swamp the hotel. That, so far as plot goes, is *Party Going*. It is irradiated by what, for want of a better word, one is tempted to call a mad poetry. There is, for instance, the episode of the spinster-aunt at whose feet a dead pigeon falls. She takes it to the ladies' lavatory, washes it and makes it up into a brown-paper parcel. The repercussions of the incident sound and resound through the novel. It disturbs the party and it disturbs the reader too. While the episode is funny in itself, it is more than that; it cannot be paraphrased or its meaning neatly summarised. *Party Going* established Green, or Yorke, as perhaps I should call him, as one of the very few successful symbolists in the English novel; and like *Living* and indeed all his novels, it is both gay and sad.

When Yorke wrote to me suggesting we should meet he had ceased, temporarily, being a production engineer in the family business in Birmingham, which made beer-engines and bathroom fittings, and was serving in the Auxiliary Fire Service in central London. There is a swipe at him in this capacity in the first paragraph of what I think is the second volume of Waugh's *Sword of Honour* trilogy. I remember that in his letter Henry promised, if there should be a blitz when I met him in London, he'd take me out on his fire tender. I had to reply that, having been through blitzes on Bristol, dashing round on fire engines in air raids wasn't my idea of fun.

A few weeks later, I met him at his fire station, which proved to be a garage in Davies Street, just off Oxford Street. We spent the afternoon in the canteen, drinking tea. He had warned me on no account to divulge to his mates that he was a novelist. He was a tall, film-starishly handsome man not unlike, I thought, Eliot as he appears in photographs of the 1924 period; he laughed a good deal, and the laughter struck me as slightly hysterical. He told me funny stories that seemed always in character, to be his and no one else's. On this occasion, there was one about Antony Eden, to whom, I think, his wife was related. When Eden had gone to Russia in 1935, he had been the first British cabinet minister to visit the Soviet Union officially since 1917. Waiting to change trains at the Polish-Soviet frontier, he was intrigued by the spectacle of a crate of bananas being transferred from the Polish to the Russian train. A night or two later, at the inevitable banquet Stalin gave for him in the Kremlin, two stalwart flunkeys ceremoniously bore into the chamber what evidently was the same crate of bananas; whereupon the oldest old Bolshevik present, a very old man indeed, clapped his hands with glee and piped: 'Goody goody! The first bananas I've seen since the Revolution!'

And I recall a story he told my wife and myself when he came to dinner with us in Birmingham after the end of the war in Europe. He had discovered that my wife worked at a hospital specialising in industrial accidents and financed largely by Birmingham industrialists. One of the doctors, it came out, was the daughter of an executive in Henry's firm. One day, a Birmingham business man walked into the hospital and asked her whether she'd mind looking him over, since he felt a bit under the weather. She did so and found nothing wrong with him. He then said his wife was also a bit under the weather. She was waiting for him outside, in the car. Would the doctor care to come down and look at her? She did – and found in the car the corpse of a woman four days dead.

On this first meeting, when his shift ended, we walked back to his temporary living quarters. His wife and small son were evacuated, and he was camping in a borrowed house. There was no staff. We came to an enormous house in, I think, Rutland Gate. We sat in a vast drawing room most of whose furniture was shrouded in dust sheets. It was, he explained, Sir Austen Chamberlain's town house. He produced a bottle of gin, a jug of water and glasses and we drank gin-and-water. He was very proud of being in the Auxiliary Fire Service and hated it when it was confused with the London Fire Brigade. But now he was trying to get permission to return to industry and his foundry, where he was always referred to as 'young Mister Henry'. All his attempts were being blocked by the Home Secretary, Herbert Morrison, against whom he seemed to have a bitter grudge.

We went out to dinner at a restaurant in Knightsbridge and then went back to Sir Austen's and resumed our gin-and-water. After that meeting, I generally saw Henry when I was in London. His family came back from the country and they moved into a house in Belgravia. He was always very funny and always both gay and sad, like his novels. I don't recall his talking about any book except Doughty's *Arabia Deserta*, about which he was very enthusiastic. He did not seem much interested in other writers, though I remember he assured me I would not like Evelyn Waugh. Regardless of anyone else and of current taste, he ploughed his own furrow. He wrote his novels in his office in the lunch-hour of his Birmingham factory. Some years later, I ran into an old University friend, who proved to be Henry's solicitor. He had been with Henry to the United States, where in the immediate post-war years his novels were briefly but intensely fashionable. He refused, according to my friend, to allow them to be reprinted, for he planned to live in his old age on the royalties from his paperback editions. It is pleasant to see, at the time of writing, that some half a dozen of the novels are now in paperback and that he is highly regarded again, by the young especially.

He was, I gathered, a great man for night clubs, and this, I felt, went with what seemed to me an underlying melancholy. There was the famous line, under 'Recreations', in his potted biography in *Who's Who*: 'Romancing over the bottle, to a good band'. This was a side of him I never saw, but I do not doubt its existence. He might have cried with Swift *'Vive la bagatelle!'* for small things often absorbed him. He described eagerly how he taught his cat to retrieve, and I remember the pride with which he put the animal through her unnatural paces in the drawing room of his house in Trevor Place, time and again making her bring back to him a ball of paper he had thrown into the corner of the room. It must have been at much the same time that he bought a cage of white mice at Harrods for the delectation of his small son and found that he himself was spending endless hours watching them as they ran up and down the little steps that led from one level to another. The absorption did not last long; the mice multiplied so rapidly that he was forced in self-defence to return them to Harrods.

He was a very different man from the one I had ten years before imagined the author of *Living* to be. I don't remember ever talking about politics with him but I sensed his attitude to them was of sceptical amusement. Where the working classes were concerned the impression he gave was that he found them comic rather than not. But then I think he found most people comic. He assured me solemnly that his stock among his employees had risen astonishingly after he was seen escorting a Soviet trade delegation round the foundry and machine shop. He pretended he would die a poor man, ruined by the excesses of the welfare state. I took this to be an exercise in the whimsical akin to his story, which he told me with some pride, that his father held the record for bringing in the smallest amount of money ever realised in a BBC 'The Week's Good Cause' appeal – something less than a pound in response to a broadcast for the restoration of, I think, Tewkesbury parish church.

On one visit to London he invited me to lunch at the Ritz, which, as the last novels show, was a favourite place of his. I was one of a party and I found myself sitting next to a girl of perhaps seventeen. She told me she worked in the War Office. Idly, I asked her what she did there. She told me with some frigidity that she was not allowed to divulge her work to anyone. It was the end of our conversation, but I still suspect she was in the typing pool. What mainly impressed me at this lunch was that, wartime or not, the lives of the wealthy had not changed much.

During the last year of the war I saw Henry two or three times in Birmingham and perhaps two or three times in London after that. He was always funny and always, it seemed to me, almost manic. I remember how excited he was by the Moscow Dynamos in their game against Chelsea in 1945 or 1946. No one could have written his novels but he, and they were unpredictable from novel to novel, except for being surprisingly and originally beautiful, like *Loving*, that fairy story of wartime life set in a castle in neutral Ireland staffed mainly by English servants. There are magical scenes, as of the two young housemaids waltzing among the dustsheet-shrouded furniture in the deserted ballroom:

> They were wheeling wheeling in each other's arms heedless at the far end where they had drawn up one of the white blinds. Above from a rather low ceiling five great chandeliers swept one after the

other almost to the waxed parquet floor reflecting in their hundred thousand drops the single sparkle of distant day, again and again red panelled walls, and two girls, minute in purple, dancing multiplied to eternity in those trembling pears of glass.

Again, as so often, there are the birds, in this instance the peacocks and doves whose presence and display irradiate the novel, at the centre of which is the butler Raunce, an Englishman, glad and guilty because he is out of the war, out of the blitz, out of danger. He seems at first no more than a petty fiddler, then a hypocrite, then a lecher; but as facet after facet of him revolves before us we realise that he is more complex than our preconceived notions have allowed for and exists completely in the round, so that disconcertingly he takes us by surprise as from time to time people do in life.

I am not sure that *Loving* is my favourite novel of Green's, but it is the one in which all his talents come together. After it, there was a kind of fissure. In *Back* and *Concluding*, the novels that followed, there was a concentration on the poetry of the visual to the virtual exclusion of everything else, so that they seem to be literary equivalents of French Impressionist paintings of ballet scenes. In the last novels, *Nothing* and *Doting*, this visual poetry disappears almost entirely and Green relies solely on his uncannily accurate ear for speech. They are wonderfully entertaining, these novels of upper-class life in London in the first years after the war, but all the same something has been lost.

I think his last years must have been sad. He became very deaf and was a sick man. He retired prematurely from business, and in vain one waited for a new novel from him. The last time I saw him was at a soirée at the Royal Society of Literature. He was sitting alone and apart, and few people knew who he was. I talked to him a little, though whether he heard what I said I had no idea. He was still gay, ruefully so.

From one point of view, Green was a variant of the perennial figure the eccentric Englishman, who almost by definition is upper class. But that is the least important thing about him. He was obviously not a great novelist but he was as original a one as anyone of our time. In a way, he was the purest: he seemed to owe nothing to anybody. His vision, at once poetic and comic, was his own, and for me at any rate the novels it inspired have been a never-failing delight.

These war years possessed a singularly lunatic quality; the adjective indicates a despair of being able to find any more precise definition. At the time, I thought the feeling was personal to me and bound up with my civilian status and my having to live outside my normal condition. I now believe that the feeling was general and shared by men in the services and civilians alike, for quite the most accurate renderings of the quality of British life during the war are to be found in Waugh's *Sword of Honour* trilogy and Julian Maclaren-Ross's collection of short stories *The Stuff to Give the Troops*.

One or two personal experiences will pinpoint what I mean. It does not seem to me remarkable that I was once blown off my chair in an air raid while manning a telephone in the wardens' post: it does seem to me remarkable, even extraordinary, that in something called Unarmed Combat I should have learned to kill people. A length of cheese wire, I learnt, was a very useful thing to have: you crept up behind your enemy, flung it round his neck, twisted it and pulled on both ends as hard as you could. Whether I successfully mastered what I was taught I shall never know for practical examination, as it were, was ruled out; but though I had some scepticism, I took it seriously enough. I thought it was quite within the bounds of possibility that one day I should have to use the cheese wire. In the same way, it is almost incredible now that I once possessed a dagger, a terrifying lethal-looking weapon about eight inches long and with a very sharp point. I knew the precise spots of the body into which it could be most efficaciously driven. My friend the instrument maker at the foundry made it for me lovingly from an old file. My request that he should run me up a dagger seemed entirely reasonable to both of us. It was not until some years later that it struck me it was not something one should have in a house in which there were small children.

We were all, of course, suffering from wartime hysteria, though the threats seemed and were real enough. One was conscious of the hysteria and of the element of play-acting. I recall a Civil Defence exercise I took part in. We had to imagine that a shop in the Queen's Road had been hit by a bomb and behave accordingly. The chief warden spurred us on with cries of 'The flames are leaping up, the flames are leaping up!' He waved his walking stick like an English general in the Crimean War; he had worked himself up into a fine lather of excitement. It was difficult to remember that he was a highly civilised stockbroker, an *aficionado* of advanced music and modern painting, with the bearing of a particularly keen prep-school master. There was the constant gap between one's idea of oneself and the world one found oneself in. It was only by a conscious commitment to fantasy that one could reconcile oneself with the lunacy in which one lived and to which, in a sense, one was pledged.

Humour was everything, and I can see that, knowingly or not, I sought out situations where humour could operate. I found them in the warden's post. By that, I do not mean that everybody spent his time making jokes or looking on the bright side or seeing, as we say, the funny side of things. I mean, indeed, something rather the reverse of that and much more serious, something more akin to what is called gallows humour. Perhaps it was pure luck that I found it. We were certainly lucky in the two 'paid' wardens who were the backbone of the post. Both were ex-service men, old sweats. One had been a sergeant in the Indian Army; the other, who lived in a boat on the Avon, had been a gun-layer in the Royal Navy in the first war. They were, one felt, professionals in an amateur war who submitted with good grace to taking orders from amateurs. I remember being instructed by the ex-sergeant when on patrol with him one night in a raid. We were making our way to a spot where a shower of incendiary bombs had just fallen. It was about two hundred yards away and, alone, I would have run there as fast as I could. As I pressed forward, he appreciably slowed down, so that I had to adjust my pace to his. 'Remember,' he said, 'we never run as long as we can walk.' And the old gun-layer would sit in the post during raids manning the telephone switchboard and ask each warden as he came what conditions were like outside. The answer was usually melodramatic or self-consciously nonchalant. In either case, it evoked the response: 'Yes. But what I want to know is this. Is it safe for the wardens to be out?'

I made a very good friend at the Post and we generally went on patrol together. In the first instance, we drifted together, I suppose, because we were obviously the two 'educated' ones in our company. He was an Anglican curate, chaplain in fact, to the Bishop. I do not think I had known a curate before, and my normal reaction to clergymen of any kind was to give them as wide a berth as possible. I found Woods, who was about my age, a delightful man; and then, on patrol one night, I discovered what seemed to me an extraordinary thing about him: he had not read a novel in his life. I found this truly extraordinary. What had his schoolmasters been thinking of? What had Cambridge University been up to? Immediately, I realised the naivety of my expostulating. Mildly, he defended himself. He had nothing against novels; it was simply that they played no part in the life he had embarked on and he read theology to the virtual exclusion of everything else. We struck a bargain: I would recommend some novels I admired and he would introduce me to theology. I lent him *Tess* and *Jude*, which seemed to me to have some bearing on the theological. He saw the point and was much impressed with them. He lent me Reinhold Niebuhr's recent Gifford lectures, which I read with profit.

On one occasion we were officially rebuked for frivolity. There was a combined Army and Civil Defence exercise in which we were on continuous duty for twenty-four hours. The first stages in the invasion of the West Country were simulated. It was assumed there would be non-stop strafing and bombing for two or three days. Elaborate 'incidents' were devised and authority told us we should use our imagination to the full to achieve the utmost in realism. George Woods and I remembered Alfred, the pride of Clifton Zoo, an enormous and infinitely sad-looking gorilla calculated, we thought, to strike terror into Nazi invaders and Home Guard troops alike if encountered wandering round on the loose. According to popular legend, during air raids chosen marksmen from the Zoo staff surrounded Alfred's cage with their rifles at the ready. We therefore telephoned Report Centre that Alfred's cage had been hit in the aerial bombardment, that Alfred was at large and when last seen had been shambling down the Whiteladies Road towards Park Street and the Tramway Centre. The message was solemnly acknowledged, and we recorded its transmission in the logbook.

An hour later, we telephoned Report Centre with the information that Alfred had been sighted in Hotwells and was rumoured to be striking terror into women and children. An hour later, we reported a fresh rumour: faced with the apparition of Alfred, a platoon of Home Guard at the docks had turned and run. Alfred was assuming King Kong-like proportions in our minds. An hour later, we reported again, to have our message interrupted by a male voice which said brusquely: 'Look here, we've had a bloody nuff of fucking Alfred, see.' Some hours later, Report Centre's weariness with the anthropoid was formally expressed to the post warden: we were officially reprimanded. It was almost suggested that we didn't know there was a war on.

After I left Bristol I saw Woods only infrequently. The war over, he went back to Cambridge, and I visited him once or twice at Downing, where he was chaplain and then dean. He became Professor of Theology at King's College, London, and died at an absurdly early age. I remember him as a good man who was at ease with his goodness and made you at ease with it, too.

Another friend I made in Bristol was Gwilym James, D. G. James, Professor of English in the university. I had known of him before, since he had been a WEA lecturer in Birmingham, where my father was in his philosophy class. My father talked of him with the warmest admiration and, indeed, with something more than that, with the affectionate pride with which a father might speak of a son, so that I felt that in some sense my father saw him as a surrogate for my brother Charles, who had been killed in 1918. When I found myself in Bristol I sent him a note making myself known to him. He was some years older than I and Bristol was his first Chair. He had come to it a few months before from a temporary secondment to the Board of Trade, where he had been concerned with the devising of clothes rationing. At that time, he was the author of one book, *Scepticism and Poetry*, a learned and eloquent attempt, written from the standpoint of Christian orthodoxy, to refute Richards's *Principles of Literary Criticism*. Richards's book was more sympathetic to me, but I found Gwilym a wonderfully entrancing man. His mind fascinated me, partly because it was so unlike my own. He approached literature from a philosophical angle, as is evident in his books on Francis Bacon and Newman, while mine was a practitioner's interest. In some ways, he reminded me of my old tutor, A. M. D. Hughes. He had a beautiful mind, which had its counterpart in the beauty of his eloquence and expression, which quite transcended what passes, vulgarly, as Welsh.

That I benefited by glimpsing writers and writing through his very different mind I do not doubt at all. He wrote poetry, though I did not see anything of it, which I very much regret. I do not think he ever published. Once – quite unintentionally, I think – he quoted a line which proved to be his own. I was arrested by it and asked where it came from. He said it was from a long philosophical poem he was writing, and the line was: 'The long cylindrical hoot of the owl.' He quoted it, I remember, as we were listening late on a warm summer evening to an owl. I do not much believe in mute inglorious Miltons, but that Gwilym was a real poet I am absolutely certain.

After the war, when the University College of Southampton was raised to university status, Gwilym was appointed its first Vice-Chancellor. In its first year, he invited me to deliver a public lecture, and when years later, I found myself in academic life, he was a firm and invaluable partisan of mine. He retired from his vice-chancellorship early, in order to return to teaching and scholarship. He was learning Irish and Old Welsh for the books he was intending to write. Then after a year as visiting professor I think at Princeton, he died very suddenly towards the end of 1968.

It was Gwilym who told me, the information having come his way in his capacity as Professor of English, that the RAF was calling for volunteers to learn Japanese. The invitation was for 'recent' graduates, and I was scarcely that; nor did I have either linguistic capacity or secret ambition to learn Japanese. But the notion seemed to fall into the pattern of the current madness and, besides, learning Japanese would mean a year in London, which was what really swayed me. A year in London! It was the promise of a new enfranchisement. I applied, and the Air Ministry sent me a travel warrant. I duly made my way to a branch of the Air Ministry in the Horseferry Road, Westminster, which proved to be a line of Nissen huts.

I was ushered into the presence of the man who was to interview me and was abashed by his being not only several years younger than I but a squadron-leader with the ribbon of the DFC on his tunic. He was as much embarrassed as I was, as though it was the first interview he had conducted. He called me Sir and was obviously puzzled that anyone should be so eccentric as to wish to learn Japanese. But his manners were impeccable. He suggested with great diffidence that I was rather old to be thinking of learning Japanese. I demurred. 'Our experts,' he said, 'say you can't learn it after the age of twenty-two.'

I made more attempts during the next months to put myself in the forces, all farcical and all ending in the same way. I set out to be a meteorological officer in the RAF, to join Field Security Police, to get into a section of Intelligence which I was assured was the opposite of MI5 and for which you had to be very good at crossword puzzles, the Army Education Corps and the Army Bureau of Current Affairs. The men who interviewed me, charming men all of them and invariably captains or majors, seemed genuinely keen that I should join them and, when they finally came up against the obstacle that was insuperable, wracked their brains on my behalf, as though it was my personal happiness that was primarily important. All, their faces illumined with pleasure and relief, suddenly saw the solution to my problem. The BBC! Had I thought of the BBC? Alas, I was a year or two below the reservation-age for the BBC and on this the Ministry of Labour and National Service was inflexible.

I decided to let authority do with me what it would. I'd just go on living from day to day, on suspended service, as it were. A week or two after having come to the decision, I had to go to Birmingham on business for the factory, to secure some information the nature of which I have completely forgotten. It meant, among other things, attending a trade luncheon at the Midland Hotel, and there I ran into a man whom I had known slightly at the University. He had been a research student in metallurgy. He was now director of a research and development organisation. We talked, and by the end of the meal I had been offered and had accepted a job with him as a technical writer. I spent the rest of the war translating the findings of experts into terms the layman could understand, writing for the aircraft industry and especially for firms doing work under contract to the industry a series of little handbooks on the properties of aluminium and how to cast it, forge it, machine it, weld it, stamp it and shape it under the rubber press. I became a master, you might say, of the hundred-and-one things a bright boy can do with aluminium. It was knowledge that vanished overnight when the war was over.

By the beginning of 1943 I was back in Birmingham. I settled into a bedsitter in Edgbaston, near Five Ways, and resumed a private life. True, I became a warden at a post in a cellar under a shop in Colmore Row opposite the Cathedral but I saw no action of any kind and made no friends there. So far as Birmingham went, air raids seemed to have ceased and a warden's job was merely an impersonal chore. All I remember about the post now is that there was a lugubrious paid warden who prided himself on his facial resemblance to Lord Montgomery, with whom no man could have had less in common. He boasted of his petty crookery and scrounging, by which he lived in peacetime. 'If there's a blitz on I usually go looting,' he told me gloomily one night.

And I was writing a novel again, though not with ease, because I did not quite know what I was doing, except I'd sworn to myself that it must be quite different from anything I had done before. Almost as a deliberate exercise I set out to write a classical comedy, by which I meant one that could have tragic conclusions but would resolve itself into a relatively happy ending. I was much mortified when I realised that I had been writing pastiche Virginia Woolf, pastiche *To The Lighthouse* and *Between the Acts*. For a time, the novel was in abeyance. In the end, I think I wrenched myself clear of Mrs Woolf. At any rate, when it was published in 1946, I do not recall any reviewers spotting her presence in the novel. But all novelists, I imagine, cherish to themselves influences on their work which may be entirely illusory and certainly go unrecognised by their readers. When *Blind Man's Ditch* appeared in 1938, more than one reviewer cried in triumph 'Graham Greene!' and pointed an accusing finger, but no one mentioned André Gide or Wyndham Lewis, who seemed to me as evidently there as Greene.

I began what proved to be the final draft of the book on VE Day, in greatly changed circumstances. I was now married and had been since Easter of the year before. Three weeks before that, I had met my future wife at a party in Hampstead and within twenty-four hours we had decided to marry. We had nothing, one would have said, in common and we came from entirely different backgrounds. By profession, Peggy was a physiotherapist, something which I had scarcely heard of. Marrying her was far and away the wisest thing I have ever done.

We were married by special licence at the Hampstead register office, which proved to be in the basement of the Town Hall, in Haverstock Hill, in a ceremony of almost inconceivable rapidity and against the noise of incessantly ringing telephones; the registrar, I recall, was chasing a bridegroom who had failed to turn up from Aldershot. Peggy was wearing the clothes in which I'd first met her, which I suppose must be called walking-out uniform of the Red Cross, with a flash saying Physiotherapy on her shoulder. She was on embarkation leave — hence the speed. After the ceremony, we adjourned with the witnesses to Soho, where we lunched at a Spanish restaurant. We had a few days together. London was full of men and women in uniforms bearing strange flashes. In a pub in Rosslyn Hill, a man pointed at Peggy's and said: 'What's that? Where is it?' I explained that Physiotherapia was the forty-fourth or possibly the forty-fifth member of the newly-formed United Nations, was to the east of Jugoslavia and contiguous with it, a tiny, rarely visited and fertile country on the flanks of the Massage Mountains. This statement was received with complete trust.

Within a week or so, embarkation had claimed Peggy, and when I next heard from her she was at a base-camp in Algeria, whence she travelled up the spine of Italy in the wake of the Allied advance. After some six months, she was released from the Service and joined me in Birmingham. I was lucky enough to find a mouse-infested but furnished flat to rent in a rundown though well-treed road in Edgbaston. Looking back at those last months of the war against the Nazis, I marvel now at how industrious I was. In addition to writing the novel, I was kept busy by all sorts of miscellaneous writing. I was writing critical essays for *Penguin New Writing* and for a half-yearly book-magazine called *Janus*, edited by the distinguished Indian scholar B. Rajan. I was contributing a fortnightly 'London Letter' on life on the home front to the *Palestine Post*, an assignment Reggie had obtained for me. I had begun reviewing novels for *Time and Tide* regularly, and poetry, too, from time to time. I was on my way to becoming established.

The war seemed never-ending; the years seemed to contain many more than twelve months. Nevertheless, life was recognisably returning to normality, and officially so. There was a growing recognition that a state of war was the exception, not the rule. Progress in this direction was admittedly spotty but for me, a sign of this progress towards a future peace was the coming back to life, on a larger scale than before, of BBC Midland Region. I found myself in demand as a writer both of feature programmes and of talks. The Birmingham *Evening Despatch* invited me to become its radio critic. So long as I remained in the city, I contributed a weekly article of eight hundred words, which I dropped in at the *Despatch* office at nine o'clock each Monday morning, having written the piece last thing on Sunday night.

I was conscious of having lost time because of the war and conscious, too, that my coevals in the Services had lost much more time than I had; and though I was being carried forward almost involuntarily, as though on the crest of a wave, I could not tell whether the success was real or illusory. In pessimistic moments, I thought it might be due only to lack of competitors and rivals. I soon knew. The war ended and as soon as I could get release from my job we returned to London. Theoretically, it was impossible to find anywhere to live, but Michael Joseph came to the rescue. He offered us, until such time as he needed it for himself, the flat at the top of the blitzed Georgian house in Bloomsbury Street, almost on the corner of New Oxford Street, which housed his trade department. That was on the ground floor. Above it, until one reached the top floor, all the windows were glassless, and the house itself was encased in a network of tubular scaffolding.

We established ourselves there, I remember, on the first day of December, 1945. I cannot say that we were excessively comfortable in our new quarters. We had very little furniture. We were visited from time to time by black rats. It was a hard winter, and fuel was hard to come by. The wind swept upwards through the paneless windows below and through the cracks in the floorboards, for which we had quite inadequate coverings. Once, very early on, I scoured London for coal, for we were without fuel of any kind and my wife was down with influenza. Hampstead, which I had been assured was a veritable Tom Tiddler's Ground of coal, failed me, and I took the tube to Covent Garden, where my agents, who have come to my rescue in all sorts of situations over the years, lent me a bucketful. I bore it back to Bloomsbury Street in a taxi.

And I remember, one bitterly cold evening, the front door bell ringing. Descending the stairs, I wondered who it could be, for no one had called before. It turned out to be Donald Allen – the American critic and anthologist D. M. Allen – who had been a graduate assistant in English in the University of Iowa in the summer when I had taught there and a student in one of my classes. Since that time, I had heard nothing of him; and now, here he was, in the uniform of a lieutenant in the United States Navy and cradling in his arms a bottle of bourbon whisky. He had seen a review of mine in the *Spectator* and walked round to the office to get my address. He joined us for dinner, after which he sat in his Navy greatcoat shivering over our meagre fire.

VIII

The years immediately after the war were packed years. Overnight, one felt that the bloodstream of one's world was circulating again, in full flow. Yet I think there was no sense of rivalry or competition: there seemed room for everyone, though this may merely have been one of the illusions necessary to the literary life. Reggie and Olivia Manning came back from Palestine, their lives since 1940 having traced a course resembling that of the Pringles in Olivia's superb *Balkan Trilogy*. Reggie was about to join BBC Features. Henry Reed had been demobilised from Intelligence, whither he had been seconded from the Army. Among other things, he had learnt Japanese, which in turn he had taught to Wrens. He intended, he said, to devote every day for the rest of his life to forgetting another word of Japanese.

His reputation had been made entirely in the war years. He had first gained recognition for his famous parody of Eliot, 'Chard Witlow', which appeared in a *New Statesman* competition over the initials H. R., which led to its being attributed, against all evidence and probability, to Herbert Read. The identity of its author became clear when 'Naming of Parts' was published in 1941 or 1942. It must be by far the best-known poem in English inspired by the war and it has so often been anthologised as, in a sense, to have hung round Henry's neck and made him seem too often the writer of a single poem, which is anything but true. It deserves its fame. Wittily, delicately and with exquisite lyrical beauty, it encapsulates the experience of every civilian who found himself caught up in the war-machine.

At much the time we returned to London, he retired to Dorset, appropriately, since he was engaged on a life – it was to be *the* life – of Hardy. But he was never long away from London, for he was a great frequenter of the theatre, of opera and the ballet especially. He often stayed with us on these occasions, and we stayed with him in Dorset. The life of Hardy has not emerged, though as late as 1971 he wrote that he 'still sometimes rashly' supposed he was working on his Hardy book. But a by-product of it has become famous as his celebrated piece for radio *A Very Great Man Indeed*, which in the dedicatory letter to the published text he describes as a 'small dramatic study' arising out of his researches. It is a marvellously funny comment on the biographer's art and was among the first of a series of plays that compose, MacNeice's apart, probably the most sustained contribution to radio-writing we have. In those days, though, it was as a poet and scholar that I primarily saw Henry. His knowledge of Shakespeare, Henry James and Joyce was great.

In 1946, he was on the crest of the wave, and so in my way was I. I had succeeded Hampson as a novel-reviewer in the *Spectator* and I was doing a great deal of work for radio as well, writing features for Midland Region and talks and programmes for Schools Broadcasting and for what were in effect adult education series designed for the masses of soldiers waiting to be demobilised. I had not been more than a week or two in London when MacNeice telephoned me to ask whether I was interested in a job in Features. A little earlier, I would have jumped at the offer; now, cautiously, I asked about the salary and realised I was earning more as a freelance.

I was broadcasting a monthly talk on new books for Midland, which was pre-recorded at Broadcasting House. My producer was always Roy Campbell, the South African poet, who was in bad odour generally because he had fought for Franco in the Spanish Civil War. A large, burly, bald man, he seemed always to wear a bush shirt and an Australian bush hat. He walked with a stick, for he was lame, the result of war injuries or of an accident in the bull-ring; you could decide for yourself. He was a noted literary roughneck, famous for having marched into a public hall where Spender was speaking, mounted the platform and knocked him down. He related the event to me more than once, with a gusto I found embarrassing. I was one evening in the BBC Club with MacNeice when, apropos of nothing so far as I could see, Campbell challenged him to a fight. They squared up to each other and bystanders rushed in to hold them apart. I found his particular style of bravura distasteful rather than not. He peddled a brand of Catholicism akin to Belloc's, though with Sussex replaced by the veldt and the Camargue.

He was nothing like as naive as he tried to appear. At his best, he was a fine poet, and I had admired him ever since, as a boy, I had read his 'Tristan da Cunha', in the *New Statesman*. One of the things that intrigued me was that in the early Twenties in South Africa he had been closely associated with Plomer, with whom he had edited a literary magazine consciously South African and consciously anti-South African Establishment. I could think of no two men more different from each other or, I would have thought, more antipathetic. I tried to draw him out on their South African friendship, but Campbell's delicacy of feeling was finer than mine, and though it was plain he saw nothing of Plomer he never said a word in disparagement of him.

I have said Campbell was my producer. In fact, no production ever took place. We met in the studio, I would go through my script for length, and then Campbell led me out of Broadcasting House and round the corner into the George in Great Portland Street, where he regaled me with the latest episode in the saga of his life. We would get back to the studio just in time for the recording.

One afternoon – these talks were always recorded just after lunch – he was at pains to impress on me what a nice man Mr Eliot was, more than that, a real gentleman. The day before, he and his friend Dylan Thomas had decided to spend the evening drinking but when they met in the afternoon discovered that neither had any money. Since a loan was called for, who more likely to be good for one than a fellow poet? So they went to the offices of Chatto & Windus and asked to see Cecil Day Lewis. Day Lewis turned a deaf ear to them. They thereupon went to Russell Square, to Faber & Faber, where they saw Mr Eliot. They explained their problem. No one could have been more sympathetic. All smiles, Mr Eliot took out his wallet, removed a five-pound note from it and pressed it upon them. Thanks he brushed aside.

Campbell told me how he came to get a job with the BBC. In the war, he had been a sergeant-major in a West African regiment and when he came back to England Desmond MacCarthy put his name forward at the BBC. When he went to Broadcasting House on his first morning he had assumed, he said, he was to be a commissionaire. Campbell was a joker, and I realised that one of my roles was to be his butt. Once, we met in the studio as usual, I ran through my script and he showed no sign of wishing to move on to the George. I read my script again. Then my curiosity won. Didn't he, I asked, feel like a drink? A drink? He echoed the word as though in total incomprehension. Then light dawned, and immediately he was full of concern and self-reproach. 'But my dear fellow, why didn't you say? *Of course* you must have a drink. How can I have been so thoughtless?' He swept my protests aside and led me to the George, accusing himself of unpardonable inconsiderateness towards me. I realised he had turned the tables very neatly; I'd been completely fooled. At the bar, he ordered a pint of bitter for me and a small tonic for himself. 'But aren't you having anything yourself?' I asked. 'My dear fellow,' he said, as though surprised in turn, 'but I don't drink.' 'You don't drink?' 'I drink every other year,' he said 'and my non-drinking year began yesterday.'

Campbell's persona of a philistine roughneck I found bearable only in short spells. In conversation, he seemed to reveal a mind that was vulgar and superstitious. And this cannot have been anything like the whole truth, for his poetry, the early South African poetry especially, is very fine.

Occasionally, I would see him of an evening in the Soho pubs with Dylan Thomas, whom I knew only very slightly and for years by repute only. I remember running into the poet Ruthven Todd late in 1939 and his telling me with some excitement of the events of the previous night, which he had spent with Thomas. Somehow, they had snared a pigeon in Trafalgar Square, killed it, borne it in triumph to Hampstead Heath, where they had made a fire and roasted it. It was, Todd said, very tough.

Sometime in 1946, Reggie Smith asked me to come into the BBC and watch a play he was producing. My wife was away and I did so. The play was trivial enough, a reach-me-down thriller; the interest lay in Thomas, who was playing the villain. At this time, he got most of his living from radio-acting, and very impressive he was, even in the hammiest parts, just as he could make the most tawdry verse sound wonderful. After the show, we went to a pub and Thomas clowned, as was his way in bars. Then he discovered he had missed the last train back to Oxford, for he was living temporarily at Witney. I took him back to Bloomsbury Street.

Thomas alone was quite different from Thomas in a crowd. We talked for hours, and he talked seriously and passionately about the one thing that interested him, poetry. I regret bitterly now that I had no means of recording his talk, for it was brilliant. He is often seen sentimentally as a sort of holy innocent warbling his native woodnotes wild: in fact, as was implicit in everything he said, he was soaked in the English poets.

As it happened, an anthology, *Poems from New Writing*, had just been published which contained a poem of mine. That was gratifying, but whenever I read the poem on the page I was disappointed; at a certain point it began to fail, but why I could not say. I showed the poem to Dylan, which I certainly wouldn't have done if he'd been in his pub mood. 'These lines,' he said, cigarette dangling from lower lip, 'are dead. This is what you should do.' And he gave me a lesson in verse-making, showing how my lines could be given at least a shadowy likeness to life.

We talked about poetry till four in the morning, or, rather, Thomas talked and I listened. He drank the dozen bottles of beer I had and ate a Camembert cheese, for the disappearance of which I got into trouble when my wife came home. Camemberts were still very hard to come by.

It was an encounter which I gratefully remember. After it, I met Thomas only once; in a Soho pub one Friday evening. He came in with Campbell and challenged me aggressively. I had reviewed Lowry's *Under the Volcano* that day in the *Statesman*; I admired it intensely, and my notice was as near to a rave review as I thought Raymond Mortimer would tolerate. It wasn't near enough to satisfy Thomas, who was a friend of Lowry's.

A famous Soho character of this time was Julian Maclaren-Ross, whose short stories of Army life from 1940 to 1945 seem to me to be, along with Waugh's trilogy, the best and most accurate rendering of the military existence of the day we possess though Julian is always writing from the angle of the private soldier, giving the worm's eye view. Generally regarded as a paranoiac, he was certainly an egomaniac. The Army could do nothing with him, and the Army was not alone in this.

I met him when I was still in Birmingham and he in an Army psychiatric hospital waiting for his discharge. I promised to look him up when I got to London. He said he did not know where he'd be living but he could be found from six to eleven most evenings at the left-hand end of the saloon-bar of the Wheatsheaf in Rathbone Place. The left-hand end of the saloon-bar of the Wheatsheaf, I found, was sacred to him; it was there he held court. As an arty and literary pub, the Wheatsheaf had begun, I imagine, as a sort of adjunct or overflow of the Fitzroy Tavern, a hundred yards away, but it was smaller, quieter and contained a higher proportion of non-arty locals than the Fitzroy. Though I admired his writing, I thought of Julian as a curiosity, as indeed a *naif*, which in a very worldly way he was. I could not place him in any English context. He had been brought up on the French Riviera, in exile as it were, though how this came about I never knew. But, as I soon discovered, he had a positively encyclopaedic knowledge of contemporary English and American fiction, especially as it leaned towards the thriller and the crime novel; conspicuous among his heroes were Dashiell Hammett, Chandler and Eric Ambler. I think that no one earlier had the least interest for him. He had three enthusiasms: contemporary fiction, films, but only Hollywood films, and murderers. He probably knew more about Landru than anyone else alive did and at the slightest provocation would recite excerpts from the novel he was writing about him. Not that he despised more local murderers; he thought well, I remember, of Haigh and of Patrick Hamilton's trilogy based on him. I soon discovered something else: he had a phenomenal memory, the nearest thing to total recall I have ever met. One evening, he took me completely by surprise by reciting to me the whole of the last chapter of my novel *Blind Man's Ditch*.

This capacity for almost total recall was one of his tools as writer. He was relatively prolific, and people who knew the pattern of his day wondered when he did his writing. He was in the Wheatsheaf from noon until three, in a cinema until six, then in the Wheatsheaf again, then from eleven till about one belatedly dining in a Greek restaurant at the wrong end of Charlotte Street. He was always, as I have said, ready to recite from works in progress, and this, I realised, was how he wrote. Like some poets, of whom Yeats was one, he composed orally and fixed what he had written in his mind by constant repetition and constant re-phrasing. After his meal at the Greek café, he took a taxi back to his hotel, settled himself with his manuscript-book in the deserted lounge and took down his story as it were from his own dictation. His handwriting was the neatest and most legible I have ever seen; he scorned the typewriter as an unnecessary superfluity and sent his stories to editors and novels to publishers literally in manuscript.

He lived generally in hotels and went everywhere by taxi; which I thought affectation, an acting out of a fantasy of how a writer should live. It was a subject he was strong upon; he would talk eloquently on what was due to a writer from society. He would ask: 'Why can't I walk into a bank, see the manager and demand an overdraft like any other business man?' It was a rhetorical question; he could if he wanted to, but everyone knew he wouldn't get one, for he wasn't a business man. Necessity, he said, compelled him to live in hotels; too few private houses had lifts, and he was unable to climb stairs. I had, in fact, invited him to dine with us soon after we were back in

London. When from the front-door step Julian saw the staircase, which still had something of its original Georgian elegance, he looked at it with horror and said he couldn't possibly climb it. How the incident ended I have forgotten, but certainly he didn't have dinner with us in the flat.

I now think I may have been quite mistaken in assuming that Julian's way of life was dictated only by his fantasies, for I was pulled up short when I last read his story 'I Had to Go Sick'. There, he recounts the comic chagrin and dismay that befall them both when he and the Army simultaneously discover he is incapable of marching: the British Army, and the Infantry in particular, is based upon the proposition that men can march, and when they can't it is as nonplussed as I was. Perhaps he really did have something wrong with a leg that prevented him from climbing stairs, climbing on buses and going down escalators to underground trains. All the same, to live permanently in hotels and travel everywhere by taxi was not, even in 1946, a sensible way of life for a young writer without private means and dependent for an income entirely on a few highbrow magazines.

It meant his existence was dominated by the necessity of getting immediate money, money with which to pay the next week's rent. For the most part, the hotels he patronised were in that stretch of Bloomsbury between Southampton Row and Upper Woburn Place. He did not remain at any one of them very long because the day always came when lack of money forced him to do a moonlight flit. This incessant need for money made him a menace to his friends. 'He that hath wife and children,' Bacon wrote, 'hath given hostages to fortune.' So had he who had Julian as a friend. Indeed, it sometimes seemed as though he felt that because one had undertaken to support a wife and family one had also accepted a moral obligation to support him as well. But this is to be too unkind. He genuinely intended to pay one back, but he never did because he never could. Along with this went the capacity he had of making one feel thoroughly and smugly respectable.

In 1948, we left London to live in Romney Marsh, but that did not mean leaving Julian, for from time to time, always at an inconvenient one, such as Saturday afternoon, when the banks are closed and weekend shopping has pretty well cleared one out of ready money, a telegram would arrive, invariably asking for five pounds immediately, to be wired to him at such-and-such a post office. Two or three years later, I had a commission to broadcast on books every Sunday afternoon. It was a delightful assignment marred by the fear that when I came down from the studio I would be intercepted by the girl at the reception desk with a message for me. A Mr Maclaren-Ross had telephoned about something extremely urgent: would I telephone him as soon as I came out of the studio?

I did not invariably do so but on one occasion when I did he invited me to go round and have a drink with him. He was living in a furnished room in Paddington. I noticed maliciously that the only way of reaching it was by climbing a flight of stairs. Perhaps his leg was suddenly better or, as I suspect, the girl he was living with was still new enough to be able to impose some discipline on him. Before getting down to the real business of the meeting, which was to borrow a fiver, he regaled me, I recall, with rum and Coca-Cola.

In an article in *Horizon*, Julian maintained a writer needed an income of at least three thousand a year in order to live. In the late Forties, that was a very decent sum, and certainly Julian never had anything like it. But he lived as though he did. His habits consumed money. He seemed to have read every interesting new novel within a week of publication, and in fact he had done so: he could quote whole pages to you. I wondered how he got them, for he was not a novel-reviewer. It was, I discovered, perfectly simple. He bought a novel on publication day, read it that day and on the next took it to a second-hand book shop and sold it as a review copy. In other words, a seven-and-sixpenny novel cost him three-and-nine. I once hinted that he could save himself a lot of money by joining a public library. Those at Hampstead and St. Pancras, I said, were particularly good. I knew from the look he gave me that I had branded myself as irredeemably bourgeois.

He chain-smoked cigarettes through an amber holder, for Edgar Wallace was another hero. And he carried a cane with a silver knob. This, he said, was in case he should meet the critic John Davenport, who combined considerable charm with enormous strength and was given from time to time to beating up other people. I recall being at a party of Olivia Manning's, sitting in an armchair after midnight and becoming aware of a shadow looming over me. I looked up, and there was Davenport with his fist clenched above my head. I was terrified and waited for the fist to come down on my skull. Instead, Davenport leaned over and kissed the top of my head, saying, 'Walter, I love you dearly.' It has always seemed to me a narrow escape.

The silver-knobbed cane was part of Julian's style of living, part of his persona, which was that of the writer as dandy. A fairly shabby dandy, perforce. In the slang current at the time, he looked a bit of a spiv. He was arrogant with a long, fleshy face a little, I thought, like Oscar Wilde's. He was patronishing, too. Not with other writers; with them, he was merely *primus inter pares*; but people who were not writers he seemed to see very much *de haut en bas*. This went with much formality and an elaborate politeness, never more so than when in the presence of an old lady who was, so to speak, one of the Wheatsheaf's regular communicants. Night after night, she sat at her usual table with a crossword puzzle in front of her and an alarm clock and a glass of stout beside it. Julian was always polysyllabically solicitous for her welfare.

Since he could write a lively, astringent book review, literary editors were eager to have him to write for them, but to employ him meant the disruption of a paper's accounting system. He could not wait a month after publication for his fee, as everyone else had to; he demanded payment on the spot, and in cash, when he took his copy into the office. Which often meant that the literary editor, who was not earning three thousand a year, had to put his hand into his own pocket. Similarly, publishers, especially new, unestablished and therefore probably poor publishers, were eager to publish him, but since he always needed money he always demanded immediate advances, which were generally exhausted by the time he settled down to write the book. Then he needed further subsidising. The fact was, it was impossible for even the most benevolent of publishers to give a small-selling author an advance large enough to live on while writing his book and waiting for it to be published, and this would have been true had Julian not been bent on living at the rate of £3,000 a year. His intentions were always honourable, but more and more publishers who did not get the manuscripts for which they had paid advances, felt aggrieved, as did Julian himself. Every offer from a fresh publisher was like the beginning of a new love affair: it was ecstatic, and the relation was to be for life. Then he would discover that this publisher, like all the others before him, was an exploiter of authors and therefore could only expect to be exploited in his turn.

He was always optimistic, always about to make a killing, often from a film he would write. Before a word of the script was written, much less a producer found, he had cast it completely. 'Of course,' he would declare grandly, 'Dennis Price will play the lead.' Once he managed to interest a new company in my novel *Blind Man's Ditch*. He would write the script and all I had to do was to lend him a copy of the novel, which I did. I did not see it again, for within six months the new film company had gone out of business and my novel had disappeared with it. As it happened, it was my one copy, and the novel had long been out of print.

This optimism of Julian's was seen as evidence of his refusal to recognise or live in the real world. I am not at all sure that this was so. He was unlucky. When he died, suddenly and unexpectedly in the early Fifties, he was already writing short plays, little thrillers, for radio, and one can see how, when television was firmly established two or three years later, he might have established himself with it as a television playwright. Perhaps he simply did not live long enough. He was called an impossible man. He was a difficult one who made life hard for himself because he had an obstinate romanticism that caused him to pit himself against the world. He had pitted himself against the Army and in a way he had won; but he could not win against the world.

If he was impossible, it was only because he had no money. With a private income, at the worst he would have appeared only as a harmless eccentric. Whether he would have seemed any the less a bore I doubt, for that was a consequence of his self-absorption. He was amusing, so long as you did not see too much of him, and he fascinated me partly because we were so different from each other. Beside him, I could see myself as the industrious apprentice, the man without panache, but precisely because I was an industrious apprentice I could recognise another compulsive worker when I saw one. Again, I can only quote James on Flaubert, for Maclaren-Ross too was 'born a writer, grew up, lived, died a writer, breathing, feeling, thinking, speaking, performing every action of his life, only as that votary.'

No writer could have been more different than L. P. Hartley, whom I met at much the same time. They existed in almost ludicrous contrast. Hartley and I were friends for years and he puzzled me for years. At his best, he remains for me one of the finest English novelists of his time, though one of those who, as they say of wine, do not always 'travel'. Some of my closest American friends, men whose judgement I respect and Anglophile to boot, see nothing in him, and almost half his fiction remains unpublished in America; against which must be set the further fact that the only two critical studies of him are by Americans. In 1946, the *Spectator* sent me *The Sixth Heaven*, the second volume of the *Eustace and Hilda* trilogy, for review. I had not read the first, *The Shrimp and the Anemone*, and I had little reason to love Hartley, whom I saw as a slightly sinister literary pluralist who had contrived at one time to review new novels week by week simultaneously in the *Observer*, the *Saturday Review* (later, the *Weekend Review*) and a glossy society magazine. Moreover, he had reviewed two of the three novels I had written, not with much sympathy or, it seemed to me, much perception. One of these reviews, I remember, made my father very cross indeed. So I was scarcely predisposed to praise it when *The Sixth Heaven* arrived.

I was utterly disarmed by it. I rejoiced both in its humour and its moral discriminations. Eustace seemed to me a triumphantly successful creation, for all that the diffident, sensitive young man with vague literary leanings has been a stock figure in English fiction ever since Butler wrote *The Way of All Flesh*. I, who had never stayed in a great country house, could see that Eustace was every naive young man, as in the fantasy he has about the valet who has been put at his disposal:

'Did you ring, sir?'

'Yes, I did. I'm afraid I can't find my white flannel trousers.'

'If you'll excuse my saying so, sir, it's not likely you'll find them under all that mess. That mess will take me at least fifty-five minutes to clear up, and this is my evening out.'

'Oh, I am so sorry.'

'Oh, it's no good your apologising, sir. I was only saying to them in the Hall, that, of all the guests who've ever stayed here in my experience, man and boy, you've given far the most trouble. We wondered where you had been brought up, sir, we did, straight. Not in a gentleman's family, I said, believe me.'

I saw that to review it adequately I must first read *The Shrimp and the Anemone*. I was bowled over from the first paragraph, which sets, in a single incident of childhood, the whole novel before us, for who is Hilda, the dominating older sister, if not the anemone, and who Eustace, the gentle, over-scrupulous little boy already preoccupied with moral dilemmas and problems of behaviour, if not the shrimp?

How could I not write an ecstatic review? Hartley sent me a charming note of appreciation and an invitation to lunch at the Athenaeum. When we met, he seemed to dart forward to greet me with hand outstretched and head slightly to one side. He was more than a dozen years older than I, chubby, almost portly, bald and, in my eyes and as I discovered not in mine alone, very much like a benevolent H. G. Wells in appearance. In his behaviour towards me he was uncomfortably considerate, and I found his politeness and good manners altogether formidable; I felt very much a roughneck in his company.

To begin with, we talked about Leo Myers. I gathered something of Hartley's life. He had been at Harrow, gone up to Balliol and then, after two or three terms, become an officer in the first war. He had distinguished himself, he told me, in the musketry examination at Shorncliffe, or, more precisely, in the written part of the exam. He did not, I think, see service overseas and when the war was over returned to Balliol. He had been a guest at Garsington and between the wars had lived in Italy, mainly in Venice, for half the year. Now, he was a great weekender at country houses, for, like Leo Myers before his reformation, he lived in that section of English life in which society and the arts overlap. He talked of his friends, the Sitwells and David Cecil particularly, but also of the Marchesa Iris Origo, Lady Abercrombie and Ethel Sands, the American painter long domiciled in Europe, who had been a protégée of James and a friend of Bennett and whom I was soon to meet.

He was gentle and self-deprecating, so that on a first meeting it was difficult not to equate him with his own Eustace. He seemed to affect the role of an amateur with no special expertise of any kind, which is, of course, a traditional foible of the English upper classes. Where Leslie was concerned, I found I was constantly being deceived by this, though there was indeed a very real strain in his work not merely of the amateur but of amateurishness. What he did well, such as the *Eustace and Hilda* trilogy and *The Go-Between*, he did wonderfully well, but he did not always know what he could do well. His range was narrow, and when he went outside it the consequences could be disastrous. The fundamental idea of *My Fellow Devils*, for instance, is brilliant: the notion of the film star as a contemporary manifestation of the Devil. One sees in it Hartley's affinity with Hawthorne, the Hawthorne who jotted in his notebooks:

> Meditations about the main gas-pipe of a great city, – if the supply were to be stopped, what would happen? . . . It might be made emblematical of something.

It might indeed; but everything would depend on the working out and on what James called 'density of specification'. The theme of *My Fellow Devils* is of the utmost seriousness: how should we behave in the presence of evil? The answer is unequivocal: we should have no truck with it. But the fable of the novel, which should be the vehicle of its seriousness, never convinces. It is hard enough to swallow the initial donnee, a severe lady magistrate falling in love with and marrying a film star and then, disillusioned, embarking on a quest for God; but making the Devil's stand-in a film star leads Hartley into worlds where one feels he is a total stranger.

We parted after that first meeting on Christian-name terms and he invited me down for a weekend at his house on the river just outside Bath. It was the first of many visits. Charlie, his valet-chauffeur, met me at Bath Station. He was a tall, thin, very erect man, given either to neuralgia or to ulcers. As an ex-policeman, he was knowing about human behaviour and the state of the world and during the drive to Avondale he regaled me with an unillusioned assessment of things. I see him now as the embodiment of Leslie's own conscience.

Avondale, Leslie's house, was concealed from the road by a high wall. Its front resolutely faced the river. Leslie valued it because of that: he had only to walk across the lawn to reach his boat-house and the skiff it sheltered. Merely to say he was an ardent wet-bob is scarcely to do justice to his passion for the water. When he was in Bath he rowed every afternoon; and when I stayed with him he took me along as his passenger. In his skiff, he must have been one of the most familiar sights on that stretch of the Bradford Avon. People waved at him, it was plain that engine-drivers and firemen in the trains that crossed the bridge above looked out for him, and he was on amiable terms with the anglers on the banks.

The house struck me as not greatly lived in, though this may have been because of the absence of children. There seemed to me to be a lack of idiosyncracy. There were relatively few books, though they did include the only set of the Loeb Library I have ever seen in a private house. There were a great many gewgaws and knick-knacks, as in my philistinism I thought of them, though I suspect they were anything but that, tiny carvings in ivory, Lilliputian sets of books, miniscule china bouquets of flowers. The pictures, which were for the most part reproductions of Italian renaissance paintings, were quite literally out-faced and out-blazoned by Leslie's Persian carpets, collecting which, one gathered, was his great extravagance. There was also a grand piano. I never heard him play it, though he did play, and pretty well I fancy. From time to time, he still saw his old music master and spoke of him affectionately.

By my standards, Avondale was a big house, and seeing Leslie in it, I was impressed, mistakenly perhaps, by the loneliness of his life. It was a house in which only one human being lived, though somewhere, out of sight, at the top of the house or the bottom, were Charlie and his wife, who was the cook, and perhaps their son as well.

And since the grounds were several acres, enclosed on three sides by a high wall and on the fourth by the river, to enter Avondale seemed to be to enter another, self-contained, world in which the customs were different from those I was used to. When I came down to breakfast, Leslie jumped up from his chair to shake me by the hand, when he left the room after breakfast to begin his work he'd shake it again, and when we met for lunch the ritual was repeated. It was, I realised, a hangover from his long spells in Italy, and, though I was nothing like so chary of hand-shaking as MacNeice, it was forced upon me that in the ordinary way of things I scarcely shook hands from one week's end to another.

As I have said, he was diffident and self-deprecating, qualities he turned into a source of humour. You would have thought he was defenceless against the world. A wealthy bachelor – in an interview he gave the *Guardian* a year or two before he died he said he thought he was probably not far short of being a millionaire – he seemed always at the mercy of servants. Not that his were the usual tiresome middle-class grumbles about those paid to attend on them, for they were always translated into humour and when they appear in the novels they sometimes border, I'm tempted to say, on the metaphysical. The sensitive young men, embarrassed by underlings, bullied by them and apologetic towards them precisely because they are underlings, were kin – remote kin, no doubt, but still kin – to Kafka's nameless heroes. He was, I suppose, generalising from his own experience. Before the war, there was the greatly cherished gondolier who, he discovered, regularly tippled his whisky, and there seemed always to have been a cook who bullied him or was lost to him, bribed away by unscrupulous friends into their service. And in the last years of his life, I think he really did suffer from valets who turned out to be small-time con-men or would-be blackmailers.

Typical of these stories and summing them up was the one about the lady he had employed as housekeeper in the early days of the war. She was a widow with a small daughter, who lived in with her, so that it was natural, when Leslie, going to bed and finding elaborate flower-arrangements were appearing nightly on his pillows, should attribute them to the child. When one night, however, one appeared that was quite unambiguous in its symbolism – the stem of one of his pipes protruded towards him from a nest of primroses on his pillow – he was alarmed and consulted Elizabeth Bowen, who was staying in the house at the time. Her advice was immediate: 'Leslie, you must get rid of the woman at once.' To Leslie's relief, the woman accepted her dismissal without remonstrating. Next morning, as the taxi waited, she brought the little girl in as Leslie thought to say goodbye. Standing in the doorway, she drew herself up, as they say, to her full height, flung out her arm accusingly and said: 'Mark him well, Josephine. An Oxford man and a cad!'

Leslie wasn't victimised only by servants. Seeing him, many people saw a sucker and responded accordingly. When I first knew him, in London he invariably stayed at the Athenaeum; until, as he told me, while reading a book he had to review he was called by the porter to the telephone. He put his book down on his chair and went to the booth. When he came back, the book was gone. Another member was reading it. Leslie asked for it back. The man maintained that the book was his property and would not return it. Leslie, convinced that the Athenaeum was a haunt of thieves and liars, transferred his London headquarters to a small, exceedingly comfortable hotel in South Kensington with a remarkably good kitchen. A man I knew well, a barrister of some standing, delighted in being invited by Leslie to lunch there. He always, Leslie told me, suggested that since it was such splendid stuff, shouldn't they begin with caviare, but since a single helping was such a measly amount, shouldn't they each have a double portion? Leslie always agreed but he was not in the least deceived.

On that first visit to Avondale he gave me a copy of his first novel, or rather novella, *Simonetta Perkins*, published in 1925. The story of a girl from Boston abroad for the first time who, reacting against her Puritan background, falls in love with a Venetian gondolier but does not quite yield to him, it is brilliantly executed and would indeed be perfect if it were not so thoroughly a pastiche of James. For me, the *Eustace and Hilda* trilogy remains the most satisfactory and most satisfying of his works, at once the most humanistic and the most humane, since I find its moral centre in the following passage. Hilda is discussing Communism with Eustace's younger sister Barbara and her husband Jimmy, who are symbols of a happy acceptance of living denied to both Eustace and Hilda:

> 'Mind you, I don't agree with what they stand for,' Hilda continued, leaning her elbow on the table and shaking her clenched hand at Jimmy, who recoiled slightly. 'They think a thing becomes right if enough people can be persuaded to do it. They have no sense of personal moral responsibility. I hope you're not like that.'

'Oh no,' said Jimmy recovering himself. 'But I believe in sharing it. Too much responsibility does no one any good.'

Too much responsibility does no one any good. Is it not precisely too great a sense of responsibility for each other that is at the heart of the mutual tragedy of Eustace and Hilda?

That tragedy was the dramatisation, it seems to me, of a conflict within Hartley himself. It is presented in comic, though extremely autobiographical terms, in *The Boat*, which was published in 1949 and has been called, not wholly ironically, 'Hartley's war novel'. It contains some of his best and most delightful comedy, is absurdly too long and bristles with ambiguities, with what an American critic, writing on Hawthorne, has called 'alternative possibilities' of interpretation. It is the most riddling of Hartley's novels and perhaps the most disturbing.

The central character, Timothy Casson, is a middle-aged minor essayist who, until Italy's entry into the war in 1940 forces him back to England, has spent the last eighteen years of his life in Venice. He rents a furnished house in the village of Upton-on-Swirrel because of the chance it seems to promise of his being able to row on the river. But in this, the estate-agent's advertisement has been fraudulant, for the Swirrel is a trout-stream and the appearance of his boat offends not only the fishermen but public opinion. The rector rebuffs him with an icy 'A good many of us are rather busy with war work, Mr Casson', and his solicitors, when appealed to, suggest that, 'under stress of war', he too should take up fishing.

He finds himself dissociated from the local gentry who in normal circumstances would be his associates. His friends from the past are obsessed by if not committed to the war. His servants are hostile to him and threaten continually to leave his employ. Personal relations having failed, aesthetic pleasures then let him down. He discovers he has some sympathisers in the vulgar middle-class refugees from Birmingham, with one of whom, the golden-headed Vera, he falls in love. A Communist, she eggs him on to strike a blow for working-class freedom by rowing his boat down the river. He does so, and as a result both Vera and the rector's wife die.

All the same, Timothy does manage to strike a balance between the claims of personal life and the claims of the community, as I think Leslie never succeeded in doing. Politically, he called himself a Liberal, though his beliefs seemed to me much more akin to those his Puritan forbears would have had with regard to the established

Church – he had himself become an Anglican on going to Harrow. I see *The Boat* as something like a gentle black comedy, the representation of a recurring pattern in his life. He was constantly having brushes with authority which, though comic in telling, indicated the slightly Kafka-esque world he seemed to live in. There was the time when the local council decided to lay a sewer across his garden and through his lawns. It became a saga or perhaps a soap-opera which went on for months and which led to vast expense in legal fees, for he was determined to fight local government all the way. In the end, he won the case; and local government, having torn up his garden and laid the pipes, was ordered to dig them up again and restore all to rights. Which meant that once again his property was invaded by workmen and his quiet, which he valued so much, destroyed.

Then there was the vendetta he had with the swans of the Bradford Avon. Rowing in his skiff, Leslie, it always seemed to me, was on amiable terms with everyone. The swans, though, regarded him with extreme dislike. They hissed at him menacingly, darted their long necks out at him in the mating season and made motions of attack. He was determined not to allow them to rob him of his recreation and prepared, if necessary, to carry the war, as they say, into their camp. But whom did they belong to? The local authority disclaimed any responsibility for them or for their behaviour and, moreover, seemed neither to understand Leslie's problems nor have much sympathy with him. He wrote letters to local newspapers and in return was denounced by nature-lovers as one who not merely preached persecution of animals but demanded the death of some of the most beautiful of God's creatures. He thought up ways of rendering swans' eggs sterile and of secretly and painlessly disposing of the birds. He told these stories wonderfully well, and I must admit that I never knew how seriously he himself took them. He retired to a flat in Knightsbridge and went back less and less often.

'The past is a foreign country; they do things differently there.' So *The Go-Between* begins; and as Leslie grew older the more he seemed a native of that country, the more alien in the present. The number of things that pained him or caused him discomfort increased, and he saw his two great enemies, Freudianism and Marxism, everywhere. It was they, he believed, that had perverted legislation and education alike, though perhaps the Roman Catholic Church was not far behind them. In the name of personal responsibility and individual freedom he epoused causes patently absurd in one of his sweetness and gentleness of character. Certain novelists, who he thought preached the futility of human beings striving to improve themselves by their own efforts, were anathema to him. On all sides he seemed to see muggers and sex-maniacs, against whom the only reliable specifics were capital punishment and flogging.

I see now that we met across a gulf which in all probability was unbridgeable. This did not prevent him from being a generous friend to me, and he was generous to my children too. To the end, he was a great party-goer, a charming host and a charming guest, carrying out both functions as it were professionally. He was a scrupulous correspondent and an indefatigable writer of Collinses. But the claims of his social life were never allowed to get in the way of his writing. Daily, wherever he was, he did his stint, writing in a flowing, extremely legible hand on lined foolscap.

I came to know a number of writers through Leslie, the one I especially associate with him being Algernon Cecil, a very old gentleman when I met him, who had been history master at Eton. He was the author of a life of Metternich and, I think, the youngest son of the Marquis of Salisbury who was Prime Minister. His manners were exquisite, and I used to watch him as it were goggle-eyed, so remote was he from any world I inhabited. He was the Highest of High Tories, and when he came to lunch at Leslie's I knew I was in for a series of small shocks. Not that his conversation was intended to shock, for he was much too well-bred to seek to shock and the utterances that I found sensational were to him obviously self-evident truths to which all right-minded people subscribed. Thus, on our first meeting, he assured me that all England's troubles and perhaps all the woes of the modern world stemmed from the disastrous events of 1832, which was when the rot set in. Another time, he told us sadly that he had discovered that his valet, who he impressed upon us was an excellent young man, had voted for the Labour Party in the 1945 election. He could only think, he said, that the misguided youth had been corrupted by Socialistic ideas acquired in the Royal Air Force. I often wondered what Algernon made of me. I imagine he hadn't the faintest notion who I was; it was enough for him that I was a friend of Leslie's.

Elizabeth Bowen I met first not at Avondale but as Leslie's other guest at dinner in a French restaurant in Jermyn Street. I greatly admired her novels and I was fascinated by her way with English prose. I think she can never have been beautiful, but an unusually tall woman, until her last years, when she was bent and bowed down with arthritis, she had a gaunt handsomeness that was striking. She talked splendidly and in no sense was she an amateur; it seemed there was nothing she didn't know about novels and how they are written. She has a valuable essay called 'Notes on Writing a Novel', which she allowed me to reprint in an anthology I edited. I greatly enjoyed talking shop with her and found her impressive in every way, not least in her having overcome a disability that could have been crippling. From time to time in conversation she was inflicted with a truly ferocious stammer. She did not allow this to prevent her broadcasting and lecturing and she made herself into a notably good broadcaster and, as I discovered by report when I was at Vassar, a successful teacher.

Vassar, indeed, gave me another association with Elizabeth Bowen, for I found myself occupying the apartment she had lived in a year or two before. I could not help wondering how she had got on there, for it must have been close upon the oldest apartment in the United States. The central heating was the most primitive I have ever encountered, the refrigerator seemed not to have been defrosted since it was installed, and the gas cooker was so old that I was terrified of boiling a kettle. Miss Bowen, I suggested to a colleague, must surely have found it very inconvenient? He didn't think so, for Miss Bowen had been in New York City more often than in Poughkeepsie, and, when there, had lived mainly on caviare and Scotch. I saw no reason to believe this.

I have other associations, too, with Elizabeth Bowen. I recall Graham Greene's enthusiasm for her in the Thirties; indeed, it was probably through him that I first read her. For five years, while in Romney Marsh, I lived on the edge of what I think of as the classic Elizabeth Bowen countryside. For some years in the Fifties, her house at Regent's Park, the house described in *The Death of the Heart*, was occupied by Louis MacNiece. I last saw her in the late autumn of 1967 at a teachers' training college at Folkestone, where I was surprised to find she was to give the lecture following mine. There was perhaps half an hour between them, which we spent talking, as it were, in the wings. She struck me as being, despite her arthritis, still indomitable. She said she was occasionally in London and I promised to write to her to propose a date for dinner. This, to my lasting regret, I failed to do, for within a matter of days I was appointed to a professorship and my way of life was radically changed.

Eddie Sackville-West is someone else I always associate with Leslie, though I had met him first in 1945 when, as radio critic on a Birmingham newspaper, I had sought him out as the author of *The*

Rescue, a feature programme on the return of Odysseus which I much admired. And before that, I had heard about him from John Hampson. But that was in Eddie's unregenerate days; when I knew him he was a devout Roman Catholic, a convert. With his carefully trimmed beard, it was not difficult to imagine him in a ruff as an ascetic, melancholy sixteenth-century Spanish grandee in a canvas by Velasquez. When I met him at Avondale he was still the heir to Knole, where he was born. This being so, he could hardly fail to appear to be slumming wherever else he found himself. Not that he was anything so vulgar as a snob. It was simply that Knole as it was when he was a child remained the standard by which he measured things. Nowadays, a private house of the scale and splendour of Knole cannot seem other than incongrous, and to me Eddie partook of that incongruity.

So I found it extremely difficult to see him as Raymond Mortimer's assistant at the *Statesman*, so striking did the contrast appear between his aristocratic languor and what the paper was popularly supposed to represent. He could hardly not be something of a legend in the *Statesman* office. My favourite story about him was of his saying, on being told that someone had a dog, 'But how can he have a dog? He hasn't got a park to exercise it in.'

Leslie, I assume, had first known him as a fellow undergraduate at Balliol after the first war. When I met him at Leslie's he was living in the west of Ireland. I remember asking him how he made the journey to London. 'Oh, nothing could be easier,' he said in his bored way. 'My man drives me to Shannon, where I pick up the aeroplane from New York.' He was terribly conscious of present deficiencies and past glories and in my memory his conversation was usually on these. I recall him preaching at lunch one day how essential it was that people like ourselves, creative writers, men who lived for the things of the spirit and the mind, should have servants. He might have been the French Symbolist hero who declared: 'Live? Our servants will do that for us.' As evidence of the decline in the standards of living he quoted the fact that nowadays even at Knole the bed-linen was not changed every day.

As a small boy, he had known Conrad, who had had a cottage on the Knole estate. I had written something in praise of Ford Madox Ford and Eddie rebuked me for this. Ford, he said, was a bounder, and I was made to feel that praising Ford was tantamount to denigrating Conrad. I find Ford a much less admirable novelist than I once did, but Eddie's remarks interested me for the light they threw on the discrepancy between Ford's reputation in the United States and his reputation here. Americans overrate him partly because they are gullible; they take him at his own valuation. The English, on the other hand, since they are English, cannot take seriously claims to distinction made by a man who among other things could not decide whether he had been to school at Eton or Westminster when, to make the offence worse, he had all the time been to University College School. What light, if any, this throws on the part played by snobbery in English life and its effects on literary judgements is something I have never been able to determine.

Given the standards that informed his conversation and the languidness of his manner of speech, it was almost impossible that Eddie Sackville-West should not have been a figure of fun. In fact, he was an extremely hard-working, wholly serious man. According to his own accounts, he had spent nearly all his time at Eton playing the piano; nobody had tried to stop him, and he had been very happy. His aim in those days was to become a concert pianist, but chronic ill-health prevented this. He became one of the most learned of music critics, an admirable literary critic and the author of a notably fine biography of de Quincey. For a man who would be a writer, it is probably fatal to be born at Knole and to be a descendant of the author of *Gorbuduc*. At least, Eddie went a long way towards surmounting these grave handicaps.

My last memory of him is of a Sunday luncheon-party at Avondale at which the other guests were Lady Violet and Anthony Powell. To my naive surprise, since they were both Etonians of much the same age and in much the same line of business, I found it strange that Eddie and Powell were meeting for the first time. It was an occasion simultaneously of great fascination and excruciating boredom, for it was dominated by their single-minded attempt to discover a common ancestor. Lithely, relentlessly, they swarmed up their respective family trees, crawled perilously to the extreme ends of far-flung branches and swung themselves across to other trees. The figure is anything but perfect, but it was the first time I had come across genealogy pursued with passion. Sometime over the coffee and liqueurs, to their satisfaction and my relief, identify a common forefather they did.

I had been an acquaintance of Powell's for a number of years, introduced to him by Julian Maclaren-Ross, who appears in *Dance to the Music of Time* as F. X. Trapnel. This was in 1946 or 1947, and Powell had been in communication with me a week or two before we met, for he was assistant editor of the *TLS* and he telephoned me inviting me to write a 'middle' on the nineteenth-century American novelist William Dean Howells, whose *The Rise of Silas Lapham* was just about to be published in the World's Classics series. I was flattered by the invitation, for it was the first time I had had dealings with the *TLS*. All I knew about Howells was that he'd been a friend both of Mark Twain and Henry James. Powell said that this was all any Englishman knew about Howells: would I look into him and see if we'd all been missing something? It was the sort of exploratory assignment I relished. I spent the next three or four weeks immersed in Howells, none of whose novels were in print but obtainable easily enough from the London Library.

Julian took us to the Powells' house at Regent's Park, We had our four-months-old son with us in his carry-cot, and the Powells suggested that any time we wanted to be free of him for an hour or two we could leave him with the nanny who looked after their children. Powell said it was a service they had often performed for the infant son of George Orwell, a friend from Eton days. Powell, I remember, congratulated us on our son's 'witty nose', a remark I associate with something Graham Greene said. He had come to lunch a few days earlier and gone through the meal under the unwavering stare of my son in his high chair. 'How,' Graham was at last impelled to cry, 'their innocent eyes bore into one!'

As I recall it, the conversation that evening was largely about silent films, about which and their silent stars Julian and Powell swapped reminiscences. Powell I remember as being especially enthusiastic about Theda Bara, the famous vamp, whom I certainly never saw.

I had admired Powell's pre-war novels, *Afternoon Men* particularly. He was generally bracketed with Evelyn Waugh, for they shared a common corner of the Twenties. When *A Question of Upbringing* appeared reviewers were taken by surprise, so different was it from the early novels. As volume of *A Dance to the Music of Time* followed volume, my admiration increased. I felt there was a falling off towards the end, but it is surely a remarkable achievement, nonetheless, for in it Powell creates a world parallel to the real world and utterly convincing. It arouses fascinating questions about the relation of life to art. The characters bear the stamp of complete authenticity, yet it is impossible to name their originals with any certainty. Widmerpool, for instance, one feels *must* be from the life, yet guesses as to his original seem entirely speculative. In the end, it is as though the character Widmerpool is the universal type, the Platonic ideal, and the alleged original models derivatives from it. So with Trapnel and

Maclaren-Ross. I did not spot Julian as the source of the fictitious character, though as soon as Powell divulged the identity of the model the relationship between them was apparent. Even so, it is Trapnel who seems the master-figure and Julian whom he inspired.

Contemplating *A Dance to the Music of Time*, I think how wonderful it would be to be an invisible guest at a cocktail party for the originals of the characters in the sequence. And I also think how disconcerting it might be.

If there is such a thing as a pattern in life it is not discernible while the weaving is in process, or at least not to the weaver. In those post-war years, I saw myself above everything else as a novelist. If at the same time I had to do other things, review books, broadcast, write for broadcasting I saw these as essentially ancillary, temporary expedients. In retrospect, I can see that all the time I was changing into something else, into what I suppose I must call a critic. It was not a word I cared to use about myself, for I felt it had been debased by the glibness with which it was used. I knew what a critic was. A critic was Dr Johnson and S. T. Coleridge and Mr Eliot. A critic was one of the greatest. I called myself a literary journalist and hoped that once or twice in my life I might write something, however small, that would be criticism.

I was searching for a theme for a new novel but at any time had at least two non-fiction books on the stocks. A new publisher had commissioned a little book on Bennett, and another new publisher, John Baker, who had founded a firm called Phoenix House, invited me to lunch at the Reform and proposed that I should make an anthology of what poets and novelists had to say about their crafts. It was a very agreeable assignment in which I re-discovered something like the excitement of my sixth-form and undergraduate years and I found out once again that I wanted both to learn and to communicate as vividly as possible what I had learned.

John Baker it was who, more than anyone else, was responsible for what I was to be twenty years later. Something like ten years older than I was, he had been in publishing since his boyhood. I know nothing of his background but from his accent put him down as lower-middle class from South London. An irascible man, he had something of a chip on his shoulder which took the form of resentment at the ease with which the comfortably born obtained success in publishing. As a very young man, he told me, he had been fired from one of the noble publishing houses for trying to unionise the packers. He had a missionary zeal and was a pioneer in promoting book clubs catering for minority tastes, though his outstanding achievement was probably in promoting interest in archaeology years before it was discovered by television.

After he had published my anthology *Writers on Writing*, he asked me to write a little book on the way novels should be read and suggested, a year or two later, that I should write a one-volume history of the English novel, since friends in the British Council had told him that something of that kind was needed. I was immediately conscious of the vast gaps in my knowledge of the novel and of the time and labour it would take to fill. Why didn't he ask an academic? I said; universities were full of people who knew more about Scott and Dickens than I did. 'And tell me,' retorted Baker, 'who among academics is going to chance his arm by going out on a limb with a book like this?' I couldn't name one, and the proposal appealed to me; so that for the next four or five years I was so busy reading novels of the past two centuries for my book and new ones for the *New Statesman* that I had no time to write one of my own.

Increasingly, my life became that of a commentator. I was continually in broadcasting studios, at Broadcasting House for the Home Service, at 200 Oxford Street and Bush House for the External Services, in a former convent at Maida Vale for the Transcription Service. I was in the dummy run and the first broadcasts of 'The Critics' programme, in which I appeared about a dozen times a year for the next twenty. It was a generally agreeable programme to take part in and it kept one in touch with what was happening outside literature. At the same time, the Third Programme was coming into being. It was a major event in British cultural life and for people like me it meant a whole new market for our wares.

At the time, though, what meant most to me was that V. S. Pritchett invited me to write for the *New Statesman* and, specifically, to review new novels. I gave up reviewing fiction in the *Spectator* but went on reviewing other books both there and in *Time and Tide* until there came a time when I found myself in all three papers on the same Friday; which seemed so silly, so monstrous even, that I decided on the spot to write only for the *Statesman* among the sixpennies. Most Wednesday mornings, when the literary and arts pages went to press, I would spend in the literary editor's office.

There was, as I recall those Wednesday mornings, an atmosphere of ordered chaos, a controlled free-for-all, with Raymond Mortimer, ironical, never ruffled, very much in command. There were three desks in the office, which looked out over Lincoln's Inn. One was

Mortimer's. Pritchett, bright-eyed, effervescing with wit, with whom I had most to do, sat at another. T. C. Worsley, who had succeeded MacCarthy as dramatic critic and who was also in charge of the arts pages, occupied the third. I was meeting him for the first time, for though he had been on the staff before the war he was only recently out of the RAF. He was very tall, erect and thin, somewhat severe in manner but with a smile of great sweetness. We soon became friends and I got to know him well. Some, I know, found him spiky; he had had an unsettled youth and never, I think, found the course of living easy. He had been at Marlborough at the same time as MacNeice and had kept wicket for Oxford on occasion. He had failed to get his blue, though he did hit a six at Lord's. He had taught at Wellington and worked in Spain in the Government's propaganda service during the Civil War. Once, he told me, when Madrid was under snow, he was deputed to show an Indian novelist round the trenches in University City. The novelist insisted on making a speech to the soldiers in the trenches, saying he brought greetings from workers of India. Would the Spanish comrades, he ended, Cuthbert translating, care to send a message to the Indian workers? An embarrassed silence was broken by a Spaniard saying: 'Please tell the Indian workers we hope they're not as cold as we are.'

He had written a book describing the retreat of the Government forces from Malaga. He then taught cricket at Gordonstoun. He first appeared in the *Statesman* with a poem. I do not remember it but I can understand his delighted astonishment when it evoked a congratulatory telegram from Walter Sickert, whom he had never met.

On these Wednesday mornings two or three others were almost always present. One was Giles Romilly, who had a retainer from the paper as a reporter for the front half and as a book-reviewer. Short and sturdy and rosy-cheeked, he was related to Churchill, to whom he seemed to bear a physical resemblance. This was something of an ironical occupational hazard of working for the paper at that time; Maurice Richardson, who was a regular reviewer, was always being taken by strangers for Randolph. Giles, who had been taught by Cuthbert at Wellington, had won notoriety in the Thirties with his brother Esmond. They had run away from school, founded an anti-public school magazine and gone to Spain to fight for the Government. This, since they were Churchill's nephews, had embarrassed both the British Government and the British Communist Party. Very early in the war, Esmond was killed flying for the RAF and Giles, who had become a war correspondent, was captured by the Germans and because of his distinquished kinsman was held in Colditz as a potential hostage.

Half an hour or so before we adjourned for lunch, G. W. Stonier would come in. As William Whitebait, he was the film critic. The *Statesman* and George alike were great ones for pseudonyms, and whenever you saw a contributor with the name of a fish you could safely bet it was George. From time to time he was also Joseph Gurnard. George was a delightful person who never achieved the success that seemed so obviously within his power; though his extremely witty *Shaving through the Blitz* which appeared, over the name of Fanfarlo, in serial form in *Penguin New Writing*, may well prove to have lasting quality. Everything about him was slightly improbable. Educated at Westminster and Christ Church, he was an Australian by birth. In terms of service to the paper, he was older than anyone else in the building, for he had joined it straight from Oxford as assistant editor and had been groomed, one understood, to succeed Clifford Sharp, the first editor. It seemed characteristic of him that he should once have been a demon googly bowler for the Hampstead Cricket Club. Lunching together once, we evolved a theory that everyone was either the kind of person one met in an Ibsen play or the kind of person one met in a Chekhov. Though I admired Chekhov more, it was in a world like Ibsen's that I thought I belonged. George agreed that he could only be a Chekhov figure. He was slight, gentle, melancholy, witty, with a wispy moustache and a bald head like a tonsure. Kingsley Martin once told me that Stonier was the only man he had ever met totally without ambition. He married late and, when he finally gave up film criticism, set out to fulfil a lifelong aim to travel the length of Africa, from Cape to Cairo, by car. In the course of his journey, he came across his Great Good Place, which was Ian Smith's Rhodesia. After forty years in Chelsea and Bloomsbury, he settled down outside Salisbury to raise turkeys, though he was living at the Cape when last heard of.

And, as I have said, Maurice Richardson was often in, though we were not on much more than nodding terms until close on ten years later. He, too, I suppose never fulfilled his early promise, though he was a wonderfully good journalist writing elegant and witty pieces and book reviews until he died in his late seventies. I see him very much as a man of the early Twenties and the early post-war period. It was an eclectic time, and Maurice remained faithful both to Freud and to Marx. He had, too, a store of esoteric knowledge in the bypaths of natural history. In his own way, he was something of a dandy; the bow tie he invariably wore was in some sense his trademark. He was also what one might call a cultured bruiser. His characteristic expression must have seemed to those who did not know him one of lowering defiance: when he and his great friend John Davenport were on the town together they must have been a formidable pair. He had, I believe, boxed for Oxford. He had a great knowledge of low life and delighted in going round London at night in police cars. My abiding memory of him, though, is somewhat different.

I was with him one afternoon in Fleet Street with a number of other men, of whom one was John Raymond. I fancy we had just come out of El Vino's when Maurice gave vent to a delighted 'Look!' pointing to two nuns who were walking a few yards in front of us. The significance was lost on the rest of us, but Maurice darted ahead and somehow with the utmost dexterity and courtesy threaded his way through the people on the pavement and insinuated himself between the two nuns. Then he walked briskly on and appeared to turn into a shop. Mystified, we followed him, and suddenly he emerged from a shop-doorway smiling with gratified delight. It was, he assured us, awfully lucky to walk between two nuns.

At about one, we drifted away to lunch. Mortimer went his own way but the rest of us usually lunched together, often at an Italian restaurant in Frith Street. I felt very much that I was part of a team, and that the 'Mag', as we always called it, was more important than any of us individually and had an identity that transcended that of each of us. It was like being part of a great foundation, a college perhaps, which was also the embodiment of an almost mystical ideal.

I did not often catch sight of Kingsley Martin but for a year or so, whenever I did, I invariably found myself being introduced to him afresh. Comprehension seemed to dawn on him when my name was uttered, and he would always say something complimentary. I had in fact met him in Birmingham one Christmas late in the war at Philip Sargant Florence's. I had gained an impression of enormous vanity. The charm seemed to come flooding in as at the pressing of a switch. He had an actor's profile, and it seemed to me that from whatever angle you looked at him he was always in profile. I had got him, as I realised later, quite wrong, or, rather, I had isolated and exaggerated only one aspect of him. His faults stood out as plain as warts on a face, but in spite of them I found him a lovable man.

In 1946 and 1947, I was very conscious of the *Statesman's* divided nature; it seemed to exist in two parts, like a pantomime horse, and one often felt that the back half would dearly like to take off in a direction different from that of the front. For me, of course, the second half of the paper was the real paper, and it was galling to feel that it was looked upon as frivolous by Kingsley and the boys at the front, as a sop, perhaps, to forces that had to be pandered to and placated, at least for the time being. While they were saving the world at the front, we at the back were fiddling away like so many Neros. I doubt if Kingsley ever quite managed to reconcile himself with what more than one market survey established, that at least as many readers bought the paper for its coverage of books and the arts as bought it for its politics. So it is even more to his credit that he never interfered with the way the literary and arts pages were conducted. Occasionally he made a protest. He would plead for a respite if the name of Kafka, which was anathema to him, was invoked too often. If he had known it, he would have delighted in Anthony Powell's rhyme, which appeared at about this time in a review he wrote for the *Spectator*, I think:

> It was a summer evening,
> Old Kafka's work was done . . .

He thought that readers could have enough of James and Proust, and, once in a while, he had to be satisfied that a poem that had been published was not nonsense.

He was not a simple Philistine. He had had it on the best authority that the arts were important, though I suspect that he thought they were especially so as a kind of therapy; he was an enthusiastic Sunday painter himself. But I think he had little real feeling for the arts and he could easily be led into expressing the most absurd conventional opinions; I once heard him telling Pritchett that Henry Moore was a charlatan, this on the strength of the holes that appear in some of his sculptures. It was not, I imagine, a view he held for long, for he moved habitually among men and women of much greater sensibility than himself and he was, I think, a genuinely humble man. As soon as he knew that Morgan Forster or Leonard Woolf approved of a writer, he was happy to approve too. Forster and the Woolfs, along with Roger Fry and Lytton Strachey, were sacred cows, and I remember how disturbed he was when John Raymond attacked Strachey in a 'Books in General' article. Whatever had come over John? he asked me anxiously, knowing I was a close friend. It plainly seemed to Kingsley a monstrous, well-nigh blasphemous article. I more or less agreed with it. Fortunately, I was able to say it was a reputable view, because it was F. R. Leavis's, and I think Kingsley was a little comforted by this, for he was a loyal Cambridge man.

That was perhaps ten years later; in 1946 and 1947 it was a source of comfort and assurance to know that Raymond Mortimer, who carried great authority with him because of his associations with Bloomsbury, was always prepared to do battle with Kingsley, even, according to the folklore of the paper, to the point of marching in to his office on occasion and rebuking him for something in the front half that he had found displeasing or wrong-headed. I think few men can have had less in common, but they always spoke of each other with respect and generosity. It is indeed, as I know myself, a simple fact that no literary editor could have worked for a less overbearing, more loyal superior than Kingsley.

He was, I think, a simple man and often a naive one. I am sure that those who found him disingenuous were quite wrong, as were those who accused him of meanness. He was tremendously self-centred, but this stemmed not so much from selfishness as from a total indentification with what was dearest to his heart, which meant the *New Statesman* and all it stood for. This made him, at the worst, a master of rationalisation, and it was compounded by his heritage: he had been nurtured in the traditions of Nonconformity, and though he had early lost his religious faith it was second nature for him to behave as though he had a hot line to God or whatever had taken God's place. Also, so far as I could judge, he was totally without a capacity for introspection, which meant his own actions were constantly taking him by surprise.

His alleged meanness – and, by extension, that of the *Statesman* – are worth looking at. Obviously, it could not be expected to pay comparably with the *Daily Express* or *Vogue*, but by 1946 I knew by experience that its payment of reviewing was higher than that of the *Spectator*, *Time and Tide* or the *Listener*. I knew enough to discount the received view. At about this time I was invited to contribute to a new, rather expensive periodical called *Contact* and I was called in to meet the editor, who was a man called George Weidenfeld, a name which meant nothing to me. At the end of our conversation, he said, a trifle smugly, I thought: 'I think you'll find we pay rather better than the *Statesman*.' I was not surprised when this proved not the least true.

All the same, a policy of stinginess and cheese-paring was associated with the *Statesman* and therefore with Kingsley. When he took over the editorship, this was probably necessary, but in the latter years of his editorship the paper can have been anything but poor. It had, in fact, attained a prosperity Kingsley had great difficulty in believing and did not trust, and contributors' rates and staff-members' expenses continued to be rigorously scrutinised. This was in line with the paper's traditions, part of which was that payment was the last thing contributors expected. It had begun as a politically radical, missionary journal, and some of its early contributors, Shaw and Bennett among them, one was given to understand, had always refused payment. Similarly, it was taken for granted – and experience over the years had helped to confirm it – that the turnover of contributors to the literary and arts pages was large and that as soon as a young man had made his mark there he would move on and be snapped up by the *Sunday Times* or the *Observer*.

This unformulated but strongly felt tradition I have no doubt Kingsley sometimes exploited, as I have no doubt it was a bad tradition. When I joined the literary staff in 1959 Cuthbert Worsley had just left us to become drama critic of the *Financial Times* and we were faced with the task, which went on for months, of finding a new critic who would not seriously let down the traditions established by MacCarthy and Worsley. I recall Kingsley saying to me in exasperation: 'I'll *never* understand why Cuthbert wanted to leave us!' and he plainly couldn't. But I could have told him why. If Cuthbert had been offered a salary approaching that the *Financial Times* had offered him he'd have stayed gladly.

Over the years, there was, I think, a perceptible change in Kingsley. I once read a book by Gilbert Murray on Liberalism which began with the bald assertion that Liberals believe in high thinking and plain living, a proposition which effectively put me off Liberalism. When I first knew him, Kingsley was a Liberal in Murray's sense. He was always being shocked, or pretending to be shocked, by other people's extravagance, by the appearance of conspicuous waste. Thus, seeing George Stonier, who was a modest man, wearing a suit he hadn't noticed before, he is reported to have exclaimed: 'Not *another* new suit, George!' And Cuthbert Worsley told me of how he had once been complimented by Kingsley on a new shirt. Kingsley was loud in his admiration and enquired where he could buy one like it; until he was told the price and was then horrified. Later, doubts seemed to have dawned about the validity of the premises on which much of his life had been based, and these were accompanied by feelings of bewilderment and the reluctant recognition that possibly he had been wrong for years. This I found endearing and disarming.

I recall two conversations I had with him in 1959 or 1960. We were talking desultorily in his office one morning and he told me that he had walked home to his flat at Charing Cross from his club at half past eleven the night before. He had stopped to look at the goods in a shop-window in New Bond Street, an incident revealing, I thought, considerable depths of innocence, especially since recounted quite unselfconsciously. The inevitable happened: a tart had come up and said: 'Are you coming home with me, darling?' Kingsley had replied: 'Oh, I couldn't do a thing like that.' 'Why ever not?' asked the girl. 'And do you know?' Kingsley said, with considerable astonishment, 'I couldn't think of a single reason I could give her.'

The other time, he was expressing his envy of those people who were not oppressed by conscience, who lived free from feelings of guilt. He had never found this possible, and as the man he especially admired and envied in this respect he instanced Compton Mackenzie. I knew Mackenzie in much the same way as Kingsley did, and for me he was a performer whose reminiscences and anecdotes were often amusing, sometimes boring but always needed taking with a grain of salt. And I am not at all sure that he was the happy hedonist of Kingsley's imagination. Nevertheless, as a psychological type he was different enough from Kingsley to appear his mirror-image and therefore seductively attractive to him. For Kingsley, Mackenzie was the epitome of the free spirit, one might say of the impossibly free spirit.

There can be scarcely such a person, from the nature of the trade, as a representative journalist. In my time, I have thought my early mentor H. S. Cater was one and I have thought Kingsley one as well, and they had almost nothing in common. Kingsley had begun his career as a journalist, if not at the top precisely, at least in its higher reaches. He had come into the profession as a Cambridge don and professional historian recruited by the *Manchester Guardian* as a leader-writer. But vastly different as he was from Kay, he shared a common quality, the one which above all others is the journalist's *sine qua non*: curiosity. It was not especially selective, but it was unceasing, and it made Kingsley as little susceptible to boredom as anyone I have known. Once, when he was at a loose end one evening, he tried to persuade me to go with him and see Agatha Christie's play *The Mouse Trap*. It was then in its tenth year perhaps. Why didn't we go and find out what accounted for its popularity? I didn't accompany him, for, though I too was at a loose end that evening, I couldn't conceive of its being as boring as I assumed *The Mouse Trap* would be. But Kingsley didn't find it so, even if, as I suspect, he was as much interested in the audience as in the play.

His unfailing curiosity meant that it was always an adventure to be with him. The most run-of-the-mill, banal taxi-ride became exciting. He seemed to enter instant rapport with the driver; within a matter of minutes, he had gauged the man's politics and views on the matters of the day, and his questions, which were uninhibited by self-consciousness or considerations of conventional good taste, never seemed to give offence. Which underlines the quality that seems to me most characteristic of Kingsley, an innocence that beguiled and was redeeming.

IX

In the midst of all this activity, the circumstances of my life suddenly changed. We decided that central London was not the place in which to raise a family. We looked for somewhere to rent in the country and with great luck I found a pleasant little Georgian house in the high street of Lydd, in Romney Marsh in Kent. It was a country quite unknown to me and, though only sixty miles from London, it felt very remote. The Marsh I found enchanting. The flatness of the land, the distance of the horizon, the height of the sky and the constantly changing cloudscape gave an impression of great expanse. The feel of life was different from anything I had known before, and so were the literary associations. Looking out of my study-cum-sitting room on to the high street, with Wells's *Experiment in Autobiography* in mind, I could fancy that at any moment James and Gosse might pedal by on their bicycles on the way to visit Wells, less than four miles away in New Romney. This was Wells country. I could walk along the shingle beach from Dungeness to Littlestone and have a drink at the hotel where the First Men in the Moon had stayed and look out to see the spot where their balloon came down.

Half a dozen miles away to the west lay Rye and Henry James's Lamb House, and not far away, the villages where Conrad, Stephen Crane and Ford Madox Ford had lived. There were more recent associations. The beaches and coast beyond Dymchurch towards Hythe were Elizabeth Bowen country: it was there that the graceless Heccombs had their bungalow 'Waikiki' in *The Death of the Heart*. And Dungeness, whither a secret passage from my garden, which I never found, was supposed to lead, seemed in its romantic isolation created to be the scene of a thriller that only Miss Bowen could write.

No sooner were we settled at Lydd than I was invited to act as a tutor at an Oxford University summer school in twentieth-century

English life and literature of which Helen Gardner was director. It was designed exclusively for foreign students. For a fortnight, I lived and conducted tutorials in Worcester College. It was very agreeable, even exciting, discoursing on modern literature with French and Italian students who had been more or less barred from English studies for five or six years and discussing matters of common interest with American graduate students, for the majority of the students were young American officers waiting to be demobilised and return to graduate school. It was valuable, too, for me to come into contact as a colleague with young English scholars, junior lecturers at British universities, from whom the tutors were largely recruited.

The most rewarding experience that this Oxford venture gave me, though, was meeting Joyce Cary. We were not unknown to each other, for it fell to me, as Michael Joseph's literary adviser, to be the first reader of his manuscripts, and I gathered he always wanted to know what I had said of them. I had known his novels since the early Thirties, for John Hampson had introduced them to me. Cary was little known then. The only thing John and I knew about him was that he was completely unlike any of his contemporaries. In many ways, his work seemed to contradict most of the qualities that for us made a novel modern. He seemed an odd-man-out, but his power was unmistakable, and we admired him greatly. He did not achieve anything like adequate recognition until the war-years, though by 1947 his reputation was higher in America than it was at home. In that year, I remember going with Robert Lusty, Joseph's partner, to visit the man who was to be my American publisher in his London hotel. He had just read the typescript of my new novel and was flattering about it, but he had reservations. 'I certainly hope we can do it,' he said. 'The trouble is, it's too British.'

At the time, the comment seemed stupid. Ten years later, when I was teaching in Iowa, I was to realise what he meant. To many Americans, perhaps, indeed, to a majority, the world depicted in British fiction, the manners and institutions, the way of life described, is utterly foreign. In Cedar Rapids, Iowa, the population was predominantly Czech. There were sizeable Norwegian and German minorities, too. The overwhelming mass of the population were without link of any sort with Britain. They referred to the 'Old Country', but Britain was not what they meant.

Bob Lusty was anything but sympathetic towards Thayer Hobson's reaction to my novel. 'Yes,' he said, 'and look what happened to the last novel you turned down because it was "too British".' It had been

Cary's *The Horse's Mouth*, which, published by another house, had been the choice of the Literary Guild and a best-seller for many weeks.

It took Cary ten years to establish himself as a novelist and, even so, he was a late starter. He was forty-four when his first novel appeared, by which time he had been retired from his first career, in the Nigerian Political Service, for twenty years. As we know him from his novels, he was essentially self-made. In *The Case for African Freedom*, he wrote that he was a man who,

> after ten years of active, thoughtless, and various experience of the world, began, rather late in youth, to ask what it amounted to; to dig up all his foundations, to find exactly what they were; who discovered then as you might expect, that some of them were mud, some were hollow caves of air, others sand; and who then slowly and painfully rebuilt them, as far as he could manage the task, as a coherent whole, on which to found a new life and a new mind.

It was from his transvaluation of values, following the life of a man of action largely removed from literary preoccupations, that his fiction sprang.

Until 1932, when *Aissa Saved* was published, his life must have seemed a series of false starts. Born of Anglo-Irish stock in Londonderry, he had been sent to school at Clifton and then gone first to Edinburgh and then to Paris as an art student before going up to Oxford. There, he told me, he had had a chicken omelette for breakfast every morning. After Oxford, he had spent a few months working with Sir Horace Plunkett in the Irish co-operative farming movement and thence to Bulgaria as a member of a British Red Cross unit in the Balkan War of 1912–13. A year later, he joined the Nigerian Political Service, fought in the campaign against the Germans in West Africa and was then a magistrate and executive officer in a remote district of Nigeria. He was invalided out of the Service in 1920 and settled himself in Oxford with his wife and growing family to make himself a novelist.

It was a ten years' struggle and for years he seems to have had no close friends there outside members of his wife's family. By 1948, things were very different: he had warm friends and admirers in people like Lord David Cecil, Enid Starkie and Helen Gardner. He invited me round for drinks one evening. He was, I think, the handsomest man I have ever met. With his lofty brow and Roman nose, Cary looked proconsular: it was not difficult to imagine him ruling alone over thousands of natives in a country the size of England. He looked a ruler and a wise one at that. Meeting him, it was impossible, I think, not to be convinced of the beauty and loftiness of his mind.

I was struck, too, by the impression he gave me of certainty. Here, it seemed to me, was a man who never had to question himself, who *knew* as by direct intuition. Alert and wise, he sat there in surroundings which were his own and in which he was at home. I seem to remember there was a grand piano in the room, the walls of which were hung with his own paintings. He spoke rather jerkily in a lightish voice, a jaunty voice, which in retrospect reminds me of Lord Montgomery's as we used to hear it in the war. Whether this similarity, if indeed it was a fact, was due to their common Anglo-Irish origins I do not know, nor do I not know whether Cary thought of himself as Irish. I am inclined now to think the similarity of voice may have arisen from their being both men of action used to command. That he was a writer would not, I think, have been your guess on meeting him for the first time.

He asked me how my new novel was coming along. I replied that it wasn't; I was still waiting for an idea. This seemed to surprise him. 'Why,' he said, pointing to the ceiling, 'I've got twenty-five novels up above, in various stages of readiness.' He explained to me his way of writing. 'I do not,' he wrote somewhere, 'write one novel at a time. The process is more like collecting . . . I have a great number of . . . manuscripts in every stage of development.' When he had an idea for a novel he would set aside a special folder for it. The idea might be implicit in a report that had caught his attention in a newspaper or be enshrined in a scrap of dialogue. He would put it in its folder and add to it in the course of time any notes he might acquire towards it, sketches of characters, impressions of scenes and so on, until the material accumulated to the point where it needed only to be edited into a whole, as it were.

He made writing novels sound easy, much easier than he can actually have found it, but the method was one that he had developed for himself out of his own experience, for his early years as a writer were strewn with more or less abortive novels. The method also throws light, I feel, on the nature of his novels, which strike one as somehow improvisatory or at least very fluid. They are, so to speak, in no way set; one feels that scenes could be transposed from one to another without much difficulty, and though this contributes to the strong sense of life they have, their apparently provisional nature was not something a writer who had tried to bring himself up in the manner of Flaubert could easily adapt himself to.

I cannot pretend I knew Cary well. My meetings with him were more or less casual, at the cocktail parties Michael Joseph gave at, I think, two-yearly intervals, and at the Society of Authors. At the cocktail parties, he was usually accompanied by one or other of his sons and their wives, which throws light on a comment on himself he once made to me. He did not belong to a club, he said, because he was a 'domestic man'. In memory, his house in Oxford as I saw it in 1948, struck me as being very much lived in; one felt it was shaped very much by Cary's tastes and his wife's, and though I forget whether I met any of his children then, one felt their presence everywhere. One felt a web of family activity, with Cary very much at its centre.

I think it must have been after his wife died that he told me he gave all rights in his new novels as they were written to his children. He maintained himself on the earnings from his lecture-tours in the United States. He was in great demand, and he must have been rewarding to see and listen to, though he was not a good lecturer. At least, he was not on the one occasion I heard him, at the Oxford summer school. Indeed, I was disappointed, even somewhat mortified, for I had urged my students, most of whom were hearing his name for the first time, on no account to miss his lecture. He had thought long and deeply on novels and art, on the nature of government, on religion, on the whole range of human activity and the part the creative impulse plays in it. He spoke without notes, which is always dangerous, though wonderfully impressive when it comes off. He was obviously relying on his ability to tap, as it were, his consciousness and his unconscious as the discourse flowed. This he did not manage to do. He sounded as though he were talking from the top of his head, as they say. He talked jerkily and disconnectedly and did not seem to be doing much more than repeat the proposition that the novel was important because it celebrated life and that life must be reverenced because it was life. I suspect he misjudged his audience, which was a specialist audience seeking knowledge and specialist also in that it was composed of men and women who had experienced war at first hand, as combatants or as inhabitants of enemy-occupied countries.

I did not see him at all during the last three years of his life. I was in America when he was struck by creeping paralysis. He struggled against it with great courage and ingenuity – he devised ways and means of continuing his work as his control of movement decreased – and against all odds was writing to the end. Dan Davin, whom I introduced to him and who became a close friend, has a most moving account of the last years in his *Closing Times*.

Having seen the film of *The Horse's Mouth*, Kingsley Martin asked me about Cary. What was he like? What were his beliefs? I answered him as best as I could. He could scarcely wait to hear me out. 'Oh, Schopenhauer,' he said, disappointedly. No philosopher, I do not know whether Cary was influenced by Schopenhauer or not, though I suspect not. Both as novelist and thinker, he was, as I have said, a self-made man, what Eliot, writing of Blake, called a 'resourceful Robinson Crusoe'. But he was also, of all our contemporaries, the novelist and celebrant of the creative imagination. That for him, was the central factor in human life, since it made every man the creator of his own life and destiny and, as he shows in such novels as *Mister Johnson*, *Charley Is My Darling*, *A House of Children* and *To Be a Pilgrim*, the protagonist in tragedy and comedy alike. Tragedy and comedy are, indeed, reverse sides of the one coin. My memory of him is of nobility.

The move to the country changed my life little, for I could still be in London by mid-morning. It was more affected by changes at the *New Statesman*, for Raymond Mortimer was giving up the literary editorship to join the *Sunday Times* and Pritchett wished to devote all his time to writing. As I discovered over the years, it was the kind of internal crisis Kingsley Martin was rarely graceful in solving. Worsley took over, but the unconditional title of literary editor was denied him; he was merely 'acting'. Kingsley, I suppose, had a sneaking hope that someone with a greater name might present himself, and certainly the oddest and most impossible names were bandied about. Cuthbert invited me to come in and help him, which I did for some three or four months. I found him extraordinarily sympathetic and congenial to work with. He suggested, indeed, that I should be literary editor and he assistant, for he saw himself primarily as dramatic critic. Elsewhere, decisions went on not being made; from week to week, one had a sense of intense activity going on offstage, of enormous wheels and sprockets spinning and whirling in the void.

Then, quite suddenly, it was announced that Cuthbert was to be literary editor and his assistant, Janet Adam Smith. Since she could not join the paper for some weeks, would I, I was asked, carry on in a temporary capacity?

I did not know Janet, whose husband, the poet Michael Roberts, had recently died, leaving her four children to bring up. Of course, I knew of her reputation. She had been Ackerley's predecessor at the

Listener, a valiant and discriminating champion of contemporary poetry, and she had written well on James and Stevenson. It seemed to me that no appointment could be more sensible, and I was perfectly willing to carry on till she arrived.

I was responsible for a coup or two. I induced Graham Greene to write for us occasionally, which was regarded as a considerable achievement since his affiliations had always been with the *Spectator*. We entertained him to lunch at a restaurant in Percy Street, Worsley, Giles Romilly and George Stonier and I. When we got to the restaurant, he said, as though sniffing a challenge: 'Isn't this the place where they wouldn't serve George Orwell because he wasn't wearing a jacket?' We took our cue from Graham. It was a very hot, humid day, and when we were ushered to our table, we took off our jackets and loosened our ties. Nothing, of course, happened; the waiter took our orders and in due time the dishes arrived. I suspect we all felt some slight disappointment, imagining the paragraph we would have telephoned the *Evening Standard's* 'Londoner's Diary'.

It was about this time that I set a competition still often remembered when Graham is mentioned in print. In a curious way, it seemed as if Green had become the contemporary novelist's occupational name, for besides Graham, there were Henry, F. L. and C. F., as well as the distinguished Franco-American Julian. I offered the usual prizes for the best first or final paragraph of a new novel by any Green. None of the competitors attempted parody of anyone but Graham. I judged the competition and announced the winners. By first post next Monday a letter had come to the editor from Graham thanking him for the present of an unsolicited guinea. I had at least had the gumption to award him the second prize, for what he assured me was a genuine paragraph from a discarded novel.

That evening, I had drinks with him at his flat. A number of people were there. He produced a razor he had just bought and was very proud of. He demonstrated it in action. It didn't need lather, it wasn't powered by electricity, you could use it anywhere. I was unimpressed: what was the point of it? 'But think,' he said, 'how useful it will be in an aeroplane?' There, he had me.

In August, the slackest month of the publishing year, Worsley went off on holiday. By the time he got back, Janet would have joined the paper. Meanwhile I was in charge. There was little to do; all the reviews we would use were set up; no new books were expected. Any new play was unlikely to demand more than a shorter notice, and if I didn't cover it myself I knew that Kingsley adored nothing so much as deputising for the dramatic critic. I was rather bored, indeed; and then the month was made memorable by my meeting John Raymond.

I do not think he can have published more than a couple of reviews in the *Statesman*. He was a mysterious Golden Boy who had appeared out of nowhere, the discovery of Desmond MacCarthy, who had been so impressed by something John had written in an obscure magazine circulating among second-hand booksellers that he had urged the *Statesman* to take him up. It was my task to see through the press John's first 'Books in General' piece, a consideration of Ronald Knox's *Enthusiasm*. I found it impressive in its learning and dazzling in its felicity. John came in, a much younger man that I'd anticipated, chubby, in his early twenties, with a round face that was pink and apparently still hairless. He was just out of the Army, where he had served with Field Security Personnel in Ceylon, and was now on the *Times*. Both his parents, I knew, were distinguished actors. I made one or two trifling suggestions that perhaps marginally improved the piece and made him a gift of the German word *kitsch*, which he did not know and accepted gratefully. I had never met another man I had so taken to at a first meeting. We lunched together. It was the beginning of a close friendship that lasted a decade, though all I knew at the time was that this was the most delightful of young men, the most enchanting of companions, in whom learning and sensitivity went hand-in-hand with high spirits and a champagne gaiety. These were qualities which even in later years, when he was at his most tiresome and difficult, surfaced intermittently and I think were never wholly lost.

He was more than ten years younger than I was, and when we were together I always felt we were of different generations. He was not, for instance, a Thirties man. And I was aware of other differences between us. Indeed, I found him both fascinating and disconcerting. As much as Compton Mackenzie in Kingsley Martin's eyes, he was wonderfully free of the Nonconformist conscience. At the same time, he had his own religious commitment; when I first met him, he was taking instruction from the Jesuits at Farm Street. Here, I have to confess a failure in imaginative sympathy with him. When, a few years later, I found myself briefly attracted to Catholicism, it was not from any influence of John, and in the end I saw that for me conversion was the ultimate act of desperation, one of which I was incapable.

I can see, of course, how the Roman Church spoke both to his sense of history and his sense of drama. I realised when we met that here was an extremely ambitious young man, but the nature of the ambition was puzzling. To a degree beyond that of almost anyone else I have known, his life was inextricably bound up with books. You could see this when you visited him at his flat at South Kensington. It was underfurnished, but this was scarcely noticeable since chairs, tables, chests of drawers, the spare beds, were piled with books. Books were stacked on the floor, too. He was a great raider of second-hand bookshops and seemed to buy books by the dozen. Where review-copies were concerned, he was ruthless and quick to sell, but I don't think he ever sold or threw away a book he had bought.

Part of this was simply an aspect of his loathing for libraries, though there was one of which he was a regular patron, for he held it in great respect. This was the library of the Reform Club, which is traditionally a working library for politicians, economists and journalists, a place, in other words, after John's own heart. For John, books were the tools of his trade. He was not a bibliophile and he had no reverence for first editions. For him, a book was what the dictionary says it is, 'Portable written or printed work filling a number of sheets fastened together, usually with sheets sewn or pasted together hingewise and enclosed in cover.' What gave it its value was what was written or printed on the sheets. He collected books because he had to have, immediately to hand, on the premises, as it were, his own version of the British Museum Reading Room. There was no apparent order in his collection; seemingly, its arrangement was utterly higgledy-piggledy; but he could find what he wanted in it without difficulty.

What surprised me was that he seemed to have no overwhelming wish to write books himself. He took it for granted, of course, that he would write some in the way of his trade, but he had no ambitions, as far as one could see, of writing a great novel or a great biography. He certainly didn't despise such things; quite the opposite; yet in his own way he cut the writing of them down to size. He was a journalist, it was what he wanted to be, and he saw it as the noblest, or rather second noblest, calling a man could follow.

His ambition was to write 'middles', literary causeries of the kind we associate with Desmond MacCarthy and Bennett in his Jacob Tonson guise. The 'Books in General' page in the *Statesman* was made for him. In his hands, as in those of Pritchett and two or three others, it was a minor art-form. Two qualities went to the making of his success in it. One was prolificity – I remember Pritchett telling me, in the days when he lived in the country, that he had 'an artesian well of "Books in General" down in Wiltshire' – the other was his endless curiosity.

It is in this latter quality, of course, that the journalist in him emerges. When I first met him he was on the *Times* and he always valued his association with it. He liked to see himself as being near the centre of power and always prided himself as being 'in the know': he revelled in the atmosphere of El Vino's Wine Bar in Fleet Street, in the gossip swapped there by the political correspondents. It was in El Vino's that he met and had a long companionable talk with Aneurin Bevan. I found his political stance obscure. He had voted Labour in 1945; in the Fifties, whenever success at a bye-election suggested there was another Liberal renaissance, he would talk about fighting a constituency as a Liberal; but generally he would invoke Lord Randolph Churchill and call himself a Tory democrat. In fact, he would not have made a good member of any party. He was fascinated by politics, even in a sense passionately so, but fascinated and interested in them as a spectacle. His was a romantic view of them: he saw them as a clash of personalities. His two contemporary political heroes were Churchill and Bevan, whom he plainly saw as more than life-size, latter-day Pitts and Foxes, actors on the world stage.

Characteristically, it was in times of crisis that he seemed to come most alive. During the Suez crisis he lived from day to day in a state of constant excitement, of thrilled absorption in the play of events from moment to moment, speculated on what would happen to Eden and what would be the fate of Selwyn Lloyd. It was part of his nature and of his attitude to journalism. It was that expressed in the title of Philip Gibbs's famous novel of Fleet Street, *The Street of Adventure*, which I suspect John had read as a boy.

This way of seeing politics and current events almost in terms of theatre was in keeping with his favourite reading, which was English history of the past two hundred years. For John I think politics and history were almost interchangeable terms.

It is at this point that one begins to wonder whether his idealisation of journalism was not a compensatory rationalisation. That he had not been to a university was an abiding regret; it was the nearest thing he had to having a chip on his shoulder. There were occasions when he really did seem to see himself as a deprived child. He had been to school at Westminster, whose tie he always wore, and just at the time when he should have been going up to university his parents were struck by the economic bad luck that is one of the hazards of the acting life. Instead of going up to Oxford, he joined the staff of the *Daily*

Graphic as an apprentice reporter. Thereafter, it seems to me, his attitude wavered: one day, he would think the life he lived, that of the journalist who hobnobbed with the great or the near-great and felt himself close to the centre of power, was the real life and he would dismiss any other kind of life as second-rate; the next day he would regret his was not the different and perhaps more subtle form of power that was the don's. He conducted something like a long love-affair with Oxford, and if there was any man you might have thought was born to be a fellow of All Souls, poised between the world of scholarship and the world of affairs, it was surely John Raymond.

One got near the heart of him, it seems to me, when he revealed himself as the secret diarist of his times. I did not see his diaries, of course, but there were times when one was made very conscious of them; as when he shared a holiday in Rome with my wife and myself. My wife had known the city during the war, but for John and me it was a first visit. It was, needless to say, a wonderful experience, and for me it was heightened by John's open, entranced response. He carried with him everywhere, I remember, a copy of Stendhal's *Rome, Naples et Florence*. He was as enterprising as he was delightful. He got us an introduction to Alberto Moravia, who invited us to his flat for a drink. It was kind of Moravia to see us and difficult not to feel that he accepted the task of presenting cocktails to visiting English and American writers as a chore inseparable from being an international figure. For both of us, Moravia embodied in himself, in his wit and his world-weariness, the spirit, unillusioned, cynical, of the ancient and ageless city, which we saw very much through Jamesian eyes.

No matter how early my wife and I got up, we always found that John had risen hours before us and had already walked the city, Stendhal in hand, and though we were not early bedgoers, we were aware that when we retired a significant part of the twenty-four hours was just about to begin for John. He would walk the streets once more or sit in a café drinking grappa. However late he turned in, he had first to write his diary for the day.

It was not until we went to Rome together that I took it seriously. It could not, he assured me, be published in his lifetime, for it was a daily and totally frank, uncensored record both of his own behaviour and of the doings of his time. He made the writing of it sound a whole-time job, for, almost, it seemed, it out-Boswelled Boswell or was Haydon's journals, Crabb Robinson's diaries and Creevy's memoirs rolled into one. It seemed to be a desperate bid for immortality of a kind I could scarcely understand, for fame which by its nature could only be posthumous I could see no point in.

Now that John is dead one wonders what has happened to the diaries. They were not mentioned in any obituary articles on him I saw. I would like to think that, devastating as they may prove to be, they exist and will one day be published. In any case, one can see how the keeping of them satisfied his deepest nature. It placed him at the centre of the world and gave him Godlike power, made him the supreme historian, the supreme journalist, of his time, gratified his passion for being in the know and gave him the last word on everything that interested him.

I knew of John's habit of not sleeping long before we went to Rome and often envied him it. No matter how late or in what condition he went to bed, he woke early, usually about five, and always fresh and bright. 'Wasn't that a splendid evening we had last night?' he would say with enthusiasm, quite oblivious of the two or three eminent critics he had insulted before passing out. He suffered neither from hangovers nor from alcoholic remorse, and an hour's sleep wiped out of his mind all memories of drunkenness as the tide cleanses and smooths a beach. At the time, one envied John his freedom from hangovers. Now, I see it called for anything but envy.

Gradually, it became more and more apparent that John was living, at any rate on occasion, in a world of conspiracy, one in which he was both a victim of conspiracy and a conspirator. I was first fully aware of this in the autumn of 1956, when I returned from a year's absence in the United States. I saw as much of John as I had done before. He was very successful. He was assistant literary editor of the *Statesman* and seemed to be in demand by almost all its rivals as well. He rejoiced in all this and often seemed poised on the verge of the manic. He seemed to think in terms of enemies who were waiting to get him or at least were standing in his way. He would, for instance, talk with dark suspicion of Cyril Connolly. Osborne's *Look Back in Anger* had just been put on and it made a great impression on him. At last, his generation had found its authentic voice! He saw himself as an Angry Young Man who had declared war on the old and on the Establishment, a word and concept that came into currency at this time through the brilliant political journalism of his close friend Henry Fairlie. After a certain point in the evening, he would change without warning from a deferential, charming young man into a blustering bully. I recall him being gratuitously and contemptuously offensive to the old poet Richard Church, who may have taken himself over-seriously but was totally without malice, and to the old drama critic Ivor Brown, simply because he was a drama critic and had therefore from time to time pronounced judgement on John's parents.

By the late Fifties, he had become, I think, very much a split personality and a source of worry to his friends. After a certain amount of drink he was impossible, and of this the next day he would have no memory. There were two Johns, the one one thought of as the real John and the doppelganger within who was his mirror-image. The John one thought of as John it was impossible not to love. He was the charmer with an infectious appetite for life. He transformed, by his response, the commonplace into something rich and strange, and with this quality of magic he had a simplicity that was childlike and touching. It was impossible not to warm to his enjoyment, for he was a great appreciator, of book, of figures in history, but also of smaller things, of claret, for instance, of the cold table at the Salisbury in St. Martin's Lane, of the musical comedy *The Boy Friend*, which he must have seen getting on for a dozen times. He existed, it often seemed, on the edge of self-parody. It was wonderful to see him being the man of action. Normally, his voice was a light tenor, but put him on a street kerb at night and show him a distant cab, and his eyes would light up, he would raise his arm and brandish his umbrella peremptorily and bellow 'Taxi!' like any bull. Hotel porters apart, no one in London could get a cab like John.

The doppelganger, his mirror-image, was a ruthless, contemptuous swashbuckler knocking down anyone who stood in his way and vowing vengeance on all who seemed to be doing him down. In a way, the link between the two was the furled umbrella he always carried. Maybe I make too much of it, because it had after all been part of his ritual dress since boyhood, along with the topper, part of the uniform of the Westminster Schoolboy of his day. But that was not how he answered, when, never having seen him holding the umbrella raised and open against the rain, I asked him why he always carried it. He assured me it was for self-defence; if ever set upon, he'd be able to hit back. There was a kind of sense in this, for there was a *louche* side of him that manifested itself in his saying from time to time at ten or eleven at night: 'Look. Do forgive me. I've got to go down to Soho. I'll be back in an hour. I promise you.' He always was. What he was up to one can only suspect. I doubt if it was especially dangerous. The umbrella, I think, was a property belonging to the mysterious underworld he carried within him.

In these years, too, his Catholicism flourished, one might almost say rioted. He was, I am convinced, sincere in his devotions but he was also at times too obviously, to exhibitionistically devout. He was a member of the Gargoyle, a bohemian nightclub in Soho known now as a haunt of Guy Burgess, whom, I sometimes think, I was the only man of my age in London never to have met. I would sometimes go there with John for supper after the theatre. There would come a point, brandy having been called for, when the world, the flesh and the Devil were denounced and renounced and out would come John's rosary. To the accompaniment of a dance orchestra but oblivious of it, he would tell his beads fervently. At such times, there was nothing to do, I found, but to get up and leave him to it.

One of these times sticks in my memory because it was a very special occasion. We had been invited to a late-night party at the Savoy Hotel given by Sidney Bernstein to welcome Charlie Chaplin back to England after he had been declared *persona non grata* by the American government. Why we had been invited we did not know, for neither of us knew Bernstein or had associations with Chaplin, and clues were not immediately apparent. People I would have expected to see were not there and some I would not have expected were. Mr Eliot was one of those. Otherwise, all the guests we recognised seemed to be vaguely of the Left; for instance, what seemed the whole editorial staff of the *News Chronicle* was present. We concluded that in some sense we were there representing the *Statesman*.

We sat at a small table more or less alone. It did not make it any the less a good party that I did not meet Chaplin. It was a splendid supper and, afterwards, we sat back and watched the dancing and suddenly John made the sign of the cross, fished out his rosary from his back pocket and began to say his aves. The comedy of the incongruity did not strike me; I felt only embarrassment. I desperately did not want to leave the party, but there seemed nothing else for it. I remember John now as the one genuinely tragic figure of my life.

I realised I was on kissing terms with the Establishment when, in the autumn of 1949, the British Council invited me to undertake a fortnight's lecture-tour of Czechoslovakia. At that time, currency for foreign travel was severely restricted; a week or two in France or Italy was all most people managed. By contrast, Czechoslovakia was exotic, *terra incognita*. For me, it would have been so at any time, for the language was impenetrable. Much more important than this was the sense one could not avoid feeling that one was venturing among enemies: Czechoslovakia had been taken over by the Communists a year before. I was in Prague for a week and then toured the country for another week, speaking at provincial centres. It was difficult to get one's bearings or to hold on to any one thing that seemed true. Wherever I went, people would tell me I must on no account fail to see the library and then lead me into the more remote stacks, where they would ask me to tell them about Orwell's *Nineteen Eighty-Four*. Had I read it? Or they would assure me that they were not Communist but were married with small children: what else could they do but submit and connive? One was in a world haunted by rumour and atrocity-stories.

When I got back to Prague after my week in the country I found Alexander Werth, the *New Statesman's* Paris correspondent, established at my hotel. He had left messages for me: would I get in touch with him as soon as I was back. He said he had a bottle of Scotch, but much more important was the prospect of getting hard news, reliable information. But Alex proved just as eager to have my news and views of the state of the country as I was to learn from him. He was in something like despair. He knew the country well, his books were bestsellers, and he was getting nowhere; nobody would see him or talk to him, for he had come in from Belgrade, and Jugoslavia had just broken with Stalin. I was infected with the hysteria that seemed to grip all Westerners in the country at the time and said something about the Terror and how dreadful it was. Alex snorted: 'Terror? What Terror? They've only got 15,000 in prison. I don't call that a Terror.' By birth, he was a White Russian and, despite his Scottish education, was anything but British in his manner. I took him to a reception the Council gave for me that evening. The guests were pro-Westerner almost to a man, but at last Alex met Czechs who would talk to him.

I was to have flown home next day, but my flight was cancelled because of a snowstorm, and in the evening I was taken to a party at the British Embassy, a party for Embassy personnel: English girls who were secretaries, disabled British ex-servicemen who were porters, minor officials. It was, I gathered, a normal Saturday-night hop. Nothing much happened. There was some dancing, some singing round the piano; one had the sense of being in a beleaguered garrison. They were living in siege-conditions or thought they were, which comes to much the same thing. Talk was mainly of rumour and conjecture, of what They would do next, of how the American Ambassador had invited five hundred Czechs to a cocktail party and how only one had turned up; of how the Czech administration couldn't understand the British and Indian diplomats being close friends and allies; of how Western diplomats, invited to State shoots, found they were expected to buy the game they shot and of how at one of these shoots a Western ambassador had shot the Bulgarian ambassador in the buttocks, or it may have been the other way round.

It was my only glimpse of life as it was lived in the lower ranks of the Embassy: one had the sense of people making a life for themselves in the face of continual frustrations and restrictions, and one could only admire. In my first days in Prague, I had been to a house-warming party at the Military Attaché's new quarters, a lively and gay occasion because it was assumed the Russians hadn't yet had time or opportunity to bug the premises. And on my first morning in the country, I had been received by the Ambassador, Sir Pierson Dixon, who was later British representative at the United Nations. He was a figure I found attractive and impressive. He told me that as I was the first English lecturer the Council had imported into Czechoslovakia since the Communist *coup*, he proposed to use me as a guinea-pig: my presence gave him a good excuse to give an official luncheon party to which he could invite Czechs. He proposed to invite twenty. It would be interesting and perhaps instructive to see how many turned up.

In the event, three did. I had met them all before. One we picked up in the official car which was taking me to the Embassy. The Ambassador had told me something about him, for he was much admired by the British, Professor Vocadlo. He had a brief-case with him, which, when we arrived at the Embassy, he ceremoniously presented to one of the Czech policemen outside for safe keeping. Another was a short-story writer I had met once or twice in London during the War, when he was an officer in the Free Czech Army. The son of a world-famous Czech painter, he was essentially a cosmopolite who had been educated in England and America. He sought me out at the Council offices at Prague, and we had a long talk in a small inner room that was deemed not bugged, either because of technical difficulties or because it appeared hardly bug-worthy. He was bitterly regretting the patriotic impulse which had sent him back to Czechoslovakia in 1945. He was not, he complained, allowed to travel. I in my naivety assumed that at least he had the freedom of the countries in the Communist bloc. But no; the only place he was allowed to go to was Bulgaria. And what was Bulgaria? He told me: 'the arse-hole of the universe'.

The third Czech guest was there because he could not avoid it. He was the man at the Ministry of Information in charge of cultural relations with the West, a man held in contempt by the British because he had been in London throughout the War with the Free Czechs, a Jesuit priest who, when the Party took over in Prague, promptly unfrocked himself. He had received me in his office a day or two after I arrived. He was given to head-shaking and the expression of pious regrets. He asked me, horror written large on his face: 'Mr Allen, is it true that Mr T. S. Eliot is a Fascist?'

That luncheon at the Embassy was the most splendid I ever attended. There was an impressive number of footmen. The pheasant was excellent. I sat over coffee with the Ambassador and his three Czech guests. Would we, Dixon asked, care to try 'our only British liqueur?' They recoiled at the notion: I was patriotic and rewarded with a glass of Drambuie. Gently, Dixon began to bait the man from the Ministry of Information. 'Tell me, Dr —,' he asked him, 'what do you think of *Nineteen Eighty-Four?*' Back came the blandly innocent answer; 'But what is 1984, Your Excellency?'

One took it for granted that as soon as one left one's hotel room it was searched. Whether this was really so, there was no means of knowing. One could well have been the victim of a vast illusion. And was one followed? Obviously, in Prague it was impossible to tell. In the country, it was otherwise. I recall I went to Bratislava, the capital of Slovakia, to give a lecture in the University, and from there I was invited to be the guest of the Slovak Writers' Union for lunch on Sunday at the Slovak writers' castle. The Council regarded this as a signal honour. On Sunday morning, we set out for the castle, two car-loads of us, all British except for our interpreter. I was in an Austin 16, which seemed to be greeted with interest, even enthusiasm, in the villages we passed through. We were tailed all the way by a little Skoda with two men in it. We had a puncture and had to stop to change the tyre. The Skoda stopped too, and the two men got out and watched us at work from a distance of two hundred yards.

When we got to the castle, which was not a castle but a nineteenth-century country house, the Skoda waited for us at the gates. I wondered whether we should tell someone to be sure to see that sandwiches were sent out to them.

We had a memorable meal, the seven or eight of us, in a large house that seemed otherwise deserted. The only Czechs I could see, apart from the interpreter, who had singularly little to do, were the steward and the waitresses. In Bratislava next morning, I was received by the Slovak Commissar for Education, a man named Novomesky. Since he spoke no English and I no Czech, we relied entirely on our interpreters. Even so, he struck me as an eminently sympathetic man, someone with whom in other circumstances one could have had a genuinely friendly relationship. Before the war, I found out later, he lived in Paris, the most distinguished of the Czech surrealist poets. I remember he enquired with what seemed real interest about the welfare of Elizabeth Bowen, who had been on a Council tour of the country a month or two before the *coup*. He spoke of her with great admiration. Before I left, I thanked him formally for the honour the Slovak writers had conferred on me by entertaining me to lunch, only regretting that I had been given no chance to meet any Slovak writers. Equally formally, he regretted it, too; the Slovak writers had all been called away at very short notice to a conference in Prague.

It seemed to me that Prague of all great cities in the world was the most fitting birthplace that could have been found for Franz Kafka.

I was also entertained to lunch by the staff of the English Department of Charles University. It was an uneasy occasion; everybody seemed under constraint, watching and taking his lead from Professor Ventura, the Professor of American Literature. He was not the titular head of the department but, according to Council lore, the resident Party man. It was true that he had the largest office and the thickest carpet. He regularly attended Council functions and in the question-period after my lecture he called the straying sheep round him, corrected their aberrations and drew the Party line. At the end of lunch, my colleague from the Council said that he was driving me into the country that afternoon, that we had a capacious car and would be delighted to have company. Silence, while everyone looked at Ventura. He thanked us. There was nothing he would love more to do than show me the Bohemian countryside, than which there was none more beautiful, but we must forgive him; could we but see the pile of papers on his desk, all of the greatest urgency . . . All said there was nothing they would love to do more than show me the Bohemian countryside, but, alas, they were so busy; I must forgive them. All said this except Vocadlo, who said simply: 'I've nothing to do that can't equally wait till tomorrow. I'll be delighted to come with you.' Thus, he gave notice that he proposed to be alone for the next three hours with two Englishmen in a closed car.

It was a brave and characteristic gesture, but then I suspect Vocadlo was the bravest man I have known. We set off. He talked with great animation. He was passionately eager for news of friends in England. How was Kingsley Martin? Did I know J. T. Sheppard, the Provost of King's, Cambridge? How was Elizabeth Bowen, who was the last Britisher he had seen and of whom he spoke with warmth? How was

Edwin Muir? He said he'd do his best to answer my questions, but in fact his story and his comments on the system poured out.

From what I had heard of him from Peirson Dixon and from what he told me himself I got some idea of his past. He had an international reputation as the greatest Czech Shakespeare scholar. Most of the years between the wars he had spent in England, working first as a lecturer in Czech at the School of Slavonic Studies at London University. He was closely associated with King's and he was spiritually a Cambridge liberal. He reminded me, indeed, of MacCarthy, who had been a friend of his. He had known Bennett, too, and been a translator of Capek. He had returned to Czechoslovakia in 1938 and became Professor of English at Brno. A Socialist, he had spent the war as a prisoner in Buchenwald, been rescued by the British in 1945 and sent to Cambridge to convalesce at King's, where a fellowship waited for him, if only he could get out of Czechoslovakia. Though he thought he could stand up to the rigours of escaping himself, his wife was an invalid, and he could not leave her.

He didn't think he was in any physical danger, if only because many members of the Government had been prisoners in Buchenwald with him, and he had taught them Russian, but he thought that he was slowly being pushed out of Charles University. He said, with genial scorn, that he was supposed to attend weekly classes in Marxism-Leninism. He would not co-operate. A year or so after I met him, he was, I believe, deprived of his Chair, though apart from that was not persecuted. In his forced retirement, he settled down to translating Shakespeare into Czech.

I was evidently not entirely *persona non grata* to the English Department at Charles University. I was invited at very short notice to lecture on contemporary English writing and Vocadlo was my chairman, which meant, I suspect, that no one else was willing to commit himself to the West by association. I remember that at question-time a bright young man, who was plainly bent on doing a job of exposure, asked me in a voice that rang with self-congratulatory superiority whether they could assume that *all* literary criticism in Britain was subjective. I replied that I believed that in the last analysis, whatever theory of criticism was dominant, all good literary criticism was subjective, essentially so. And at that, Vocadlo jumped up to say how profoundly he agreed and how heartened he was to hear such words spoken in Charles University.

Vocadlo, whose Christian name I don't think I ever knew, is at the heart of my memories of Prague and Czechoslovakia in 1949, and my memory of him symbolises my visit. It was exciting but overwhelmingly sad. Vocadlo quivered with life. I have never known anyone who responded more eagerly or sensitively. I only wish I had met him at a happier time, as I wish I had seen Prague, which is the most beautiful city I have ever been in. Throughout my visit, I was conscious of being present at a tragedy. The usual patterns of blame and condemnation were quite transcended. I was conscious all the time of meeting men whom I liked and in normal times would have been friends with. Now, one was on different sides of a chasm that could not be bridged. One could do no more than gesture across it. Thus, I recall that on my last morning in Prague Professor Ventura went shopping with me to find a good book to buy on the architecture of the city; I remember, and somehow his confession, which seemed significant and to suggest something less than total Marxist conviction, that he told me he had never been able to understand the economic determinism of the baroque architecture of Prague. I have heard nothing of him since.

Novomesky, who I believe was Clemanti's brother-in-law, was involved in Clemanti's downfall and, soon after my meeting with him, found himself in prison for a number of years. What happened to the people I met who were still sanguine about the future I have no means of knowing, for I have not heard of them since.

When I got back home I found a letter waiting for me from my Chinese friend Chun-chan-Yeh, the only Chinese I have ever known. Don Allen, who had known him in China, introduced him to me in 1946 and I had seen a considerable amount of him and stayed with him once or twice in Cambridge. E. R. Dodds had met him during the War in Chunking. He was already regarded as one of the best of the younger Chinese novelists, and Dodds had brought him back to England to lecture on the Chinese war-effort for the Ministry of Information. He told me when we met that he had been entertained by resident Chinese throughout the provinces of Britain; they were almost invariably restaurateurs and many of them believed they were still living in China, on the frontier of the far-flung empire close to the Barbarians.

Yeh was a most engaging man, of exquisite courtesy and of great ability. He had been taught in his university in China by Julian Bell. During the three or four years in England he published three or four novels in English which seemed to me very good indeed. Studies of peasant life, they struck me as having been written under nineteenth-century Russian influence, for they had something of Turgenev's lyricism. He wrote to me from on board ship in the Indian

Ocean. It was a letter of farewell. He had decided to throw in his lot with Communist China. He wrote that he did not suppose we would ever meet again. He was right, and from that time on I have not heard a word about him.

I had intended, of course, to write some articles about my impressions of Czechoslovakia. They would have been unpolitical; but try as I might, I found it impossible to be neutral and objective, and I was far from sure that my reactions went beyond the trite and superficial. I took Vocadlo's greetings to Kingsley and explained why I couldn't write the articles I'd promised him.

I continued to be much caught up in the novel. My fifth, *Dead Man over All*, appeared in 1950. The sales were short of brilliant, but it had a pretty good press. It seems to me now the best novel I have written. I managed to crystallise in it my experience of the aircraft factory near Bristol in the early years of the War, and it still seems to say something about those years besides saying something about the nature of British industry generally and the influence upon us all of our Victorian forbears. I took it for granted that I would go on writing novels but for the time being that had to take second place to reading them. I had, it seemed, become a Strasbourg goose condemned to consume novels unceasingly. I read against time and with growing desperation. My life became geared to the production of the commissioned history of the English novel. I realised more and more keenly how poorly equipped I was to write it, and it was no comfort to think, as was probably true, that everybody else was as poorly equipped. If I hadn't had a saving passion for the novel I would have dropped the project; as it was, I seemed to be holding a novel in one hand, reading it, while with the other hand I was putting my reaction to it down on paper. It had long been evident that I would have to select rigorously among the works of the novelists I read, but I had to do so in such a way as to make my verdict on them credible and convincing not merely to the reader but also to myself. It was not easy. How do you cope with a writer like Scott, for instance? I came to him with hazy memories of *Ivanhoe*, *Quentin Durward* and *The Talisman*, books read without much interest as a schoolboy of thirteen or fourteen, and with something like a contemptuous disregard for him, which books like *Aspects of the Novel* hadn't precisely discouraged. Where Scott was concerned, modern critics, I found, were scarcely any help at all, but a Victorian like Bagehot was, and better still was the enthusiasm of George Eliot and Thomas Hardy. No man is more keenly aware than I am how much of Scott I haven't read, and I do not think it likely that I shall ever repair the omissions; but at least I read enough to understand why Scott's reputation in his own day and for most of the nineteenth century was as transcendent as it was and why it was deserved. I was never convinced that Scott was a great novelist as I understand the word but I was soon convinced that he was a great writer, one who re-shaped the world for his generation and for his descendants.

If I often cursed the fact that I had been made to read so little classic fiction in my undergraduate years I never ceased to be grateful for the accidental steeping I had had in the background to Victorian fiction, in Carlyle and Ruskin, for instance. And I was helped, too, in my reading in the fiction of the past by my monthly task of reading and writing a review of newly published fiction for the *Statesman*. There was a continuity in what I was doing: reading novels old and new and trying to write them as well, I was conscious that I was tracing a tapestry still being woven.

Nevertheless, it was daunting to realise how slowly the book was progressing. I felt the reading for it and the writing of it would never end. I was constantly being distracted from both tasks; necessarily so; I had a young family to support and I had to turn away much too often to write an article or to broadcast simply in order to ensure that the rent was paid and there was something in the pot. I reached and passed the deadline and I saw that I needed at least another year. John Baker was infinitely patient but the American publisher I was contracted to was not; as far as he was concerned, I had simply broken the agreement and he wished to have nothing more to do with me. In fact, it wasn't difficult to find another. He was Elliott Macrae, who was president of the old New York house of Dutton. He happened to be on his annual visit to London. I met him, and it seemed only fair to explain to him the plight I was in. Within a day or two, he had seen John Baker and Allen Lane of Penguin Books, who had bought the paperback rights, and persuaded them to pay me the advance on publication due to me in quarterly instalments beginning immediately.

It didn't entirely solve my problem but it greatly eased my financial situation and it was a boost to my self-confidence. I had complete faith in John Baker, and it was splendid to realise one could have similar faith in one's New York publisher. Elliott was a highly successful publisher. I was never persuaded that he knew much about books, but his dynamism was self-evident. He was a short, erect man who bristled with energy. It was difficult not to see him in some sense as a figure of fun, which was, I think, how he was often regarded on both sides of the Atlantic. I doubt if this worried him much. I don't suppose we would have agreed on many things; he was an old Southern conservative and, I fancy, a Presbyterian; but he was unfailingly kind to me, and I owe him a debt of gratitude. He was in his way Napoleonic, as was Allen Lane.

The pressure upon me of extraneous work was partly eased in 1952, when I was commissioned by the BBC to do a weekly talk on books for a year. In many ways, it was the most agreeable assignment I ever had. I had pretty free choice of what I should talk about, though it was generally a new book I chose or a reprint. I gave up reviewing for the year, and the assignment also prevented me appearing in the BBC programme *The Critics*, for which, temporarily at least, I was glad, for though it was always a pleasant task, it was inevitably a great time-waster. And particularly I enjoyed my weekly programme, which was called *Talking of Books*, because it allowed me discreetly to propagate my enthusiams.

I thought of such attempts as missionary enterprises, and one of them had consequences I'd never imagined. A new book by Wyndham Lewis had just appeared, together with a reprint of his novel *Revenge for Love*, and they gave me the chance to talk about Lewis, who I thought was stupidly underrated, either out of prejudice or ignorance. I recall Kingsley Martin being amazed at my enthusiasm for Lewis, whom he had not read because he had been assured he was mad. Of Lewis as a human being I knew only the commonplaces of gossip, which all boiled down to the belief that he was paranoiac. As a writer, however, he had fascinated me for years, at times almost to the point of engrossment. Though no one else seemed to notice it, I even thought he had influenced me. The fascination he exercised upon me was that of the mirror-image: intellectually, his beliefs were precisely the opposite of the tradition in which I'd been brought up. He placed a spell on me, a spell the power of which I can indicate by reporting that as an undergraduate sometime in 1930 or 1931 I read his book on Hitler and for the best part of a week was convinced that I too was a Nazi. I couldn't sustain my faith longer than that, but all the same it was a great relief to learn a year or two later that Lewis himself had admitted he'd been taken in by Hitler and had felt compelled to take his book back.

But the spell Lewis had on me was not simply that of the attraction of what one knew to be wicked. Behind him, I felt the power of a whole body of thought unEnglish in the sense that it had influenced the English very little, though it had dominated the Continent. I suppose the shorthand expression for this would be Cartesianism. He drew upon and appealed to a body of theory and practice which had no counterpart in English. He was indeed, it seemed to me, profoundly unEnglish in his manner of thought, so that for me he was the embodiment of the Great Outsider, and it seemed to me, when I discovered it later, beautifully fitting that in fact he was not English by birth but North American and that, further to clinch the extraordinary nature of the man, he had been born in a yacht in the Bay of Fundy.

All this, what I thought of as his extraordinariness, was summed up in his prose style, which for me was the most powerful, the most graphic, the most arresting, of our time.

Something of this is what I sought to communicate in my talk on Lewis. Whether I succeeded at all I have no idea. For all I know, no one heard it; except the one man who had no need to hear it. Within two or three days after the broadcast the BBC forwarded a letter to me. It was from Lewis. Would I care to go round for a drink after my broadcast next Sunday? The invitation was utterly unexpected; it had never struck me that he might hear my talk; in my mind, he was already with the illustrious dead. It was, it seemed to me, as though one had been invited to drinks by Jonathan Swift.

The evening came and I went along to Notting Hill in awe. I was terrified as I think I would not have been had I been going to meet any other living man. The studios where he lived with his wife have been long pulled down; I carry in my memory an impression of steep flights of stairs and long corridors, blank impersonal walls behind which Lewis lived. I presented myself. Lewis was sitting in an armchair, an enormous Buddha of a man behind his dark glasses, for he was now almost blind. I had been very moved by the farewell to art criticism he had written a year or two earlier in the *Listener*, in which he announced with great dignity that he could no longer see well enough to look at pictures. Now he wrote his books in an enormous angular scrawl on large sheets of paper.

My memories of Lewis are inevitably tinged and perhaps distorted by my preconceptions of him, which were based on my reading of his books and current gossip about him. The first time I saw him I was struck by what I thought of as a quality of stoic melancholy in him. I was struck also by the fact that his teeth seemed unusually large and I remembered the self-portrait of Kerr-Orr in *A Soldier of Humour*:

I am a large blond clown, ever so vaguely reminiscent (in person) of William Blake, and some great American boxer whose name I forget. I have large strong teeth which I gnash and flash when I laugh. But usually a look of settled and aggressive naiveté rests on my face. I know much more about myself than people generally do. For instance I am aware that I am a barbarian. My body is large, white and savage. But all the fierceness has been transformed into *laughter*. It still looks like a visigothic fighting-machine, but it is really a *laughing* machine. As I have remarked, when I laugh I gnash my teeth, which is another brutal survival and a thing laughter has taken over from war. Everywhere where formerly I would fly at throats, I now howl with laughter. That is me.

. . . So I move on a more primitive level than most men, I expose my essential *me* quite coolly, and all men shy a little. This forked, strange-scented, blond-skinned gutbag, with its two bright rolling marbles with which it sees, bull's-eyes full of mockery and madness, is my stalking-horse. I hang somewhere in his midst operating it with detachment.

That was written sometime before 1914, when the author was a young man. The Lewis I was meeting was in his late sixties and much more accepting, more settled, less frenetic. All the same, meeting him, I recalled the passage as a still recognisable self-portrait. And I also remembered Auden's line on him: 'The lonely old volcano of the Right' and was struck once again by the fact that though he was commonly shrugged off as a fascist, which of course he wasn't, the men and women who most admired him were themselves anything but fascists and generally of the Left, people like Geoffrey Grigson, Naomi Mitchison, Michael Ayrton and Julian Symons. He had as I had come to realise, been a formative influence on the men and women of my generation.

It was not an easy session; I was abashed and thus inhibited and Lewis, as I expected, was a man quite without small talk. A few years later, Rebecca West, whom he had published before 1914 in *Blast* and whom he greatly admired, told me that in those *Blast* days he had taken her out to dinner *tête-à-tête* and spoken scarcely a word to her. We drank, I remember, gin-and-French from little glasses whose rims were coated with sugar; it was the way, he assured me, that the Spanish drank. He told me, with great pride, that Mr Eliot visited him every Thursday evening and read to him. We talked about his painting. Had the British Council, I asked, thinking of the exhibition of Henry Moore sculpture the Council was sending round

Europe, ever put on a show of his work? 'Good God, no,' he replied. 'Eliot and Herbert Read would never let them do a thing like that.'

I stayed, I suppose, for about an hour and when I left he invited me to dinner one or two Sundays hence. Next morning I went back to Lydd. Julian Symons and his wife were driving over for lunch and I got back just before they arrived. Julian was laughing as they entered the house. Just before leaving, he had had a telephone-call from Lewis, who wanted to know whether Walter Allen was an honest man. It was, I saw, wryly funny. All the same, it came as a warning that I must step with caution, for I realised that to know Lewis inevitably meant that you had entered a morass of suspicion.

Two or three Sundays later, I duly went to dinner at the studio at Notting Hill. I felt Lewis was a little easier, less strenuously on guard, or that I had become less an object of suspicion. In the beginning, I realised, I could hardly expect not to be that, if only because he saw the *Statesman* as part of the conspiracy against him. It was a splendid meal: Froanna Lewis was an excellent cook. After it, without any preparation or beating about the bush that I recall, he asked me if I would write a book about him. I was flabbergasted. For some years, it had been a private dream that one day I'd do a book on Lewis, a very private dream that I'd not mentioned to anyone and indeed did not take entirely seriously myself, for I saw it as an expensive luxury that I'd never be able to afford. I played for time, for I found the suggestion, coming from Lewis himself embarrassing. The proposal would have been wholly acceptable and in order if it had come from a publisher: from Lewis himself, it seemed rather different, and doing a job of public relations was the last thing that interested me.

I temporised. I suggested there were other, more obvious candidates for the task than I. Such as who? Lewis wanted to know. I instanced Grigson. He'd just write a pastiche of me, Lewis said. Then Julian Symons. Symons was just waiting for him to die; then he'd have a book out on him in no time. I was, naively perhaps, rather horrified at Lewis's cavalier attitude towards men who had shown themselves over the years his honest admirers. I said I would think over the proposal. I also said that if I agreed to write the book, I saw no possibility of being able to begin for at least two years.

I did think about it and in the end decided to write the book. It would be, I hoped, a straightforward work of exposition. I told Lewis what I had in mind, he did not dissent or indeed attempt in any way to direct my mind, and I came to the conclusion that there would be no interference from him. I was swayed in my decision by my liking for Lewis's publisher, Alan White, the managing director of Methuen, who was a great admirer of him and worked hard on his behalf. The book was never written. Lewis died before it could be begun, and I was then invited to write an autobiography instead. Rashly, I agreed to do so but I had only approached the first essential preliminaries when the enormity of what I had undertaken dawned upon me. It was the old problem: how do you keep yourself and your dependents alive while you are writing the major work? I did not see how books of the kind I had in mind could any longer be written by Englishmen without private means or the resources of great foundations behind them. It so happened that an American friend, whom I had met through our common interest in Lewis, Professor W. K. Rose, of Vassar College, was preparing a collected edition of Lewis's letters. He did the job in exemplary fashion and with speed: he was able to do so because he had a year's sabbatical leave from Vassar and a substantial grant-in-aid from one of the more substantial American foundations. With the edition of the letters behind him, he seemed to me the obvious person to write Lewis's biography. We discussed it but he decided against it, for in the event he had found that he had not been allowed a wholly free hand with the editing of the *Letters*. Mrs Lewis, backed with the authority of Mr Eliot, had prevented his publishing some letters. In the conventional sense, Lewis's life was not unblemished, and he did not see how it could be written while Froanna was alive. This was my conclusion, too. The great enemy of the honest biographer who would set out to write the life of a subject recently dead is the subject's relict, who for the most worthy of motives does not always want the truth about her late spouse made public. Here, there is an obvious conflict of loyalties. In our time, the great example of this, even though it took a slightly different form, was the destruction at the behest of Lady Churchill of Graham Sutherland's portrait of Winston.

Lewis died before I was in a position to begin the study of his work I had in mind. I continued to see him from time to time. To say his opinions were idiosyncratic would be accurate enough but, all the same, an under-statement. They never failed to surprise me. I found, for instance, that he had a great scorn of Edmund Wilson, who, he told me, was always called Bunny. The derision he managed to get into the way he said Bunny was formidable. He dismissed Evelyn Waugh as though he was a popular best-seller of the calibre of Warwick Deeping or A. S. M. Hutchinson. He was, I found, still in touch with Ezra Pound and he surprised me by deploring the attempts being made to get him out of St Elizabeth's Hospital in Washington. Pound was much better off where he was, he said. If you let him out, he'd only go back to Italy, where he'd commit some appalling indiscretion that would probably endanger his life or cause an international incident. When he arrived in Italy he'd almost certainly be interviewed by the press and he'd probably publicly denounce the Jews . . .

I was interested in Lewis's background. He told me of his father, a Canadian who had the distinction of having been an officer in both armies in turn in the American Civil War. He said he thought he was probably related to the Canadian bestselling novelist Mazo de la Roche. I interpreted this merely as an indication of his belief that the population of Canada was so small that everyone knew everyone else. The last time I met him was at a party given in Broadcasting House to celebrate the conclusion of Geoffrey Bridson's adaptation for radio of his satire *The Human Age*, the commissioning and broadcasting of which were among the BBC's greatest contributions to culture. He was, I remember, alone, sitting on a sofa, a blind titan. I went over to him. Pritchett, he said, had just been talking to him. 'Pritchett says he thinks my books are very funny. Funny!' There was, again, a wealth of derision in his enunciation of the word.

Work for the biography I abandoned did not add greatly to my knowledge of Lewis. The men and women who were close to him in the early days, the years of *Blast* and Vorticism, were most of them dead, though my first tentative researches did give me the chance to meet Dame Rebecca West, for which I was glad. Reginald Pound, who had been literary editor of the *Daily Mail* in the Twenties, told me of his contacts with Lewis, which seemed wholly in character. From time to time he had commissioned articles from Lewis. This was at the time when Lewis's concern for his privacy was at its most obsessive, though I suspect that it was bound up as well with a wish to avoid his creditors. His postal address was the safe deposit at the Hotel Cecil. He and Pound would meet at the Café Royal for dinner, after which Pound would solemnly escort him back to the safe deposit and say goodbye to him there. Where he lived, Pound didn't know.

Lewis remained essentially a mystery to me, and I suspect he always defied knowledge. By the time I met him he was, I think, comparatively mellow, at any rate to the extent of no longer fighting the world. He was old, and I assumed the time of his great works was past. I was wrong, for *Self Condemned* did not appear until 1954 and

The Human Age until some time after that. The latter seems to me the most sustained tour de force to have appeared in English since *Ulysses*. It is magnificent and dreadful, in the strictest and purest sense of the word, as the last pages of *Gulliver's Travels* are dreadful. *Self Condemned* is the most moving, the most affecting of the novels because it largely presents a full-length portrait of a character obviously in many ways close to a portrait of the author, firmly and classically controlled and rendered with the remorseless objectivity Lewis praised in Chardin and Flaubert. The note of personal anguish sounds through it all the same. Satire is purely incidental; the book strikes one as a considered attempt at self-judgement, and the nature of the judgement made may be seen, perhaps, in the punningly ambiguous title of the novel.

I imagine that people like myself, who knew Lewis only after his return from his Canadian experiences during the War, saw a different Lewis from the one both of *Blast* and of *The Apes of God*, a Lewis in a sense of more human. It was in my attempts to lay the ground-work for the biography that I had my one meeting with Mr Eliot. I was put in touch with him by Janet Adam Smith and he invited me to have tea with him in his office at Faber's. His charm was such as almost to disarm criticism. He had met Lewis in 1915 when he had arrived in England but he didn't, he said, think he could help me, for he felt he had never known Lewis. At the time, I took this as an instance of the bland disingenuousness one had heard Eliot was capable of; I knew that Lewis himself thought of him as a close friend. Now, I believe Eliot was telling nothing more or less than the truth.

Lewis was a man of genius, one of the two or three I have met. Whether he was the greatest of them I do not know. Baffling as I found him there was a tragic dimension to him that I never found, for instance, in Auden. One could regard him only with awe, and this made ordinary moral judgements on him or criticism on the score of paranoia seem trivial. He was not a man given to praise, and of all the praise I have had from anyone for anything I have done the most precious was when Lewis gave me to understand he thought well of my history of the English novel.

X

In 1955, twenty years after my first excursion to the United States, I was quite unexpectedly invited to take up a visiting professorship at a liberal arts college in the Middle West. That it was in Iowa, in a city not twenty miles from where I had taught before, was entirely by chance. I had no associations of any kind with the college, which, so far as I know, had no English connections. I can well understand why the group of academics and their wives who met me that September evening off the plane from Chicago should have seemed so apprehensive.

I was not entering entirely unknown territory when I disembarked at Cedar Rapids, for I had spent a weekend there when I was at the Univeristy of Iowa and I knew a little of Coe College by repute. I was, of course, eager to see what differences the passage of twenty years had made. The College found me an apartment over a plumber's shop just across the road from the campus, and it was there I first knew the pleasures, enervating though they are, of floor-heating. My memory of Cedar Rapids was hazy, and the city proved to be utterly different from what I anticipated. For one thing, it was four or five times bigger than the town I remembered and was no longer only the home of a company making a famous breakfast cereal but had become a centre of the electronics industry. The inter-urban railroad – a grand name for the tramway linking it to the much smaller Iowa City – had disappeared, and though, as I lay on my bed at night above the display of water-closets and bathtubs, I could hear the melancholy *poésie de départs* of the bells tolling on passing locomotives, I speedily discovered there was no passenger railway connection with the outside world.

Change glared at me. Negroes, who in my past experience had been scarce in Iowa, were much more evident. In the department stores there were Black sales clerks, which I think would have been impossible twenty years earlier. And I was aware for the first time, though they must surely have existed in England in 1955, of supermarkets: the Piggly Wiggly was three blocks up the avenue from the plumber's shop. But Iowa was still a semi-prohibitionist state, though you no longer had to pay a dollar for a licence to drink. When I applied for one, the clerk snarled: 'What's your number?' I was nonplussed. What sort of number? I asked. 'Gotta driving licence, ain't yer?' He said. I explained I didn't drive. He looked at me pityingly. 'Social security number'll do,' he said. I wasn't a citizen, I was a temporary visitor, I had no social security number. We had come to what my old tutor called an impasse: all we could do was stare at each other. I had an inspiration. Would a British passport number do?' I asked. He exploded in exasperation. 'Any goddam number'll do,' he said.

By American standards, Coe was tiny; there were fewer than a thousand students. It was a liberal arts college, which meant that all its students were undergraduates. I knew it had a good reputation academically and socially. It was a member of the Mid-Western Conference, a select body of colleges in the upper Mississippi valley which played one another at football. The most prestigious of them, I imagine, is Carleton, which has provided Harvard with presidents, though the most widely known is probably St Olaf's, in Minnesota, if only because it was, Scott Fitzgerald tells us, the alma mater of Jay Gatsby.

Coe was a Presbyterian foundation, and the Presbyterian ethos was still powerful. I had a letter one morning from the administration wanting to know my religious affiliations. Taking the view that this was no one's affair but mine, I ignored it. A week or two later, I had a letter from the President of the College himself repeating the request. I consulted the chairman of the department, a man I liked enormously, and he thought it would probably mean an easier life if I gave the information. Very consciously tempering the wind to the shorn lamb, I stated that I was agnostic. My chairman said I was lucky: I'd be able to get away with it because I was an Englishman and a visitor. Usually, I gathered, those of my beliefs, or lack of them, styled themselves Episcopalian or, if very daring, Unitarian or Quaker. In fact, I don't think I met anyone without formal doctrinal affiliation, for not to profess church membership was tantamount to declaring oneself an outlaw. The nature of the church did not seem to matter; membership was all. It was, I very soon realised, a conforming society, though what you conformed to was pretty much irrelevant.

The pressure to conform was considerable. The banks, insurance companies, real estate people, took advertising space every Saturday in the newspapers urging you to go to church next day, and billboards proclaimed the same bidding from the same sources. It wasn't necessarily a Christian country you were in, but by God, it was a religious one. You went into a restaurant for a meal, and there, beside the menu, was the card setting out recommended graces for Protestants, Catholics and Jews. And no one seemed to find it funny that throughout Advent the banks resounded with carols. They seemed to go with the enormous cut-outs of the Three Wise Men and their Camels that were everywhere, the Christmas tree in every apartment window and the garland of evergreens hung on every front door.

This regard for conformity seemed to me not only real but passionately held. I had to teach Thoreau and found myself much moved by his pamphlet on civil disobedience, which I had not read before. When I came to teaching it I found myself very eloquent. This, I asserted, was where the driving force of the United States lay; this was what had compelled its founding; this, so long as its spirit was preserved, was what guaranteed its unique position in the world. I spoke of Thoreau's influence on Gandhi. And then it dawned on me that such of my students who were listening were doing so with horror. No one, I found, had a good word to say for Thoreau. He only got what he deserved. Refusing to pay his taxes when the country was at war, indeed! He was no better than a Commie.

The McCarthy era was only recently over, and it could be taken for granted that for the parents of most of my students McCarthy was a hero. It was a time, it seemed to me, when above everything else it was the great and sole end of man for him to keep, in the felicitous American expression, his nose clean. I found it depressing. When I compared it to the country I had known twenty years earlier I could only think that America in adversity was a nicer place to live in than America prosperous. It had become less generous and therefore, it seemed to me, less American. Its climate I found more and more defined by the lists that appeared in the local papers every day of the people who were being sued and fined for not having paid their hospital bills. That was something I couldn't stomach.

It was a society impossible not to be critical of, a society that, by and large, seemed never to have suffered. For the first time in my life, I found myself feeling consciously European. I don't want to be misunderstood. I was nothing if not contented with my lot. I liked my colleagues and enjoyed my work. I enjoyed particularly having to teach Shakespeare, which I had not done before, and having to come to terms with modern American poetry. Nevertheless, I was thankful that I didn't have to be there for good, for while the standard of living was appreciably higher the quality of living was even more appreciably thinner. I was sounded out as to whether I would accept a permanent appointment. I said I would think about it, and think about it I did.

I reached the conclusion that I could make a pretty comfortable living on either side of the Atlantic. I did not see how, without the sort of luck that cannot be bargained for, I could make a living either in Britain or the United States from novels alone; in Britain, the crutch I used to support myself was journalism and broadcasting of a kind that did not exist on anything like a comparable scale in the United States; in the United States, the crutch could only be college teaching. Materially, I decided, the profits and losses from my transferring my family and myself to America would more or less cancel one another out. I saw it boiled down to a question whether I wanted to see my children brought up as American, and, when all rationalisation was stripped away, I knew I did not. I did not wish to find myself playing the part, central to so many American novels, of the immigrant father forced by the circumstances he finds himself in to abrogate his rights and responsibilities as a father out of a desperate anxiety to avoid doing something *wrong*, something that would hinder his children in the arrival at an American identity. I would be forced to embrace the conformity which seemed to me the curse of contemporary America.

I could, I thought, live happily enough myself in America, but to do so with a family was another matter. I knew that, in any real sense, I was ignorant of America's 'hum and buzz of implication.' The phrase is Lionel Trilling's, in his essay 'Manners, Morals, and the Novel'. The passage runs:

> What I understand by manners . . . is a culture's hum and buzz of implication. I mean the whole evanescent context in which its explicit statements are made. It is that part of a culture which is made up of half-uttered or unuttered or unutterable expressions of value. They are hinted at by small actions, sometimes by the arts of dress or decoration, sometimes by tone, gesture, emphasis, or rhythm, sometimes by the words that are used with a special frequency or a special meaning. They are the things that for good or bad draw the people of a culture together and that separate them from the people of another culture . . .

They were the things in American culture which I had not got and would never have, for one had to be born into them.

This was brought home to me on my second or third Saturday afternoon in Cedar Rapids. My colleague Vernon Lichtenstein took me, as a kind of initiation ceremony, to the first football game of the season. I was prepared to be fascinated, excited: I was about to see, for the first time, things I had only read about in fiction or been shown in films. I was about to see America, no less. And, predictably, the drum majorettes paraded, twirled their batons, performed cartwheels, somersaults, handsprings, incited their menfolk to prodigies of valour. The ROTC band marched and burst into music at points in the game of, I assumed, special significance even if I could not see it. We, the spectators, stood up from time to time as though by unspoken command in tribute to the feats we were witnessing. It was novel yet utterly familiar, just like what one had seen in the movies, pure Scott Fitzgerald. The only things missing were the hip-flasks circulating in the stands, which wouldn't have done in Puritan Iowa. It was the American way of life made flesh, and as I watched all I could think was *How bloody, bloody, bloody silly!*

I divulged nothing of this to Vernon, who seemed totally caught up in the spell of the game. My attitude, I needed no telling, could not have been more deficient in imaginative sympathy, more irrational, pharisaical. In my time, I had been a frequenter of Lords and I loved the game of cricket and everything about it. At that time, I did not know a single American who did not react towards cricket in any way except boredom and good-natured contempt. I could see why, though I assured them that if they did not understand cricket they could not understand the English. I still think that by and large this is true. I knew, too, American intellectuals who discussed American football with the enthusiasm that others bring to chess or the late quartets of Beethoven. I saw that where American football was concerned I would always be an alien in the United States; which seemed to rule me out as a prospective citizen.

Not entirely to my pleasure, I found that I was something of a public relations property of the College. It was taken for granted that I would speak at a Cedar Rapids Rotary Club lunch, and though talking to Rotary Clubs is not my notion of fun, I did so willingly enough. I wasn't prepared, however, for the telephone call I had at the College a few days later from Des Moines, the state capital. The caller introduced himself as president of the Des Moines Rotary Club and told me peremptorily that I was due in Des Moines on Wednesday week to address the Des Moines Rotarians; the Hotel Roosevelt, 12.15 sharp. I was somewhat taken aback by this arbitrary disposing of me but merely said that, while of course I'd be happy to talk to the Des Moines Rotarians, Wednesday was quite impossible, since it was my heavy teaching day. 'Young man,' the man at the other end of the telephone-line said, 'you go and ask President Brooks. I guess he'll be pretty happy to have you give up your classes to talk to Rotary here in Des Moines. Call me back.' The President told me he would indeed be grateful if I went to Des Moines to address the Rotary Club there; poor man, like most American college presidents, he spent most of his time engaged in the effort to whip up funds.

Since there was no rail service to Des Moines, I took a stopping plane from Chicago, which got me in soon after nine, having taken less than an hour from Cedar Rapids. It was the beginning of a singularly accident-ridden day. I had three hours to kill and I thought I should first find out where the Roosevelt was. I had been told that the State Art Center was well worth visiting, so I took a cab there. Des Moines is a city, I suppose, of a quarter of a million and, as is the way of American cities, its suburbs seemed vast. When I got to the Center I found it didn't open till 11.30, so I still had two hours to kill. I wandered round the suburbs and saw no other pedestrians. I began to realise that, since I was walking, I was being looked at askance from passing cars and the windows of ranch-style bungalows. I took refuge in dodging whenever I saw one into drug-stores and drinking coffee. I got to the Center just as it was opening and had a positively splendid exhibition to myself.

'Modern European Masterpieces from Mid-Western Collections' it was called, and it was a stunning display of privately owned sculpture and paintings. Picasso, Matisse, Modigliani, Bonnard, Utrillo, Braque, Brancusi, Moore, all were there. And I had to leave almost as soon as I'd arrived to get down to the Roosevelt. I got there with fifteen minutes in hand. As I was fishing in my pockets to pay off the cab I discovered I had lost my wallet. The cabby was sympathetic and we proceeded to retrace my morning progress through the suburbs and round the drugstores. I did not find the wallet. Back at the Roosevelt, I borrowed money with which to settle the fare and then sat down for the Rotary lunch, flanked by Old Glory. I was introduced by someone who had adopted what he fancied was an upper-class English accent, which the serried ranks of Rotary found excruciatingly funny. They were plainly what are called in the Middle West just a great bunch of kidders. It was appalling, but I bore it as gracefully as I could. At two o'clock exactly the meeting ended with everyone dashing back to business. I was left with three hours to get through before catching my plane. I could not fail to think it had been a thoroughly exasperating, fruitless day.

I was looked after by a very nice stockbroker, who was solicitous on my behalf. In quest of my wallet, he telephone the Art Center, the cab company, the police. It seemed lost without trace. I consoled myself with the thought that I had my return air ticket, which I'd stuffed into my breast pocket, and had lost not more than twenty dollars. I sat in the stockbroker's office and read the *Wall Street Journal* without much understanding until he drove me to the airport.

The following Sunday, I went with my colleagues to the opening in the Cedar Rapids Public Library of a memorial exhibition of the painting of Grant Wood, whom I had known in Iowa City. He had been a Cedar Rapids boy, and the show was opened by another, Coe's one Rhodes scholar and a well-known poet, who was one of the luminaries of the University of Iowa. I was introduced to him, and my surname obviously triggered off a memory, for he turned to my colleagues and asked with some excitement: 'Have you heard the latest about Allen Tate?' They shook their heads. 'He was in Des Moines and he lost his wallet. Poor old Allen; drunk as usual.' Tate, whom I never met but had a high regard for as poet, critic and novelist, had rather disgraced himself the year before when Coe had given him a doctorate. I amused myself and my colleagues by speculating on the course of action etiquette dictated to me. Ought I to write a letter to the *TLS* warning putative biographers of Allen Tate that stories of his visiting Des Moines, Iowa, getting drunk and thereby losing his billfold were untrue?

As for my wallet, a few days later I had a letter from a lady in Des Moines inviting me to identify a wallet, containing papers bearing my name and address, which she had found on the seat of a cab she had travelled in.

The man who looked after public relations at the College was, naively, I thought, much tickled that I, a Limey, was teaching the history of American literature and on the strength of it tried to get me on the television programme *What's My Line?* Rightly, the producers were not impressed; I was relieved, all the same. I found the work of preparing lectures for the course tremendously exciting. I was reading Whitman pretty much for the first time and, knowing Eliot's antipathy towards him, I was fascinated to find things in common between the two poets. I was led to realise Eliot's Americanness as a poet. I realised, too, that Tiresias in *The Waste Land* and the 'I' of *Song of Myself*, 'I, Walt Whitman, a cosmos,' who says in one of the great lines of poetry 'I was the man, I suffered, I was there,' in the roles they played in the poems were similar figures. I was greatly excited, too, by the poets I was reading for the extension lectures I was giving, particularly by Edward Arlington Robinson, Ransom, Tate, Hart Crane and Wallace Stevens. Intellectually, my year at Coe was intensely liberating.

We had a week's holiday at Thanksgiving and I took myself off to New York to stay with Don Allen, who was with an avant-garde publisher and had an apartment in East 9th Street in Greenwich Village. I had seven or eight crowded, eventful and rewarding days. Someone at home had told me to make myself known to Harvey Breit, the assistant editor of the *New York Times Book Review*. I knew nothing about him except that Don described him to me as one of the few Americans who could be regarded as a real *boulevardier*. What that meant I did not know, but it sounded impressive. Breit invited me to call on him at the *Times*. He spoke warmly both of MacNeice and Henry Green and seemed to be acquainted with everybody on either side of the Atlantic. He introduced me to the editor of the *Book Review*, Francis Brown, and soon after five he took me round the corner for a drink at Sardi's, which hitherto had been for me an entirely legendary place but now seemed merely the local bar of the *New York Times*.

He suggested I should go home with him and take pot luck. He was an unaffected, friendly man, and I was surprised to find how impressively he lived, for he and his wife had a whole house in one of the Fifties just off Fifth Avenue, in the 'Silk Stocking' district in fact. It was a comfortable, relaxed evening, which I remember with pleasure and with gratitude, for, though Harvey did not remain with the *Times*, for me it was the beginning of an association with the paper which lasted fifteen years.

Don gave a cocktail party for me. I had found out that my friend George Lamming, the West Indian writer, was in New York, and he came. I had known him four or five years, ever since reading the manuscript of his first book, *In the Castle of My Skin*, for Michael Joseph. It seemed to me the most original work I had read for them, a work of genius. George himself, who came from Barbados, I found as impressive as his book. Don's guests seemed to find him different from any other Negroes they had met, nothing like an American Negro. Later, George and I compared notes and agreed we had met as though we were the only two Englishmen in New York City.

After the breakup of the party, some of us went together to a restaurant on Sixth Avenue for dinner. I was sitting next to Philip Rahv, the literary critic who had been brought over to the United States from Russia as a child and epitomised for me the New York Jewish intellectual, ruthless in argument, abrasive, contemptuous of what are generally considered the graces, and geared, it seemed to me, to Paris, Berlin, Moscow, to anywhere but London. I was confounded when he demanded of me brusquely: 'Why do you Britishers make such a fuss about Lionel Trilling?' It seemed a somewhat odd question for the founder and editor of *Partisan Review* to ask about one of its most distinquished contributors. I stammered something that seemed wretchedly lame and unsatisfactory even as I was saying it. Rahv brushed it aside. 'You've had one Matthew Arnold,' he said. 'Why do you want another?'

Next day, I went with Elliott Macrae to dine with him at his house in New Canaan, Connecticut. I called for him at his publishing house on Fourth Avenue just up from Union Square. It was larger than any London publisher's I knew and seemed to have a much bigger staff. It was the day before Thanksgiving and the Thanksgiving break, and it was impossible not to be struck by the warmth with which Elliott and his employees exchanged the appropriate farewells. This was obviously an old-established family business, and I felt that if Elliott was not referred to as 'young Mister Elliott' he ought to have been.

We made our way up the Avenue to Grand Central and the train to New Canaan. We sat ourselves down in the club car. It was my first encounter with this American institution, which is precisely what the name denotes, a railroad car rented by a group of men organised as a club. The atmosphere was that of a club. Negro waiters patrolled the aisle with trays of drinks. One of them brought Elliott his customary highball, and I chose the same. As the train drew out of the station, Elliott looked up and down the car approvingly and said with some complacency: 'If the Russians dropped a bomb on this train there wouldn't be much left of Wall Street.'

The train emptied at New Canaan, which even I knew was a preserve of the conspicuously well-heeled. The first thing that greeted you when you went into Elliott's house was an enormous Teddy bear propped up in a wooden armchair. It was the original Winnie the Pooh, and the sight of it reminded me that Elliott was especially proud of his imprint's association with A. A. Milne, to the memory and to the furthering of whose children's books Elliott was dedicated.

Elliott, I recalled, had published a Latin version of *Winnie the Pooh* and before many years were out he was to publish a learned literary joke in which various schools of academic literary criticism were parodied called *The Pooh Perplex*. The taste for Milne was not one I shared, and I thought it politic not to divulge this. I was all for publishers being enthusiastic about the authors they published and I had already realised I stood high in Elliott's esteem, as was made clear when I learned the other dinner guest was to be Orville Prescott, the chief book reviewer of the *New York Times*. I did not think highly of him myself, though he was an agreeable dinner-table companion. But ever after, when Elliott and I met, he would recall the dinner-party and describe it enthusiastically to anyone else who was present. You'd have thought from his account that Prescott and I were two latter-day Shakespeares and Ben Jonsons at the Mermaid Tavern. With the best will in the world, I cannot believe that the conversation round that dinner-table in New Canaan can really have been quite the feast of reason and the flow of soul that Elliot made it out to be.

For Thanksgiving dinner, I was the guest of another publisher, one very different from Elliott — Victor Weybright, the founder and president of the New American Library. I had met him a number of times in London, for his visit every September was one of the events of the literary season. He was a great Anglophile, almost, you might say, an honorary Englishman. During the war, he had served under Winant at the U. S. Embassy in Grosvenor Square. I suspect he was the only New Yorker habitually to wear a bowler hat, which he bought at Lock's in Piccadilly. He was also, one understood, a great rider to hounds and had his own pack in Maryland, which was his home state. After the war, he had worked for a time for Allen Lane, promoting the American end of Penguin Books. Invevitably, it now seems, they quarrelled, and Victor started the New American Library, which was as remarkable in its way, which was distinctively American, as Penguin Books. In some ways, it was much more revolutionary, for the books it published were mass-produced, printed on newspaper presses on newsprint, and distributed through the media for mass-consumption, notably drug stores. It changed entirely the relations between authors and the traditional publishing houses, which in many instances were forced into a secondary position to the paperback houses. In this respect, it seems to me, it went far beyond anything we saw in Britain. Book and paperback in America became synonymous terms. But it also took advantage of the enormous increase in college education, furthering it as it did so, in the publishing on an unprecedented scale of both the accepted European and American classics and the most highly regarded twentieth-century writing.

Weybright, who was always kind to me, told me he made a practice of always having at least one Englishman among his guests at Thanksgiving dinner; the year before it had been Victor Pritchett. So for the second time that week I found myself being entertained in the Silk Stocking district of Manhattan. The special place Thanksgiving holds in American life was beginning to dawn on me; I can think of nothing in English life comparable with it. All the same, I was dismayed by the grandeur and apparent formality of the occasion, for I found that I alone among the male guests was not wearing morning clothes. We were waited on by two men servants; the dinner, of course, was traditional, turkey with oyster stuffing and cranberry sauce, and Brussels sprouts, provided, I learnt, especially for me as an Englishman. I don't think I let on that among vegetables the Brussels sprout is far from my favourite. After dinner, I walked the fifty or so blocks of Fifth Avenue down to the Village through a Manhattan quieter, more deserted, more Sabbath-like, than I have ever known it.

The day after Thanksgiving, winter began. When I landed at Cedar Rapids it was snowing and so bitterly cold that I wondered whatever could have induced otherwise sane men from Europe to settle in the Middle West. In fact, I knew that in this part of the world most of them had come from a Europe of similar climatic conditions; if you are born in Bohemia or Slovakia, neither the winters nor the summers of Iowa will seem to you out of the ordinary.

It was in Cedar Rapids that I got some insight into the class-structure of the United States. I had, I think, accepted quite uncritically the popular American view that class scarcely existed in America, except, perhaps, as divisions between ethnic groups or successive waves as immigrants. If there were a class system at all, it was certainly very different from that existing in England: to that, the English novelists, Jane Austen, Thackeray, Trollope and the rest, offer a pretty reliable guide. There is nothing comparable to them in American writing.

I wouldn't wish my experience in Cedar Rapids to form the basis of a generalisation about class in the United States as a whole. For one thing, the United States is too vast a country, containing too many regions dissimilar historically and geographically. Nevertheless, the pattern in Cedar Rapids is scarcely likely to be unique. On the surface, it is predominantly a Czech city. There were sokols, and in the Fifties at any rate the great Iowan composer seemed to be Dvorak. When I visited the local travel agency, I learnt that the 'old country' meant Moravia or Bohemia, anywhere but the British Isles. Besides Czechs, there were Germans and Norwegians, but the predominantly Czech nature of the city seemed even ritualised in the tradition that the mayor, the chief of police, the fire chief and the district attorney all had Czech or Slovak names. This was by no means true of the trustees of the College, and to be a trustee, I learned, was a sure sign that a business man had arrived socially. Early on, one of the trustees was pointed out to me as being a particularly wealthy and powerful member of the community, president of one of the three or four banks, owner of the newspaper, a director of the company that owned the local broadcasting station, and so on. Like a reigning monarch, he had Roman numerals after his name, III or it may have been IV, and to my fascination, part of his name was Van Vechten. I knew Carl Van Vechten came from Cedar Rapids and I had often wondered how it came to be so, for as a novelist he was a dandiacal old bird whose values seemed far removed from those of Iowa. I associated him particularly with Ronald Firbank, whom he introduced to America and by whom I fancy he was influenced. When I met the Cedar Rapids business man who incorporated his name in his I asked him whether he was related to Carl. He replied that indeed he was: Carl was his uncle.

I learned something of the family background and, by implication, of the structure of social and political life in Iowa. His family was one of three or four which had migrated from New England, where they had lived since the seventeenth century, to the lands beyond the Mississippi and founded Cedar Rapids in the eighteen-forties. These founding fathers of the city and the state had, it seemed to me, gone on behaving seigneurially, like their analogues the great European families that claimed whole regions by right of conquest or occupation. I had no doubt I was talking with an American aristocrat. Despite all appearances, his family retained its power, which was not so difficult since it controlled the agencies that projected the appearances. Members of the family did not often figure publicly, so that their power was largely unsuspected. But they and their relations controlled the Republican Party in that part of the state, and the Czech mayor and the rest were their puppets, the stalking horses behind which they concealed themselves and ruled. They had, it seemed to me, an aristocractic disdain for the people, popular institutions and public opinion. The centre of their world, their standard of reference, was still New England. When their sons came to prep. school (*anglice*:

boarding school) age, they were sent East to somewhere like Groton or Kent, whence they proceeded to Dartmouth; and their daughters, too, were sent East to school, though after a semester or so in one of the city high schools, whither they went briefly as a sop to democracy.

I do not suggest that the pattern I stumbled on is general but I fancy it is duplicated many times through the United States and I am sure that the power and influence of New England are still inestimable. At the same time, I am pretty sure that the pattern I discerned is unsuspected by perhaps a majority of Americans. You may catch glimpses of it, though, in American fiction, notably in the otherwise disparate novels of Willa Cather and John O'Hara.

It was an insight, I realised later, that I could have got only in a small college like Coe, where one was always aware of the pressure of the community in which it existed bearing down upon one. I often thought, on subsequent visits to America when I was attached to much larger institutions, it would be possible to spend one's life in a university in America and not at any time come in contact with ordinary life or sense at all at first hand what is called grass-roots opinion. Indeed, the American intellectual, ivory-towered in his many-acred campus, seemed to me often to live in a fool's paradise. I have no doubt that the gulf between intellectuals and the people as a whole is greater than in Britain, and one's consciousness of the gulf was intensified by the very size of the universities, with their student-populations of twenty, thirty and even forty thousand and faculties in proportion. At Coe, one could well feel the world too much with one, but there were compensations, of which the chief probably was the closeness to ordinary, non-academic life. Cedar Rapids had its college, and a distinguished one, but was anything but a college town.

In my eyrie above the plumbing shop on B Avenue I managed to get a fair amount of work done. I wrote a first draft of a new novel and a few pieces of reportage for the *Statesman*. I even contributed a couple of pieces for *Punch*, which, under Muggeridge, had once again become a magazine serious writers could write for. Journalistically, however, this American sojourn was noteworthy because it saw the beginning of my association with the *New York Times Book Review*. I had reviewed two or three books from them when Francis Brown telephoned me to ask whether I'd review Robert Graves's lectures as Professor of Poetry at Oxford, which had just been published as *The Crowning Privilege*. Graves, Brown added, almost it seemed as an afterthought, was still little known in America as a poet and if I cared to use the occasion to write about his poetry, I could have two thousand words.

I could not have wished for a more agreeable assignment. After publication, it brought a letter from Graves in Majorca which seemed utterly in character, and graceful besides:

> Very many thanks for your very kind review of *The Crowning Privilege*. The Trinity College lectures should really have remained unpublished; but I think libel is an honester crime than slander, so I published, and hoped for the forgiveness of honest men like yourself who know how the temptation is to protest against the worshipping of idols — especially if one is born a black Protestant as I was . . .

A year after I got back to England there was a curious tailpiece to my trip to Iowa and the excursion to Des Moines. I was invited to a reception at the American Embassy under the auspices of the United States Information Service. It was a six o'clock to eight o'clock affair and was very crowded. MacNeice, who was also there, told me that Robert Frost, who was in England to receive an honorary degree from Cambridge, was expected to look in at about eight. Was I, he asked, interested in meeting him? I was indeed. I had known Frost's work since my first visit to America in 1935 and liked it enormously. I thought it was generally misunderstood on both sides of the Atlantic, partly, perhaps, because of its great popularity, thought it much more complex than it was assumed to be and often of a disturbing ambiguity. In other words, Frost seemed to me to be anything but an American counterpart of the Georgian poets.

At eight o'clock, he had not appeared and the throng was thinning out. If I had been alone, I would have gone. But Louis said we should hang on a bit longer. He seemed to know Frost's habits. And suddenly, as though out of nowhere, Frost materialised. The old countryman's white thatch was unmistakeable. Louis introduced me. I said something about having been in Iowa recently. He seized on this. 'Then you know —?' he said in a gruff voice, naming the man who had confused me with Allen Tate. I said I did. 'He's a phoney,' Frost growled with great conviction; and I realised I was seeing the old poet in characteristic form.

In retrospect, it is easy to see my year at Coe as an experience decisive for my future. At the time, it seemed no more than a pleasant interlude in my life as a freelance writer, and when I got back to England I took up my work again at the point where I had left it. The scene had changed to some extent. It can be summed up, perhaps, by the staging at the Royal Court of *Look Back in Anger*. It was not a play that meant much to me, and I was puzzled by what seemed to me John Raymond's immoderate enthusiasm for it. It presented him with a gesture and a pose he found eminently satisfactory, and with hindsight one sees that it chimed with the times, with the Suez débâcle and events in Hungary.

The English Novel had been out for a year in Britain and was now published in the United States. I became used to hearing waggish professors of English in whatever country I might be saying to me: 'Ah, Mr Allen, I was reading your book only yesterday in a student's essay.' I was working on my novel *All in a Lifetime*, which was published in 1959 to a modest acclaim and made me for a month, so my publishers assured me, a bestselling author. As though I had learned nothing from the experience of writing *The English Novel*, I had embarked on a sequel to it, a survey of British and American fiction since 1920. I persuaded myself that a fair amount of the work was already done and that it would be largely a montage of material already written for other purposes. The task, of course, was nothing like so simple. I was forced to the realisation that of the novels of the last ten years which deserved consideration less than half had come my way: a regular reviewer's knowledge is not selective so much as spotty, necessarily. Then, how far could my judgements on authors made fifteen and twenty years ago still be relied on? When I was nineteen, no contemporary novelist had meant more to me than Aldous Huxley: when at thirty-two I wrote an essay on him for *Penguin New Writing* he had seemed almost unreadable. Plainly, considerable resampling was called for, and where the Americans were concerned, many novelists, Willa Cather, for example, and Nathanael West, had to be read for the first time.

All the same, writing *Tradition and Dream* proved a light labour compared with that of *The English Novel*. Partly because, totally unexpectedly, I found myself with a monthly salary. One afternoon in 1959 while in London, I found myself being pursued by telephone. Wherever I went, messages awaited me; would I go round and see Kingsley Martin immediately; it was most urgent. At Great Turnstile, I found a considerably concerned Kingsley. Would I, he asked, come in straight away as Janet Adam Smith's assistant, for John, they were driven to conclude, could no longer be relied on?

This was the time, of course, when I saw most of Kingsley and was closest to him. Two or three times a year, he and Dorothy Woodman gave a party in their flat at Charing Cross. The guests would be members of the staff, some contributors, a scattering of MPs, left-wing journalists, some academics and sociologists and inevitably the great Patrick Blackett and the great Professor Titmuss. The leader of the Labour Party was always invited but was not seriously expected to show up, for the *Statesman* did not invariably approve of the leader, nor did he of the *Statesman*. Janet tells a story of how, in her early days at the paper, she found herself sitting at a dinner party next to the Prime Minister's private secretary, who, learning what she did, said; 'Mr Attlee prefers the *Spectator*.'

I turned up at one of these parties held towards the end of 1959 or early in 1960. The drinks served were invariably red and white wine. The party was well under way and I edged myself into the throng. I heard someone whisper to me: 'That traitor's come!' They were not words that lend themselves to easy hissing, but hiss them Dorothy Woodman did. She passed me holding a tray that bore a tumbler, a syphon of soda and an unprecedented bottle of Scotch.

I watched where she was heading, and there at the end of the room, surrounded by a group of people, was Hugh Gaitskell. I had not met him, nor had C. P. Snow, whom I was with. I asked Kenneth Robinson to introduce us. Gaitskell, it seemed to me, was working hard to make his corner of the room neither controversial nor provocative. He had recently been in Ghana and was giving a vivid exhibition of dancing the dance called highlife. I was fascinated by the enthusiasms he showed and the zeal with which he was making himself agreeable to people who he must have known were largely hostile. It put him for me in an attractive light. Charles Snow, however, was obviously impatient of such frivolity. 'Mr Gaitskell,' he barked, 'have you read Walter's new novel yet?' He replied that he had it on his library-list but didn't know when he'd be able to read it, for he was still only half-way through Professor Marchand's life of Byron.

Such was my one meeting with Gaitskell, though I had one or two glancing encounters with him at about this time. He seemed suddenly to become a familiar in the London scene. Thus, stepping into a compartment of a tube train at Camden Town at about half-past nine one morning, I was puzzled to find that, though it was crowded and passengers were standing, two seats remained empty, one on each side of an occupied seat. The man sitting on it had his closed eyes shadowed by his hand. I stepped forward and then drew back, for I saw it was Gaitskell. At every station in turn until I got off at Leicester Square, I watched newcomers to the compartment make for the empty seats and then draw back as I had done. And it seemed to me the passengers fell into two groups, those who almost superstitiously avoided looking at Gaitskell directly and those who stared blatantly. What political conclusions, if any, could be drawn from this observation I never determined.

I last saw him when we passed in the lobby of an hotel in St James's. A week later, he was dead. In the last analysis, one chooses and follows one's political leader by faith: I followed Gaitskell.

Late in 1959, I was struck down by a literary ailment of great antiquity: like Pepys, I was cut for the stone. Kingsley decided I had gone back to the paper too soon after my operation and I was handed a cheque for £100 for an immediate holiday. By the end of March of the next year I was in Greece on a three-weeks excursion. It exceeded all my expectations and I was sharply aware all the time of how lucky I was. I was haunted by the thought that I was where Shelley, to whom I owned most of my notions of Greece, had never been. My itinerary was ordinary enough: five days in Athens, three at Delphi, three each in Mytelene and Chios, three at Nauplion. I was quite uncritical and I could not be otherwise, for I was not classically educated and could not speak or read either the ancient or the modern language. The experience of Greece enchanted me. The countries I had lived in or visited were not so many, but this was unique, irreplaceable, and when I saw Delphi it seemed to me that if nothing of Greek thought or literature remained, the loftiness of the Greek genius would have been evident in this place.

In retrospect, the essence of my visit to Greece seems to be summed up in the events of my last day but one in the country. I was in Nauplion, intending deliberately to take things easy, for I felt I had been prodigiously energetic for the past nineteen days for a man who had been cut open and sewn up only a few weeks before. I had earmarked the day for a trip to Mycenae but the night before, reading paragraphs on Nauplion in the *Blue Guide*, my eye had caught the terse description of the Gulf of Tolos: 'Eight kilometers. Motorbus; seaside resort, frequented by excursionists; small restaurants, where good fish is served.' I had spent the day at Epidaurus and in the three weeks just ending I had seen more indescribably beautiful, luminous and numinous things than I'd seen in the rest of my whole life before. Now, I felt my capacity for awe was full, full and brimming over, and though I wanted to see Mycenae, after reading those three lines about Tolos, I knew I would not, at least not on this visit to Greece. After the exaltations, I needed something more humble. What better than a seaside resort frequented by excursionists, where there were small restaurants and the fish was good?

I caught the motorbus next morning. Tolos proved to be nothing at all like what one would normally associate with the words 'seaside resort' and there was no sign of excursionists. It turned out to be perhaps three dozen fishermen's cottages set between the motor-road and the Gulf which they faced. There were few signs, either, of what one normally thinks of as restaurants; in front of a few of the cottages there might be a round wooden table or so, but that was all. I walked along the beach. There were very few people about, though there was a lot of activity near a motor boat at the tiny jetty, men, women and children milling round. They didn't disturb the extraordinary peaceful air of the place; rather, they seemed to accentuate it. This strip of beach by the incredibly blue water of the Gulf of Tolos, with the almost bare mountains rising on all sides, seemed a very long way from anywhere.

It was pretty hot, though it was still only April, and I was very thirsty. I walked along the beach looking for somewhere I could get a drink. The last dwelling was rather larger than the others; a shallow flight of steps took you up to a terrace in front of it where there were three or four tables under trellised vines. It was, no doubt about it, a place where you could get a drink, but what made me walk up the steps was the sign; a piece of wood sticking out at one side of the house with some amateurish lettering on it in Greek and German and the simple statement in English beneath it: 'The keeper speaks English.' Sprawled at one of the tables, evidently engaged in improving his English, for he was reading an English or American paperback, was the keeper.

I ordered a *citron pressé*, and he joined me at a table. 'Are you,' he asked, 'English mans or American mans?' He showed me what he was reading: *No Mean City*, a title I remembered from the Thirties, a sensational novel about gang-warfare in the Gorbals. His English was not good but it was fluent and uninhibited; when he didn't know or couldn't remember the English word he wanted he made do with the German equivalent. He told me I had chosen the right day to come to Tolos, for it was the annual holiday. It was the day when the fishermen and their families went in their boats to a tiny island in the Gulf and prayed in the chapel there to the local saint and then had picnics. 'Look,' he said, 'there's a boat going now. Why don't you go with them?' And he jumped up, shouted to the people by the boat at the jetty and pointed at me. In a matter of minutes, I was in that small fishing boat with its old motor, along with I suppose twenty men, women and children, all dressed in their best clothes.

Nobody spoke anything but Greek, but I was made welcome, and when we reached the island the village schoolmaster and his wife were fetched. She spoke French and was learning English and they took me under their wing. The island was a strip of beach, a strip of rough grass, and then rose precipitously as though it was the peak of an otherwise submerged mountain. Nowadays, except for a few goats and sheep, it was uninhabited, but on that one day of the year it presented a charming pastoral scene almost impossible not to sentimentalise. The beach and every ledge of sparse grass on the mountainside were occupied by families, mothers, fathers, children, grandparents, sitting round fires, tablecloths spread out before them, eating, drinking, picnicking. It was utterly unexpected, this concentration of innocent animation in a world that seemed empty, a vast solitude of water and mountain, until round a bend in the Gulf you suddenly came to the island.

Somehow, the schoolmaster and his wife at times hauling me up, I got to the top of the mountain. There was a tiny chapel, with a shrine, where we lit our candles to the saint. The schoolmaster's wife explained to me. During the Turkish occupation, the Turks had closed the village school, and night after night, year after year, the fishermen had brought their children to the chapel on this barren islet; it had become a secret school where the children could learn their language and history, and the Turks never discovered it. Since the liberation in the second decade of the nineteenth century, the annual pilgrimage on the saint's day had gone on. I could almost have believed that the last boatload had been ferried to their clandestine lessons as recently as the day before yesterday.

I bummed a lift back to the village and the keeper who spoke English. I bought a glass of ouzo for each of us and enquired about fish. He had caught a very fine fish that morning, he said, which, if I liked, his mother would grill for me. Had he any wine? Only retsina, the taste for which I had not acquired. 'Have a glass with me, anyway,' the keeper said, and I drank it with my lunch, which was the fish and a salad and a hunk of bread. It really was a splendid fish. When I'd finished my meal the keeper asked me how I'd liked the retsina. I had found it more palatable than I'd feared and I agreed to share the bottle with him. As we drank, he talked. He was about forty, bigger and burlier than most Greeks. He'd been an officer in the Greek Army in the civil war against the Communists and he told me how the soldiers on both sides fought their bitter campaigns in the icy winter mountains on rations consisting of chunks of bread and a handful of olives. He was very proud of having met Churchill; once, when he was in the guard of honour Winston had inspected outside the Parliament buildings in Athens, and then much more recently, when Onassis's yacht had sailed up the Gulf, tied up at the jetty and Winston had come ashore.

The keeper struck me as a man of great natural energy, and I couldn't help wondering what he found to do in so remote a place. A little desultory fishing to stock the tables of his tiny restaurant and adding to his store of vividly inaccurate English by reading English-language paperbacks while waiting for patrons? It seemed scarcely enough to satisfy a man of his vigour, and as though sensing my curiosity, he said; 'Tomorrow is a great day for me!' He was off to Athens to see a lawyer and settle a dowry on his sister. To this end he had been saving for years. 'Now at last she can get married,' he said, 'and I am free tomorrow.' 'And then?' I asked. 'And then,' looking up and down the Gulf and round Tolos, he said, 'then I'll start moving.' As he saved, he had thought and planned. The Gulf was ripe for development, exploitation had hardly begun, and those who got in first would make a lot of money. He intended to be one of them. He was going to have a proper restaurant and a real hotel where he'd offer all the comforts and attractions that would induce wealthy Athenians to stay at the Gulf. The village would be a real resort.

I wished him luck, stifling my fears that exploitation would mean spoliation. I was glad at least to have seen the Gulf and the village before the keeper had got to work. I asked about buses back to Nauplion. He said he'd take me to the bus stop, the modern Greek for which, I was always amused to see, was *stasis*. 'But first,' he said, 'you must drink coffee with me,' and he led me through the patch of ground behind the house to the village street and the cafe. He introduced me to and I shook hands very formally with the black-garbed old men sitting in front of their tiny Turkish coffee cups and glasses of water. He insisted on buying the coffee and then he began to do sums on the back of a cigarette packet. 'This is what you owe me,' he said and he went through the bill item by item. *Citron pressé*, so much; grilled fish, salad, bread, so much. It came to the equivalent of between four and five shillings. I had had, besides, at the keeper's expense, half a bottle of retsina and coffee, to say nothing of a boat trip round the Gulf, an insight into history and the pleasure of his company.

Soon after my return to England, I succeeded Janet as literary editor of the paper. Some months later, unexpectedly and, I still think, ill-advisedly both from his own point of view and the *New Statesman*'s, Kingsley relinquished the editorship, something that forced me to recognise that my loyalty, whatever I might once have thought, was towards Kingsley rather than towards the paper in the abstract, for, with Kingsley gone, I realised I had become bored and needed more time for what I thought of as my 'real' work. As soon as seemed decently possible, I too resigned. I had at least fulfilled an ambition of my youth, though I was uncomfortably aware that the reasons I gave myself for resignation were probably rationalisations of a weakness endemic in me and perhaps hereditary. From early on, I had convinced myself to believe that it was intrinsically better to work for oneself than to pursue an occupation that carried with it regular working hours and a regular wage. I had come to suspect that one became a freelance at least partly because one wasn't capable of buckling down and accepting the discipline inseparable from filling a regular job.

Anyway, I went back to freelancing. I became a member of the reviewing staff of the *Daily Telegraph*, somewhat to my surprise, for it was not a newspaper which had my sympathies or in any way spoke to me. But I was with it for more than ten years and had the happiest relationships with everyone on the paper with whom I had anything to do. The most agreeable work I had at this time, though, was an assignment from the BBC North American Service to act as anchorman in a monthly programme on the arts in England. Besides holding the programme together, I usually reviewed a book and interviewed someone thought to be of special interest to our listeners, who could be identified pretty accurately because the programme, which was recorded on tape, was put out largely by American university radio stations. Often, the people interviewed were visiting Americans or people visiting from America, which is not quite the same thing. I cannot say now with accuracy who they were, for I was interviewing pretty widely at the same time in other services of the BBC. My most memorable encounter was with Aldous Huxley, whom I interviewed for three quite unrelated programmes.

What immediately struck me about him was a quality I had not expected him to possess, a quality I can only call beauty of mind. In his presence, I was persuaded I was with a man who truly had acquired detachment. His house in California had recently been destroyed in a forest fire and he had escaped with nothing except the clothes he was wearing and the manuscript of the novel he was writing, which was *Island*, his last. In one of these interviews, he told me he'd still rather be a good novelist than anything else in the world short of being a saint but he knew that he lacked invention. He hoped, however, to refute these self-doubts with *Island*, which he plainly set great store by and which from his description was wonderfully exciting. I have never waited for a new novel with more eagerness. When it turned up from the *Telegraph* a few weeks later it proved a sad anti-climax; worthy but, compared with *Crome Yellow* and *Antic Hay*, nothing.

One of these programmes, that broadcast in the North American Service, was devoted to a discussion of *The Devils*, the play adapted by John Whiting from *The Devils of Loudon*. It had just opened at the Aldwych. It was a very fine play indeed, worthy of the biography it was made from, and Huxley, who had seen it for the first time the evening before the broadcast, was delighted with it. There were four of us in the programme, Huxley and Whiting, whom I had not met before, Harry Craig, the *Statesman*'s drama critic, and I, who was chairman. It was a most agreeable occasion. Craig was an Irishman of quite ruthless charm who had raised blarney to a fine art. A little later, he became a highly successful scriptwriter in Hollywood. Before the recording session began, we were photographed standing in a group round a microphone. It was very much an arranged, studio photograph, made for BBC publicity purposes. Huxley towered above the rest of us, who were turned towards him, looking up. 'We shall look,' Aldous said with gloomy satisfaction, 'like a barber-shop quartet.'

The session ended just after noon and I conducted Huxley to the exit of Bush House opposite St Clement Dane's where the Strand runs into Fleet Street. I knew he was all but blind, though I don't think anyone who didn't know would have guessed; to the best of my memory he did not even use a stick. I asked him which way he was going and whether I could get him a cab. He said he could make his own way very well, and I watched him, tall and thin, a figure of austere distinction, plunge into the midday crowds in the direction of Trafalgar Square.

Soon afterwards, again at Bush House, I interviewed Christopher Isherwood. It was the first time I had seen him since the evening I met him at a party at John Lehmann's more than a dozen years earlier. The sight of him reminded me of John Hampson's description of him in the early Thirties as looking like a cheerful, bright public school boy who was a keen scrum half. This seemed to me still a recognisable description, though he was almost sixty. I was flattered because he said he remembered meeting me and seemed to know who I was. He was a great charmer. We talked about his collaborations with Auden and I asked him to tell me his specific contributions to *The Dog Beneath the Skin* and *The Ascent of F6*, but, as I'd expected, he was not to be drawn.

After the recording, we went across the road to a wine bar. He told me how much nicer he found England now than when he left in 1939. It was less insular, less narrow, and he approved particularly of the presence of so many coloured people. I mentioned my interviews a month or two earlier with Huxley, and he recalled the last time he had seen Aldous, whom he greatly admired though he disclaimed any special friendship with him. It had been at a cocktail party in Hollywood. Huxley had elaborated on one of his favourite topics, the uselessness of literature, and had suddenly stopped in full peroration, as though at that moment he had spotted a possible flaw in his case. In a quite different tone of voice, he said: 'You know, I've just realised I've never read anything by Lopez de Vega.' 'I have,' said Christopher, who had read two of the five hundred surviving plays attributed to the writer. 'Have you, Christopher?' said Huxley eagerly: 'Do tell me what they are like.' 'Bloody awful,' Isherwood said. Huxley smiled beatifically and said: 'Oh Christopher, I'm so glad to hear you say so.'

Someone else I met in these interviews was Lewis Mumford, who was in London to receive the gold medal of the Royal Institute of British Architects. He seemed surprised to find himself being questioned by an Englishman who knew he had written poetry and at least one novel as well as a seminal book on Herman Melville and the even earlier *The Golden Day*, which seemed to me a notable milestone in American self-appraisal. I saw him, indeed, as one of the makers of twentieth-century American consciousness. I found him vigorous and stimulating and I shall not forget the eloquence and vehemence with which he denounced the destruction of the skyline of London.

It was at Bush House, too, that I first met Richard Hughes, who had figured considerably in my early adolescence. I had read *A High Wind in Jamaica* in *Life and Letters*, to which the editor, Desmond MacCarthy, had devoted a whole issue. I had been introduced to him, I think, by Robert Graves, with whom he had been at school and at Oxford. I knew his poems, *Confessio Juvenis*, which I must have read within a year or two of their publication in 1926, had seemed to me very much in the manner of the early Graves; one could see their common enthusiasm for John Skelton at work on both of them. And at much the same time I remember seeing his play, *A Comedy of Good and Evil*, which was greatly praised by Shaw, when it was produced at the Birmingham Repertory Theatre. Two or three years after this, I heard a lot about Hughes from Martin Gilkes, the editor of *Public School Verse*, who had been a close friend at Oxford. Through Martin, indeed, I became used to thinking of him as Diccon Hughes, though it was a name I was utterly unfamiliar with as a derivative or pet version of Richard.

Interviewing him, then, was an encounter I very much looked forward to. I knew nothing about the course of his life since those early days and I found him a mysterious figure, since from being for a few years in the Twenties a very prolific writer he had become one of the most rarely published of authors: after *A High Wind in Jamaica*, we had had to wait nine years for *In Hazard*, and between that novel and *The Fox in the Attic* there were no less than twenty-three. His genius seemed to me unquestionable but of a kind that related him to no other contemporary writer I was aware of. I did not, in other words, have the slightest notion of the man I was to meet. In the event, he seemed not only painfully withdrawn but nondescript to the point of being practically without identity. He seemed such an anonymous figure that he might have been the subject in the flesh of Auden's sonnet 'The Novelist', one who had struggled out of his boyish gifts and learned

> How to be plain and awkward, how to be
> One after whom none think it worth to turn.

He was short and slight, with spectacles and a little beard like King George V's. He reminded me of men I had known as a child; he might have been, like them, a Sunday school superintendent, a man who kept a small grocer's, an insurance agent, a school teacher, the man who collected the rent each month.

He proved almost impossible to interview; words had to be prised out of him, and of all the writers I have met he was the one who seemed most impervious to praise. My review of the novel had appeared in the *Telegraph* that morning. I had admired it enormously and tried to explain why. In the course of doing so, I had found it necessary or at least helpful to refer to Tolstoy, I think in fact quite precisely. This Hughes seemed abashed, even discomforted by. It was the most difficult interview I ever had to conduct.

Ten years later, I was commissioned to interview Hughes again for an intermittent series in the Third Programme called *Work in Progress*.

Of the next instalment of the work Hughes described as 'a historical novel of my own times' there had been no sign, but when I turned up at the hotel in Harlech where I was to stay, I found waiting for me the greater part of what was later published as *The Wooden Shepherdess*. I began to read after dinner and went on until I had finished it, which was in the small hours. We were to begin the interview next morning and had allowed two days for it. And this time there were no difficulties; Hughes was unbuttoned and expansive.

He was, of course, in his own territory, where he was very much the great man. I hadn't realised how closely he was identified with Wales, in his own eyes as well as in those of his compatriots. He had been born in the home counties, and I believe his father had been a manufacturer in the Midlands. I knew that more than forty years earlier Hughes had been associated with the Welsh literary movement and I wondered what this meant in practice. I remembered that in those days Graves, too, had stressed his Welsh affiliations but, so far as I was aware, Welshness was not the first quality nowadays that either name evoked. Did he, I asked Hughes, speak and read the Welsh language? Enough, he answered, to be able to read the lessons in church. He lived in what I fancy had been a fairly large farmhouse facing the estuary immediately across which one saw Clough Williams-Ellis's Portmeirion, a 'model resort' of various Italianate follies enchanting or infuriating according to one's mood. As I interviewed Hughes I gazed at Portmeirion and at Snowdon behind it or, rather, at where I was told Snowdon could be found, for throughout the two days I was there the mists and clouds that engulfed it did not lift.

BBC engineers arrived from Bangor and Hughes's room rapidly became a broadcasting studio. When a sofa was shifted to run a cable across the room Hughes's shot-gun was revealed. It was where he usually kept it. A few weeks earlier, on the eve of the investiture of the Prince of Wales at Caernarvon Castle, the local police called on Hughes to check his shot-gun. He thought that in the circumstances it might be better if the police took it into temporary custody, but they were entirely satisfied that Hughes should keep it, and it went back under the sofa.

In order to finish *The Human Predicament*, Hughes told me he would have to live to be a hundred-and-twenty. His way of writing was such that the longer he wrote the fewer the number of words that were actually committed to paper. Writing for him was the endless process of excision, of paring down. I saw how that marvellous first section of

The Fox in the Attic, the description of young Augustine Penry-Herbert out shooting on the marshes, which I had picked for especial praise in my review, had been achieved. It was not, obviously, a method of composition that any publisher could be expected totally to approve of, and long-suffering as Hughes's were, once in a while they turned on him whatever pressure they could command.

The Human Predicament, Hughes told me, was conceived when, during the war as a temporary civil servant in the Admiralty, he had watched German bombers weaving through the searchlights above London. This, it was immediately clear to him, was the great theme that no contemporary English novelist of ambition could burke, and he saw before him what was to be the work of the rest of his life: to embody in fiction the forces that had produced the war. The whole world was embroiled in the war, and in a sense the whole world would have to be in the novel. Inevitably, it would not be less than a vast work, the thought of writing which would have daunted anyone who was not a genius or a paranoiac. Hughes, I believe, was a genius, but all the same he may still have been daunted, for he struck me as a man who knew himself pretty well and had, as they say, the measure of himself. He could *not* have known that he was doing nothing less than pitting himself against Tolstoy.

Which explains, it seems to me, his clam-like resistance to being interviewed the first time I met him. My implied comparison with Tolstoy had plunged him into extreme trepidation. In any case, he must have known that the venture he had embarked on was ultimately hopeless, for he would not live to be one hundred-and-twenty. With the vast amount of research called for and the amount of travelling which that entailed, together with his way of composing by constant rewriting and reducing, a miracle was necessary if the book was to be finished. Since he must have realised this, his continuing to write the book seems to me to have been heroic. Of the whole, we have two volumes, and there were to have been two others, though for the life of me I do not see how four volumes only would have been enough. How far or how thoroughly he had planned the book beyond *The Wooden Shepherdess* I have no idea. There were, he told me, to be sections on the Civil War in Spain written from the point of view of someone fighting with the Condor Division. It is difficult not to think that he was engaged on a work impossible of conclusion, but what we have seems magnificent. I can think of no greater achievement in the contemporary novel than Diccon Hughes's triumphantly successful blending of Hitler, Hanfstaengl and the rest with fictitious characters.

When the recording was finally in the can and the BBC engineers had taken it away, we strolled in the early August evening in the grounds round his house. It was the quietest, the most peaceful spot I have ever known in Britain. He talked of his undergraduate days at Oxford and seemed pleased to learn that I, too, had been a friend of Martin Gilkes, of whom he spoke with affection. He was proud of having graduated from Oxford with a fourth, the only man I ever knew with that distinction. He had, he said, been too busy writing to have had time to get a better degree.

XI

Through my interest in Wyndham Lewis I had met a leading American authority on him, Professor W. K. Rose, of Vassar College. In 1963, he was to have sabbatical leave, and I was invited to Vassar to teach the courses he normally taught, courses very much in line with my own preoccupations. On the evening before I left London, we gave an after-dinner party, which I remember for one reason only. Reggie Smith and Olivia Manning arrived when things were well under way with the news that Louis MacNeice had died a few hours before. I had not known he was ill.

I crossed the Atlantic on the *Queen Elizabeth* and from New York made my way by train up the Hudson to Poughkeepsie, a trip of about sixty-five miles. I was quite unprepared for the splendour of the scenery and I, who had not seen the Rhine, thought that it must be what the Rhine was like. When, a year or two later, I did see the Rhine I decided I had not been far out. At Poughkeepsie, Caroline Mercer, the chairman of the English department, met me off the train. She was carrying a copy of Mary McCarthy's novel *The Group*, which she gave me. It had been out two or three days. My first official assignment, Carrie told me, was to read it. Mary McCarthy was a Vassar alumna, and the novel chronicled the adventures of four or five young women just graduated from Vassar in the early Thirties. It was obviously construed as autobigraphical and was destined to be a *succés de scandale* and in Vassar circles was highly controversial. The word *group* itself seemed to have a special connotation at Vassar, and I knew from Bill Rose that the college had a mystique of its own. I realised I had been given the novel as part of an indoctrination process, for Mary McCarthy had reacted vigorously against the mystique and yet seemed in herself to embody Vassar's admirable qualities.

Whatever else the mystique was concerned with, it had nothing to do with Poughkeepsie, which was the seat of the college simply because Matthew Vassar — referred to in college circles as 'Ole Massa Vassar' — was a native of the town. In 1861, the year of its foundation, Poughkeepsie was known as a small Hudson River port from which whalers set out. At the end of the century, it was also famous among fans of Henry James as a place that had supplied him with the title of a short story, 'Miss Gunton of Poughkeepise'. One of the stories on what became known as the International Subject, there is no reference in it to Vassar but it does indicate what Poughkeepsie must have symbolised for the mass of Americans of the time; synonymous, as a small town in upstate New York, with what today would be called the sticks, it was the epitome of the provincial. Later, when Poughkeepsie had taken to itself something of the prestige of Vassar, the title took on overtones of irony James himself could not have anticipated. Poughkeepsie became famous to the world beyond it mainly because Vassar was there, and it was not until perhaps thirty years ago that it acquired additional fame as the site of one of the biggest plants of International Business Machines.

Wittingly or not, Ole Massa Vassar conferred renown on his town far beyond the confines of New York State. A Poughkeepsie shipowner and brewer, in college circles he was reputed to have made his money principally from the brothels he is said to have owned on the Poughkeepsie waterfront. However that may be, even though it is not the oldest of American women's colleges, Vassar speedily became one of the most eminent, one of the Seven — or is it Six? — Sister Colleges, the female counterpart of the Ivy League.

Besides its own mystique, Vassar has its special place in American folklore, as was brought home to me when, returning from Christmas in England, I passed through customs at Kennedy Airport. It was late at night and I set my suit-case down in front of a black customs officer. His eye was caught by a label. 'Say,' he asked, 'what's it like, teaching at Vassar?' Flippantly and without thinking, I answered: 'Like being the only man in the chorus of a musical show.' He roared with laughter and passed me through without bothering to look in my baggage. 'Guess you've made my day,' he said.

From their nature, mystiques defy easy definition. Vassar's, I thought, partook of many qualities. In the popular estimate of the College, there was something of the awed awareness expressed by Scott Fitzgerald when he said: 'The rich are different from us.' Something like this was pretty certainly in my Negro customs officer's mind, and it cannot be denied that Vassar was a rich girl's college —

and, as a consequence of the date of its founding, really rather Spartan. Whatever Ole Massa Vassar intended, the ethos of the college was of the nineteenth century, dedicated to high thinking and plain living, of an establishment where the daughters of the rich were made aware of their social and cultural obligations. I do not think Henry James's Isabel Archer, who 'spent half her time thinking of beauty and bravery and magnanimity; she had a fixed determination to regard the world as a place of brightness, of free expansion, of irresistible action . . . She had an infinite hope that she would never do anything wrong', was a college girl, but if she were, she might well have been a Vassar alumna.

And the ethos, it seemed to me, governed the attitudes of faculty-members not themselves products of Vassar, the men no less than the women. In my time, moral concern went mainly into the Civil Rights movement, the campaign for racial equality. There was constant discussion among the faculty of ways of increasing the proportion of black students. It was archetypal liberal discussion: how could you increase the number without lowering academic standards? Out of a student-body of perhaps a thousand, there were not more than half a dozen coloured girls, and you could pretty safely bet that they were the daughters of high-ranking Army and Air Force officers. It was the Civil Rights movement certainly that captured student enthusiasms. I myself had the embarrassing experience – I record it with a sense of its ludicrousness – of receiving a standing ovation from one of my classes when it was learnt that I with some others, one of whom was Stephen Spender, had reneged on an undertaking to take part in celebrations in the Deep South of the quartercentenary of Shakespeare's birth when we learned they would be segregated. I felt an awful fool, for I realised I had been guilty of political naivety in accepting the invitation in the first place. The truth is, I badly wanted to see the South, which was unknown to me. All in all, it seemed fitting that the wife of the President of the United States, who most of us at the time saw as a conspicuous idealist, should be a Vassar girl and that other Vassar girls should be married to rising leaders of the British Labour Party who struck one as being particularly disinterested.

It seemed proper that Vassar should have its own method of teaching, though I did not succeed in understanding it. One did not, I gathered, impart information so much as fan the students' zeal to elicit information from you in communal discussion. It all seemed summed up in an anecdote I was told by way of illustration and, no doubt awful warning. A learned Chinese lady was hired to teach the history of Chinese civilisation and was instructed in the Vassar method. What that resulted in was not apparent until, late in the semester, a wretched student had a nervous breakdown brought about by the complete silence in which the classes on Chinese civilisation had been spent, for, waiting as she had been instructed for her students to draw her out, the teacher had sat in front of them hour after hour without saying a word.

I decided not to attempt to teach by any methods but my own, which were and remained naive. One of the classes I took over from Bill Rose was creative writing, which I approached with the usual English suspicions. Auden, when I first met him in 1933, told me that *he* could teach anyone to write. I did not believe him then and I do not now. I do not think that writing can be taught in any serious sense. But the adverbial phrase is all-important. I do not believe that anything beyond what can be learnt by rote – the multiplication tables, the rudiments of grammar, the periodic tables and so on – can be taught. Once he goes beyond instruction in the ABC of things, the teacher – *any* teacher, of *any* subject – is ultimately dependent solely on the student's own interest and talent.

I was lucky in my students, of whom there were perhaps ten, all of whom had been vetted in varying degrees before being sent on to me. One girl I very soon realised had nothing to learn from me or, I suspected, anybody else: she was, quite simply, a born writer, and the most any teacher could do for her was to help her develop her critical sense and self-confidence and to show her the nature and scope of her talents. Beyond these things, it was a matter of her capacity for experience, something which cannot be taught. In 1964, I felt it was merely a matter of time before I saw her name in magazines or in publishers' lists. The fact that I am still waiting seems to me irrelevant.

I have no knowledge at all of what became of her or, for that matter, of any of the other girls. I have, so far, seen the names of none of them in print, but this does not make me think that I or they were wasting our time. At worst, I suspect that they gained in appreciation of the writing skills of others. I was surprised and impressed in the case of two or three girls by the development in the power to grasp imaginatively and to feel and express that manifested itself during the semester. In the nature of things it seemed to me extraordinarily unlikely that more than one of them, at the most, would ever write in any serious sense, and I did not conceive it any duty of mine to teach what the advertisements call 'writing for profit'. I think I failed only with one student, and even she plainly enjoyed herself and was a model of diligence in her own way. Though ignoring, as irrelevant, the themes I suggested and the exercises I set, her zeal was evident. Week in week out, she turned in her work, which, masking as short stories, were chunks of recent and undigested experience. How 'true' they were I thought it best not to know. They were, I fancy, transcripts if not of a young woman's actual weekend exploits in Greenwich Village at least of what a young woman of undisciplined and excessively romantic imagination might think a middle-aged Englishman would like to believe was typical of young female American behaviour in Greenwich Village.

It was mainly with the students of my writing class in mind that I induced R. K. Narayan, who was in New York at the time, to come up to Vassar and talk. Narayan is now over seventy, and if the Nobel prize for literature goes to India while he is alive, it seems to me axiomatic that it will go to him, for he is one of the finest of the world's novelists. I had read his second novel *The Bachelor of Arts* when it appeared in 1937 with an enthusiastic introduction by Graham Greene. Greene was in some sense his mentor, and they speak of each other with great affection and admiration, though they did not meet, I think, till Narayan made his first visit to England in the Fifties. I met him then; at a dinner party at my literary agent's, David Higham. I was greatly taken with him, and on visits to England over a number of years he dined with us several times.

He was a small man and very dark; he came from Madras. His English, both spoken and written, seemed to me flawless, though perhaps a trifle old-fashioned. It had been his language since early childhood, for his father was an Anglophile with a considerable library of the standard English writers, on whom Narayan had brought himself up. He must have been nearly fifty when he first saw England. He told me that London was just as he had imagined it; he found it faithful to its appearance in Dickens's novels, in which he was steeped. Wherever he went in the modern city he ran into men and women who might have stepped out of the pages of *Copperfield* and *Great Expectations*.

It was a great boon to me to discover that he was in New York. He was not published in America until twenty years after his first appearance in England, and he was still little known; I think none of my Vassar colleagues had read him. But *Time-Life* had begun to sponsor him, and he now spent a month every year in New York, visiting his publishers and seeing his manuscripts through the press. He stayed at the Chelsea Hotel, which, until I visited him there, I knew of only by repute as a famous bohemian haunt. Chelsea struck me as a pretty beaten-up district; it was, in fact, one of the oldest parts of Manhattan, having been staked out in the seventeen-fifties. It stretched westward from Seventh Avenue between 14th Street and 27th Street, but the bohemians had mostly abandoned Chelsea for Greenwich Village more than half a century ago. The Chelsea Hotel remained, however. It wasn't much like the Grand Babylons of Midtown but was content to be sturdily, perhaps defiantly, old-fashioned. It was not a place you could simply walk into from West 23rd and book a room: if the management didn't like the look of you, you wouldn't get one, and the number of credit cards you could show them would make no difference. But for people active in the arts rooms would always be found. Bronze plaques on the front of the building record that Thomas Wolfe, Dylan Thomas and Brendan Behan all lived there in their time; and so, years before them, did Mark Twain and O. Henry, and after them, besides Narayan, the composer Virgil Thomson and Arthur Miller.

The Chelsea was ideal for Narayan not only because it was the most private of hotels but also because it let rooms with kitchens attached. He could make his own meals, which was a great convenience, since, as a Brahmin, in the West he was always faced with dietary problems. I don't think he cared greatly for America, but New York he found in some ways more convenient to live in than London, for it had not only the Chelsea to offer but also the restaurant at the United Nations building, which catered for the large Indian delegation.

Narayan was not a man who made a practice of lecturing or any form of public speaking. You felt he was essentially a private person in whom gentleness and authority lived side by side. He was totally unaffected and disarming and he was a great success both with my students and with my colleagues. He did not lecture so much as talk easily and he re-told the legends of the Hindu gods and goddesses. He gave us a glimpse into a way of life and a civilisation so different from our own as, one would have thought, to be incurably alien, but, as in his novels of the fictitious southern Indian city of Malgudi, his characters became utterly human, instantly recognisable as akin, for all their antiquity and supernatural status, to ourselves. My colleagues delighted in entertaining him and I rejoiced in having the opportunity of introducing to an American audience a novelist who, as thoroughly as Faulkner, has created through a sequence of novels an imaginary community reflecting in microcosm a whole culture.

At Vassar, we were near enough to the city for me to be able to spend a fair amount of time in New York. My headquarters was The Players, in Gramercy Park, which is the nearest Manhattan has to a Mayfair or Bloomsbury square. Very early in my stay at Vassar, I was telephoned one morning by the college switchboard operator who told me that while I was lecturing someone had telephoned me from New York saying he was a friend of mine and would call me again after lunch. She added that he had a foreign accent. This intrigued me; the words called up vaguely Magyar or Serbo-Croat vocalisations. It proved to be Michael Ayrton, which forced me to realise that if Michael had a foreign accent I must have one too. He said that he and Elizabeth were in New York as the guests of Ben Sonnenberg, a name which meant nothing to me, and he was inviting me to a party at Sonnenberg's on Sunday evening. He explained that Sonnenberg lived in Gramercy Park, on the corner of the square and Irving Place, almost within spitting-distance of The Players. I asked him what kind of party it would be, wondering whether it called for a dinner jacket. Michael said he didn't really know but he could assure me it would be — I use his own word — a 'piss-up'.

At the appropriate time on Sunday evening I presented myself at the front door of Sonnenberg's house in a lounge suit. I say the house but I could see that in fact it was not one house but two knocked into one. That seemed to make it little less than a mansion. I was in the presence not merely of wealth but of conspicuous wealth. I range the bell and waited. I was joined on the doorstep by another man, who I recognised was British too. We introduced ourselves and burst into laughter. It was Ludovic Kennedy.

A man-servant took us up by lift to a drawing room. The walls were hung with drawings, some of which looked to my untutored eyes like old-master drawings. Michael and Elizabeth introduced us to the Sonnenbergs, a couple in their late sixties or early seventies I guessed. He, in my memory, had a curiously Edwardian or even late nineteenth-century appearance, with long sideboards and wearing something very much like a Norfolk jacket of old-fashioned cut, milk-chocolate in colour, and a high stock. Two or three other guests arrived, one of whom was Alistair Cooke, whom I had not met before. The man-servant served cocktails and after a brief interval we were led into dinner.

The dining room, too, was hung with drawings. There were place-cards on the table, but I could not see my name and wandered round peering and feeling an idiot. Mrs Sonnenberg plainly thought I was one and pointed to a chair. 'You are here, Professor Warren,' she said impatiently. The card clearly said Professor Warren. I began to explain that my name was not Warren. Mrs Sonnenberg made it obvious that she didn't believe me. As for Sonnenberg, who during the course of dinner I was forced to think was not accustomed to being contradicted or even disagreed with, he behaved as though I'd be well advised to become Professor Warren immediately. In this plight of mine, the Ayrtons were of no help: they merely stifled their giggles.

I remained Professor Warren. After dinner, we were taken up to an enormous room which ran the length of the two houses and was set up for a film show. More than a score of after-dinner guests, the men in dinner-jackets and the women in evening gowns, invaded us and settled in armchairs or on sofas. The lights went out and we waited for the film. I wondered what it would be. It was *Tom Jones*, which had yet to be exhibited in America, though Michael and I had seen it in London for *The Critics* programme some weeks before. I would infinitely have preferred to be allowed to wander round the rooms looking at the drawings. When the film ended I was introduced to all and sundry as Professor Warren. The majority inclined their heads respectfully and said 'Pleased to meet you, Profession Warren', a few asked deferentially but as though with some doubt, 'Professor *Penn* Warren?' while the truly knowledgeable blurted out, with what seemed to me some hostility, 'Not Red Warren.' Then they disappeared with the suddenness with which they had come.

Next morning, over coffee, the Ayrtons and I held a post-mortem. Michael admitted that the evening had been nothing like what he and I thought of as a piss-up. But he had worked out how I came to be Professor Warren. Rex Warner, the novelist and translator from the Greek, had also been invited to the dinner-party. He was visiting professor at Baudouin College and had had to cry off because of sudden illness. No doubt the party had to be re-arranged and what more natural than that Rex Warner and Walter Allen, who were unknown to their hosts, should have their names confused, conflated and transmogrified into that of Professor Robert Penn Warren, who must have been known to the Sonnenbergs, if only by repute?

Sonnenberg, whom I was to meet once again, seven years later, at a luncheon of the New York University Alumni Association and who plainly did not remember having met me before, was one of the several men who were said to have invented the art or craft of public relations. He was a poor boy of immigrant stock, and his success was demonstrated by his occupation of the two-houses-knocked-into-one in Gramercy Park. The basis of his fortune was rumoured to be a minute royalty, a fraction of one per cent, levied on every pack sold of one of the most popular of American cigarettes, the brand-name of which he devised. His passion for art-collecting had its origin in emulation of the millionaire industrialists who were his clients; realising he could not compete in the sale-rooms with the likes of the Fricks, Harrimans and Mellons, he turned his attention to the then relatively unattractive field of drawings. By 1963, he had a priceless collection of drawings by old and modern masters, but it was not until his death in 1978 that I realised he had been one of the legendary figures of New York within his own lifetime.

A few days later, I had to go to the New York studios of the BBC to record a talk for the External Services. The studios were in the Rockefeller Center complex on Fifth Avenue. I found the right building and took the elevator to the thirtieth floor. When I could not find the BBC I consulted my letter again and discovered that it was the thirty-first floor. Seeing on the wall a painted arrow and the word Stairs, I decided to walk up to the next storey. What, indeed, could be simpler or more obvious? But having got on the stairs, I discovered I could not get off them. The door to the thirty-first floor proved to be locked and so were the doors to the thirtieth, from which I had just come, and to the thirty-second. I laboured up and down for a dozen floors on either side of the thirty-first. All doors were locked against me. I was an uncanny experience. I was marooned on those stairs and I might have been the only man left on earth. It was conscious of the flights of stairs soaring up above me to, what was it? the hundredth storey and conscious too of the flights plunging down below me. It was chillingly Kafkaesque. I was already late for my recording: I might be madly late. Sooner or later, I knew, I would stumble upon a janitor, or a janitor would stumble upon me, but that might not be until nightfall. There seemed no good reason why I should not spend hours climbing up and down those interminable stairs, which were so impersonal, so functional and so damnably hard.

I decided to stay close to the door to the thirty-first floor and sit on the stairs and wait. I don't suppose I was on them much more than ten minutes, though it seemed hours. A man with keys at his belt descended it seemed from nowhere. He did not appear surprised to see me. I stammered out my plight. He detached a key from his belt and unlocked the door to the thirty-first floor. Finding Limeys lost and wandering on the stairs was obviously all in the day's work to him.

I got to the studio and found my producer. Alistair Cooke was with her. I made my apologies and found I was not so very late, after all. Then Cooke said he had a favour to ask of me; he was due to follow me, to record his weekly *Letter from America*, but he was in rather a hurry: would I mind if he did his recording before mine? It was all one to me, and I settled myself on a sofa in the studio. I watched him with great interest. So far as I could see, he had no script and was talking from the briefest of notes. It was not one of his more memorable broadcasts, indeed run-of-the-mill, relying considerably on stock devices, reminiscences of Thirties jazz and his adventures on the golf course. All the same, it was a most accomplished performance, just how accomplished you probably had to be a broadcaster to recognise. I had been listening seriously to radio for thirty years and broadcasting perhaps twice a week for the past fifteen and I had no doubt that Cooke was *the* master-broadcaster. There had been other superb broadcasters. I remembered with especial pleasure and affection Desmond MacCarthy, who had brought to the broadcast talk a comparable style and polish. But the great thing about Cooke was that he was the working journalist in broadcasting who could still lift the most casual piece to the level of the literary essay and had done so time after time, week in, week out, for more than a generation. One took him for granted, so uniform was his excellence; and it was wonderful to watch him going about his daily job.

He ended and, despite the favour he had asked, did not seem particularly anxious to go. I myself sat down before the microphone. What I talked about I no longer know. We left the studio together and when we reached the street discovered that the rain was pouring down as it can do only in New York City on a Friday in the early evening rush-hour. 'I must get a cab,' we both said, and we enquired the direction we were each respectively going. I was going back to The Players, thirty blocks downtown. Cooke was going uptown, so it was each man for himself. We stared into the rain which slanted down like shafts of lances and the dense traffic which edged from traffic-light to traffic-light up the Avenue. We willed but Cooke willed more strongly than I. We were standing side by side on the kerb, an empty cab materialised before our eyes, Cooke stepped into it and disappeared among the mass of surging, jostling cars. I waited for a further fifteen minutes, during which time no empty cab was seen, you would have thought, by living man. Soaked, I set out to walk the thirty blocks. When I think of Alistair Cooke nowadays it is not only the supreme master of the microphone who comes to mind but the

Cooke who is also the master at whose bidding out of nowhere and from the densest traffic on the wettest New York evenings empty taxis appear.

Another distinguished journalist I met, and this time through Vassar entirely, was Richard Rovere, for many years the *New Yorker's* Washington correspondent. He lived a few miles up the river from Poughkeepsie and, as a friend of Bill Rose's and of other colleagues', a figure often seen on the Vassar campus. He was a graduate and a trustee of our fellow liberal-arts college and relatively near neighbour Bard College, which had begun, I believe, as an outpost, dedicated to experiment in education, of Columbia University. Rovere was a thoughtful, sombre, taciturn man who told me, when I asked about his name, which I had not met before, that he had never been able to find out its origins and had no idea where in Europe his forbears had come from. As much as any American I have known, he conformed to my notion of a Yankee.

I met him very soon after I arrived at Vassar, when he rescued me from an embarrassing situation. I was invited to cocktails by a lady who was a legendary figure in Vassar circles, as she could hardly not have been, since, as the relict of a member of one of the principal American dynasties and bearing the magic symbol III after her name, she was one of the richest women in the United States. I could not fail to understand that, by being invited to drinks, I was being highly honoured. I had been invited together with Carrie Mercer, who drove me out. At the entrance to the estate, we stopped at what had plainly been the lodge. I was intrigued by it for it was older than any building I had seen in New York State, a reminder that settlement there by the Dutch had begun as early as the sixteen-thirties and that the patroons, as the proprietors of the manorial tracts granted by the Dutch West India Company were called, had established themselves along the Hudson. We were obviously visiting what had been in colonial Dutch times a manor on the Hudson River. It happened that the lodge was occupied by someone we knew, the professor of drama at Vassar, so we could knock on the door and ask to be shown round. It was built of stone, the walls were very thick, there was not, I think, more than four rooms. It could, it was impossible not to feel, withstand either a siege or a whole winter of the worst weather recorded. In colonial times it had been, we were told, a mill.

Almost the first thing my hostess asked me at the cocktail party was whether I had noticed the cottage at the gate. Did I realise, she asked, that it was three hundred and fifty years old? 'They don't come much older than that,' I said, for I was impressed. And then I realised to my horror that she had interpreted my remark as British superiority; she thought I was high-hatting her and said, bristling, 'Oh, I know in England you don't think three hundred and fifty years is old.' And then Dick Rovere, bless his memory, interjected. 'Oh come, Mrs —, the only houses they had in this neck of the woods three hundred and fifty years ago were wigwams.' She had, I reckoned, overestimated the age of the house by fifty years. All the same, it was an impressive memorial of an antique past and the oldest building I ever saw in North America until I went to Ontario in 1971 and visited a settlement established and later abandoned by the Jesuits.

In New York, I met other men I admired, Lionel Trilling among them. I esteemed him both for his criticism and for his one novel *The Middle of the Journey*, which, as a dramatisation of ideas and the clash of ideologies must be placed alongside *The Power and The Glory*, *Darkness at Noon* and *Revenge for Love*. In its own way, it is a signally daunting work, for it is as if Trilling is demonstrating, from his vast knowledge of novels and theories of the novel, just how a novel should be written. He invited me to luncheon at the Century Club, which is, I suppose, the counterpart in New York both of the Athenaeum and the Reform. Next session, he was going to put in a year at Oxford, and we talked about that. What I remember most vividly, though, was that he said he thought well of the Beatles, who that very week had taken New York by storm and, merely by staying there, had put the Plaza Hotel under siege conditions.

I had met Trilling twice before, in London. The first time was in the Fifties, when I had taken part with him and David Garnett in a discussion on, I think, the nature and condition of modern English and American fiction. It was not, I think, a very good discussion because it lacked direction; the bases of the programme had been inadequately defined. None of us knew exactly what we were supposed to be talking about. Though it was put on in a BBC studio, it was not under BBC auspices but those of an American company. It was designed for American consumption, and I seem to remember that our chairman was a journalist from the London office of *Time-Life*. What impressed me was how radically opinions differed and became polarised. Garnett, whom I was meeting for the first time, was an ancient hero of mine, but it was soon very clear that on every issue that arose or was likely to arise it was Trilling and I who saw eye to eye, in total disagreement with Garnett. He had been a friend of Lawrence in his early years as a novelist, but it was I, with Trilling supporting me, who now emerged as Lawrence's champion. Garnett seemed to reserve his praise for Carson McCullers, who he thought grossly neglected and still too little known. I thought he pitched his praise rather too high. He was delightful, a charmer, yet I could not get rid of the feeling that he spoke *de haut en bas* and, by contrast with Trilling, as the gentleman amateur in the fatal English tradition.

I met Trilling again a year or two later at a small luncheon party given for him by Janet Adam Smith on behalf of the *New Statesman* at the Escargot Bienvenu, which was where the paper usually did its entertaining. Pritchett was there, and John Raymond. It ought to have been a splendid occasion, but I remember that John and I were bitterly disappointed. All that remains in my memory now, apart from the fact that Trilling chose *moules mariniéres* as his main dish, is that he talked at length of his love for Dunhill pipes.

This is to say that my memories of personal encounters with Trilling are trivia. They suggest that he had no small talk, which is almost certainly true, and that he took himself with undue seriousness if not with downright solemnity. But this is only to remind us that it is not through meeting him in the flesh that we know a writer but through reading his books. The books are always better than the man who wrote them.

Are these trivia demeaning to Trilling? I think not. They seem to me, rather, to expose the shallowness of our customary English ways of assessing men and women. Everything about him showed that Trilling was an intensely private person, above all, the long, lined, curiously rectangular, melancholy face beneath the head of carefully parted grey hair. He seemed in some ways very unAmerican. Americans, of every class and from all parts, tend overwhelmingly to be what are called good mixers. It is something built into the American school system, a feature of the American democratic process. I doubt if Trilling ever set out to be a good mixer or was ever thought to be one. And in manners of speech, dress and deportment he approximated more than is common in America to English patterns.

This did not make him English in any real sense, and in habit of mind he was quite other than English. He was one of those, all the children of recent immigrants, who brought into the Anglo-American tradition something foreign to it and even, one would have thought, opposed to the English strands in it. Others of his company were Philip Rahv, Hannah Arendt, Saul Bellow and Bernard Malamud. What they brought into the tradition was Jewish certainly but, almost as certainly, Russian too. It sets little or no store on the sense of humour, which the English overvalue, on the idea of good taste or a sense of proportion, all of which, where the great issues of life and literature are concerned, it finds grotesquely irrelevant.

It was perhaps Trilling's good fortune that he eased himself, as it were, into English regard with his first two books, on Arnold and Forster. Both seem peculiarly English writers, and Trilling views them with sympathy and a discriminating appreciation, so that the English saw him as an American uncannily equipped to understand them. Beside him, the best English critics of his time, Leavis shall we say or Empson, appear parochial or narrowly specialist. His scale of reference was wider, and he lived in a larger field of ideas, almost, indeed, in a battlefield upon which ideas were strewn like mines or anti-personnel bombs and across which he proceeded with cautious resolution. It was difficult not to relate this to his ancestral training in catastrophe as a Russian Jew whose forbears had survived the pogroms of the tsars. It was this, one felt, that enabled him to confront, as one who had their measure, the crucial problems of twentieth-century writing, among them the problem of why, in an age dominated by the scientific temper and by democratic and liberal ideals, the most satisfying writing, in that it is the most faithful and profoundest reflection of human experience, has been written in spite of, often in defiance of and sometimes even in downright hostility towards generally accepted beliefs.

In May, 1964, my wife came out to join me for three weeks and straightaway I was made to realise how unobservant I was, how deficient in the visual faculties. I had been discussing with my students a passage in which Lawrence describes a may tree in blossom. It is a nice problem, how far the reader's appreciation of a piece of writing is impaired by failure positively to identify natural things referred to. I have always assumed that because a Burmese student, for instance, has never seen a daffodil it does not mean that he cannot respond to 'I Wandered Lonely as a Cloud'; I take if for granted that there is some flower in his own background that will be an appropriate substitute. At the same time, I recalled from my experience at Coe how shaken I had been when I was made aware by the laughter of my class that Robert Frost's katydids were not, as I had always thought, birds but grasshoppers. The sense of the poem remained the same but I could not rid myself of the notion that I had misunderstood it for years; and in one way I plainly had. And though I knew that the phoebes of another of Frost's poems were birds, I was always bothered because I couldn't accurately pinpoint them and had to be content with an image of brown blurs roughly the size of sparrows. How valuable actual familiarity with what was mentioned in a poem was had come home to me only a week or so earlier when I saw for the first time dogwood in bloom: lines of Eliot's came miraculously to life.

I therefore sounded my Vassar students: did they know the may tree? Did hawthorns grow in America? Since they seemed unsure, I launched on an elaborate account of the may tree and its significance in English life and, since the tree is one I have known from early childhood and one I have been particularly fond of – there was one in our back-garden in Birmingham which blossomed spectacularly – I thought my exposition pretty good. Judge my consternation, then, when, walking towards the building which housed the English department, my wife exclaimed to me: 'Oh, isn't that a lovely may tree?' There it stood, larger than an English hawthorn, in full blossom.

We were coming to the week devoted to revision before examinations, and I found that with some co-operation from my students and colleagues I could get away with my wife for ten days. We went sight-seeing, something I would have been too lazy to do by myself and was glad to be made to do. I had been enlisted to give a lecture at Douglas College, the women's college of Rutgers, and from New Brunswick, New Jersey, we took the train to Philadelphia. We walked, I remember, from the railway station, which seemed as vast as the Baths of Caracalla in Rome, to Indepedence Square and Indepedence Hall and we spent the afternoon in the Museum of Art, where we were impressed particularly by paintings by the Hudson River school, which was new to us, and by an exhibition of sculpture by Lipchitz. We stayed the night at Swarthmore and went on next day to Washington. We took excursions to Alexandria and Mount Vernon, which was altogether smaller and more intimate, more *bijou* almost, than I'd expected. We flew over the Appalachians, which were higher and wilder than I'd expected, to spend a weekend in Louisville, Kentucky, with friends who taught at the university. On another occasion, we made an excursion into Massachusetts to see Stockbridge, a fascinating and revealing reconstruction of a late seventeenth-century New England village. Up the road from Vassar, we visited the Roosevelt mansion at Hyde Park, which is charming, because it is as much a memorial to the squire of Dutchess County as to the president, and we visited too its near neighbour the Vanderbilt mansion, a wonderfully grandiose monument to the vulgarity of opulant late-nineteenth-century America and a prefect foil to the unaffected Roosevelt house. And we contrived to see quite a bit of New York City, particularly the Museum of Modern Art, the Guggenheim Museum and the Frick Mansion, which seems to me the most perfect of small art collections. And I remember we took a conducted bus tour of the Bowery, where the drunks were self-consciously lying in shop-doorways.

My spell at Vassar was rewarding and agreeable. I had strengthened my relations with the *New York Times Book Review* and reviewed besides for the *New Republic* and the *New York Review*. I had appeared on television with Joseph Heller in Stanley Kauffmann's programme on Channel 13, the New York public service television channel; though I reflected that I couldn't have afforded to do often, for the reward for my labours consisted of two glasses of Jack Daniels bourbon whiskey after the programme, a reminder that whereas in England one was well paid for talking in the Third Programme, in America one was expected to do cultural broadcasts out of love. It was no wonder that American intellectuals held the BBC in quite exaggerated awe; they seemed to believe it consisted entirely of the Third Programme. I had given lectures at the Universities of Illinois, where, it seemed to me, great institution though it is, everybody could have gone over to the building of tanks at the drop of a hat, it was so impersonal and functional, and at Kansas, Rutgers and New York. There I was entertained to lunch by the English faculty. It was then I first met one of my closest American friends, the poet and critic M. L. Rosenthal. I could not foresee that a few years later I should be Berg Professor at New York University. I had besides, and no less important, made friendships at Vassar which proved to be lasting. If one of the more grandiose dreams of my youth, which was to have a flat in London, Paris and New York had not materialised, I felt that in a modest way I had become a New Yorker.

One result of my exposure to America and New York was a sharpened visual appreciation of London. I must not claim too much; my visual sense remained defective, though at least I was now aware of it, and as for visual education, it seemed to me I had had scarcely any. A little judicious reading in architecture might have done something to make good my lack, but I had done almost none, for the same reason as I had allowed myself to remain illiterate musically. I knew what I was missing but, I told myself, I hadn't time to do anything about it; there were all the books to read first. I had no time, and in a sense that was true; and I prided myself, too, that I was guarding myself against what I saw as a family weakness, which was to spread oneself out too thinly, to dissipate one's energies in too many disparate activities.

Now, I am not sure that I was right and I regret opportunities not taken. As it was, coming back from New York in the summer of 1964, I found I could wander almost aimlessly through Mayfair, Bloomsbury, Belgravia, Hampstead, Chelsea and find myself beguiled constantly by unexpected and unsought delights, the facade of a terrace of houses, perhaps, or the vista of a mews, even the proportions of a door or a window. The same thing happened, to a smaller degree only, in less regarded districts, in Camberwell, Islington, Camden Town, where one saw what often seemed a palimpsest waiting to be deciphered.

And what I found in London was common, I knew throughout England. Birmingham, aesthetically, was never a highly regarded city, but I knew little corners of it, prospects, angles, façades, the contemplation of which always pleased me. It was precisely this constant and rarely ostentatious solicitation of the eye by the common scene that, it seemed to me, one didn't find in the United States; or certainly not to anything like the same degree. New York had its impressive sights and views but they were monumental, set pieces; the prospect along Park Avenue, the Seagram Building, Brooklyn Bridge, the Guggenheim, they assault the eye with altogether resounding success, as they were meant to, but the smaller beguilements, where are they? Not missing absolutely; in New York the Village has them. And they are to be found in the old towns in New England and the South. They are not conspicuous in the Middle West; there's little to delight the eye in Des Moines, Iowa, or in Cedar Rapids; nor, indeed, are they common anywhere in America.

All this is to say that in urban America, by constrast with Britain and Europe, the eye is starved. It is, I believe, although he himself does not mention it, part of the indictment Matthew Arnold makes in what after more than ninety years is still one of the most profound, searching and measured judgements made on the quality of life in America, *Civilization in the United States*. 'What really dissatisfies in American civilization,' he concludes, 'is the want of the interesting, a want due chiefly to the want of those elements of the interesting, which are elevation and beauty.'

This new awareness of the visual coincided with the beginning of three or four years marked by foreign travel, trips abroad, by which I mean into Europe, for I did not think of the United States as abroad. I saw myself as being a relatively new kind of man, Transatlantic man in what I think was Hugh Gaitskell's phrase. These trips abroad were fortuitous and unplanned, but they had one thing in common: always I was engaged in singing for my supper, so that in as far as they could be seen as holidays, they were very much working holidays. They had to be fitted somehow into the piecemeal activities by which I earned my living. And this meant I could not profit from these forays abroad as much as I ought to have done because I could not afford to do the necessary preparatory homework. I did not have time.

And so, though I enjoyed these continental excursions, I also found them tantalising, frustrating, simply because of my lack of knowledge of art, architecture and history. So, in Germany, Austria and Malta for the British Council and in Hungary, I was scarcely any better then the most gormless and goggle-eyed of tourists. I marvelled or condemned uncritically because I couldn't do otherwise. A visit I paid to Stockholm may stand as typical. I was there to broadcast fourteen talks for Swedish Radio on contemporary English writers, the last four or five of which I hadn't had time to complete before arriving. I was in Stockholm for rather more than a week and I found it congenial. It remains in my memory largely as a vast broadcasting studio traversed by canals and dominated by a city hall.

My memories of these forays are blurred and confused. I don't say that *Fidelio* seen and heard from a box at the Vienna State Opera House was entirely wasted on me but it was an experience I should have profited from more than I did. I knew I was not living up to the privileges that fortune had granted me. What I most enjoyed was talking to audiences of university students. I talked to them in West Berlin and Munich and Budapest and found that, whichever side of the Iron Curtain I was, students shared the same preoccupations as those in the United States and were concerned almost to obsession with the same cultural heroes, Salinger and *The Catcher in the Rye* and Golding and *Lord of the Flies* and, of course, The Beatles.

My most exciting and challenging excursion into Europe, however, was in a category of its own. My book on the post-war English and American novel was to be translated into Russian, and in 1966 my wife and I were invited to the Soviet Union as the guests of the Writers' Union. We were there only for a fortnight and neither of us spoke the language. Any comments of mine must be a flirtation with the jejune. We had what I suppose I must call red carpet treatment: an extraordinarily agreeable and intelligent graduate student in English at Moscow University was provided for us as interpreter and courier, and a car was at our disposal when it was needed. I spent most of my visit consumed by curiosity that could never be satisfied. For instance: had these people, who did not strike one as the most efficient in the world, *really* hit the moon? I was prepared to believe they had, if only because the Americans said so, but how had they done it? And underlying that question was another. How much of what one saw and experienced was Russian and how much the result of Communism? When I got back to England I read a book on Russia and the Russians written by Maurice Baring and published in 1912: in its light, it was not apparent to me that much had changed since then. My notions of the country had been derived mainly, of course, from nineteenth-century Russian fiction: the country I saw was recognisably the country Dostoevsky, Tolstoy and Chekhov wrote about.

The most memorable single incident that happened to me was probably that of being shown round what remains of Dostoevsky's Petrograd by one of the leading experts. Much has disappeared, of course; a children's theatre now stands, for instance, on the spot where Dostoevsky faced the firing squad. But enough remains to persuade me that, among other things, he was one of the great literalists of the imagination, one of those in whom creation is fostered by the contemplation of the actual. We were taken to the tenement building and indeed up to the room which is thought to be the model for the one in which the old pawnbroker is murdered by Raskolnikov. If it is not, all one can say is that it is a most faithful reconstruction of the scene of what is a key-passage in *Crime and Punishment*. Dostoevsky seemed to me still extraordinarily close to parts at least of Leningrad in 1966.

I was much moved, too, by the experience of visiting Tolstoy's house at Yasnaya Polyana. It was occupied by the Germans during the war and pretty badly knocked about; by the time I saw it it had been most carefully restored. I was particularly interested in Tolstoy's library and the signed presentation copies from authors throughout the world. The curator took out Wells's books for me to look at; they were annotated by Tolstoy. One was made to realise something of the immensity of Tolstoy's international prestige in the years during his lifetime. But beyond that, Yasnaya Polyana was a charming house long and lovingly lived in, not in any sense a great house but, both in scale and as a human habitation, surprisingly reminiscent of a house on the other side of the world, Franklin D. Roosevelt's Hyde Park, Dutchess County, New York.

During my two weeks in the Soviet Union, I was obsessed above anything else by curiosity roused by the spectacle of the tourists,

Soviet tourists at that, often Kalmucks, Turkomen and Kirghiz, who shuffled round the Kremlin, the Winter Palace, the Hermitage, the Summer Palace on an island in the Gulf of Finland, shuffled round and gawped day after day in their thousands. In their uncouthness, which suggested the very extreme of provinciality, they seemed to be crude, even malicious parodies of tourists as we knew them in Western Europe. What, I wanted to know, did the buildings, the works of art, the artifacts they saw, mean to them? Certainly they were doing anything but looking at the achievements of the Communist present, were looking at what Communism had repudiated and yet bade them in some sense to admire. I had no clue to the mystery; and it struck me that I too was gawping. Going round the Kremlin, George, our interpreter, who had been brought up devoid of religious knowledge but, according to himself, had read *Paradise Lost* at Moscow University, besought me to explain the ikons to him. Of course, I could not and I began to wonder about our relation to the past and especially of the Soviet Communist's relation to his Russian past. Later, I came across a passage in Auden which seemed to have some bearing on the problem: 'Tolstoi, who, knowing that art makes nothing happen, scrapped it, is more to be respected than the Marxist critic who finds ingenious reasons for admitting the great artists of the past to the State Pantheon.' But there could be no question of the pride the authorities in Soviet Russia had in the monuments of the Russian past.

Those wondering, shuffling, staring Russian tourists had inherited the things they saw, which constituted a richer, vaster, more diverse hoard of plunder than anything I had seen in the United States. But still I wanted to know what they signified to their new owners, who, theoretically, were brought up to be atheists disinfected of even the most innocuous of superstitions. Throughout my stay in Russia I was haunted by the memory of Hyacinth Robinson, the archetype in literature of the dispossessed proletarian aesthete. Hyacinth, the hero of *The Princess Cassamassima*, which seems to me in some respects the most extraordinary of Henry James's novels, is the illegitimate son of a dissolute peer murdered by his mistress, a French seamstress, who dies in jail, having given birth to him. He is brought up in the slums by a back-street dressmaker who leaves him a tiny legacy on which he tours France and Italy. Already a committed revolutionary who has pledged himself to his leader Hoffendahl to carry out assassination if it is asked of him, he writes from Venice to his patron the engimatic princess, in what must be almost the most remarkable and eloquent letter in our fiction:

> It's not that it hasn't been there to see, for that perhaps is the clearest result of extending one's horizon — the sense, increasing as we go, that want and toil and suffering are the constant lot of the immense majority of the human race. I've found them everywhere but haven't minded them. Forgive the cynical confession. What has struck me is the great achievements of which man has been capable in spite of them — the splendid accumulations of the happier few, to which doubtless the miserable many have also in their degree contributed . . . They seem to me inestimably precious and beautiful and I've become conscious more than ever before how little I understand what in the great rectification you and Poupin propose to do with them . . . The monuments and treasures of art, the great palaces and properties, the conquests of learning and taste, the general fabric of civilisation as we know it, based if you will on all the despotisms, the cruelties, the exclusions, the monopolies, and the rapacities of the past, but thanks to which, all the same, the world is less of 'a bloody sell' and life more of a lark — our friend Hoffendahl seems to me to hold them too cheap and to wish to substitute for them something in which I can't somehow believe as I do in things with which the yearnings and the tears of generations have been mixed. You know how extraordinary I think our Hoffendahl — to speak only of him; but if there's one thing that's more clear about him than another, it's that he wouldn't have the least feeling for this incomparable, abominable old Venice. He would cut up the ceiling of Veronese into strips, so that every one might have a little piece . . .

I do not know how Hyacinth should be answered, but the paradox that faced him and all of us may be seen at its most dramatic in the Soviet Union. In Leningrad, our delightful interpreter treated me to a routine speculation about the amount of human misery and suffering which must have gone into the building of the Winter Palace; but I formed no impression that he really believed that the Winter Palace was allowed to survive only as a memorial to the suffering the toiling masses were forced to endure under an odious tyrant. It seemed to me that the pious preservation of these memorials of the past in some ways could only be dangerous to the Communist state. They may tell us little about the quality of life in the past but they do, most emphatically, tell us what the past achieved; and even if we can persuade ourselves that the Russian present is necessarily better in social terms than the past, that does not help us to evaluate the monuments of the Stalinist era, which appear to most of us akin in the emptiness of their rhetoric to the architecture of Mussolini's Rome, as grandiose, tasteless and pretentious.

One chance encounter I had in Leningrad cannot go unmentioned. Whom should I run into in the hotel where we were staying but Raymond Mortimer? We were both in a hurry and did not chat for long. He lived less than a quarter of a mile away from me in Islington, and I don't suppose I set eyes on him more than once a year. We rapidly expressed our astonishment at meeting in these exotic surroundings and then Raymond, who I don't need to say was an infinitely more knowledgeable and more zealous tourist than I, asked whether we had yet seen the so-and-so monastery. No? Then we must; it was no account to be missed. He gave us directions and waved goodbye. I had not heard of the monastery, and it did not appear to be mentioned in any tourist literature we had; but, trusting Raymond, we put off our visit to the Hermitage until later and took a taxi to the monastery. We were not disappointed, for it was everything Raymond's enthusiasm had implied. It also appeared to be Party headquarters.

Of the foreign countries I visited the Soviet Union proved the most foreign and by far the most riddling; and Moscow more so than Leningrad. Leningrad was northern, a Scandinavian city in which I could find similarities to Stockholm; Moscow was Byzantine, oriental. I had practically no contact with the Soviet counterpart of the man on the Clapham bus, though on second thoughts I do remember one. Lunching in a restaurant, we were joined by a Russian, who was attracted, I can only think, by the sound of English. At a pause in our talk, he interjected: 'Bobby Charlton is the love of my life.' It sounded curiously oracular, for it had nothing to do with anything we had been saying. He was, he said, an engineer and, no, he had not been to England but from time to time he met English engineers in Moscow and he read the English engineering magazines. Almost all the Russians I met were distinguished and a few were famous both in the Soviet Union and the West. They were eager to talk, but almost invariably there came a point in our talk when I was aware of some discontinuity in our dialogue, as though the basis of understanding had suddenly disappeared. This was not, I am convinced, due to lack of goodwill on either side. I can only fall back on Thoreau and think we marched by different drums.

Within a fortnight of my return from Moscow I was in the United

States again. The contrast was extreme and my relief was considerable. I felt at home and at ease. There was not the pressure of constant and terrible earnestness that one felt in Russia, and though there was no doubt just as much gobbledegook, it was gobbledegook of a kind I was used to and therefore found easier to disregard. I was engaged on a lecture-tour of universities and colleges under the auspices of a commercial lecture-agency. I was eager to discover whether it would prove a comparatively undemanding way of adding to my income, as it had done for a few people I knew, though I was aware you did not pick up nearly as much on the college circuit as from lecturing to ladies' luncheon clubs. For, though I was earning more money than I had every thought likely, I was still finding it as difficult as it had ever been to make ends meet. Wryly, I could see what my dentist-friend meant when he assured me, thirty years earlier, that the real problems began when you begin to earn five hundred a year. To a degree one is rarely conscious of, the way one lives, one's standard of life, is shaped by one's social surroundings, friends and colleagues. My three elder children were of or were coming to university age. They were at public schools, and this was by my own choice. Ideally, I would have preferred them to be at state schools, but those easily available did not seem to me to be very good. I had put myself more or less by accident into the privileged section of society and, while I was as much against privilege as ever I'd been, it seemed to me that as long as privilege existed one had what was tantamount to a moral duty to exploit it for one's children. This indeed was one reason why I was against privilege: it put one time and again in a false position. But putting my children through independent schools made me realise that in these days, with tax as it is, no amount one earns is as valuable as a private income, and I hadn't one. Money had to be got by my own wits or not at all.

I was besides, worried about the future. It seemed to me very likely that I belonged to the last generation of the old type of literary journalist, those who number among them Fielding, Goldsmith, Johnson, Smollett, Hazlitt, Pritchett conspicuously in our time and Edmund Wilson in the States, where the breed has been less evident, those writers, in other words, who have sometimes been called hacks and sometimes men of letters. It seemed to me significant that the reviewers now making their reputations were men like Frank Kermode and Christopher Ricks, who were academics primarily. I felt, too, that while the reading public might be bigger than it had ever been, the reading public for my sort of writing was probably smaller.

The traditional literary and political weeklies were plainly running down to a slow death, and as far as I was concerned the grossly inflated Sunday newspapers, any one of which provided reading matter enough for ordinary men for the whole week, were no substitute. The existence of broadcasting had for a time given people like myself a sense of security which, I now thought, was largely illusory. We had assumed that the pattern of broadcasting was that enshrined in the BBC, which was paternalistic and elitist in the upper-class English way, but you had only to look to America to see that that was not necessarily so; the very fact that commercial television had been introduced in Britain indicated that the BBC's position was shaken.

Moreover, it was clear to me that the nature of radio programmes was changing. The fifteen- or twenty-minute talk, for instance, was being displaced by what were called magazine programmes, in which the talk was reduced to the length of a mere paragraph, and if this process was especially apparent in the overseas services of the BBC it was discernible enough in the domestic services. And dominating everything else was the stark, unpalatable fact that sound broadcasting now existed more or less by courtesy of television, and to me television appeared very much as a threat. At this time, *The Critics* programme had the largest listening figure of any programme in what the BBC quaintly called the Spoken Word, but one knew that this was simply because there was then no television to be seen at all on Sunday mornings, when it was transmitted.

Not that I didn't appear on television when the chance presented itself. I was fairly often in the book programme and from time to time in magazine programmes, but I couldn't take it very seriously, I think because no one in television studios seemed to take what was being said very seriously. Studios were full of bustle, technicians were busy at their several jobs, the speaker was only one among many, and, one felt, not of prime importance. The producer was much more concerned with your positioning than with what you had to say and how you said it. I remembered a story Pritchett told me about one of his appearances in the television *Brains Trust*. He had met an acquaintance whom I also knew slightly, an educationalist of some distinction who frequently appeared on TV. This man said to him: 'Oh, V. S., I must tell you. I thought you were so good in the *Brains Trust* yesterday.' 'Did you really?' replied Pritchett. 'I'm so relieved. I thought I talked the most utter nonsense.' 'Oh, I'm not thinking of what you said, it was the way you looked.' It was that attitude which seemed dominant in television, and it gave me great unease. My business, my life even, was concerned with words, and in television, in which you were seen as part of a pattern, a picture, words were of small account. In sound broadcasting they had been all-important.

So, with my future suddenly felt as insecure, my interest in trying a new venture will be understandable. In the event, by the end of the tour I had decided itinerant lecturing was not for me. I cannot say I was out of pocket as a result of the trip, but the profit I had made didn't seem enough to compensate for the time and energy I had put out. I found the trip extremely exhausting, so much so that when I got back home I had to take a further week off in order to recover.

Besides, while I didn't think I'd failed as a lecturer, I found the business too easy to be satisfying. On tour, I often found I was regarding what I was doing with a mild contempt. One toured with four lectures in one's bag and parrotted them turn and turn about, the obligatory jokes cunningly calculated, so that you could be certain where the laughs would come. It was a great strain, too, having to be pleasant to everybody afterwards; I particularly took against the inevitable middle-aged lady with the blue rinse who jutted out her chin and said in menacing tones that she was just an ordinary American home-maker. She made one uncomfortably aware it was no small thing to be. It was not, I found, agreeable to despise either one's audiences or oneself.

All the same, I would not have missed it for anything. It took me to parts of America I would otherwise probably never have seen. How else would I have penetrated the Oklahoma Baptist College, with the shabby, moth-eaten buffalo that was its mascot? In a period of five weeks I was on close to a score of campuses. I flew up and down the United States and considerably more than half-way across it and back again; I got down to South Carolina, to Texas and to Montana in the north-west, even into Canada, for I spoke at the University of Waterloo at Kitchener, Ontario, which before 1914, I was told, was called Bismarck.

It scarcely needs saying that tours of this kind distort one's vision. I came back with an impression of American uniformity which was greatly exaggerated; though many things went towards fostering this. Airports, for instance, differ only in size, and the same is true of universities; one Hilton hotel is almost identical with another, and Holiday Inns are interchangeable. There is a deeper reason, too, for overstressing the uniformity of America, one suggested by some sentences in Mumford's *The Golden Day*:

> If the nineteenth century found us more raw and rude, it was because our minds were not buoyed up by all those memorials of a great past that floated over the surface of Europe. The American was thus a stripped European; and the colonisation of America can, with justice, be called the dispersion of Europe – a movement carried on by people incapable of sharing or continuing its past.

This stripped quality of American life is one of the factors that makes for what Europeans see as uniformity, and in urban environments especially it is repellant enough. Nevertheless, it is one of the qualities that gives the United States its enormous attraction for me. It is the converse, I suspect, of the Old World's fascination and allurement for the educated American. With a vision in his mind of the settlement of America perhaps not very different from Mumford's, Henry James in a famous phrase spoke of the 'complex fate' involved in being an American, crucial to which complexity is the American's relationship with Europe. It is much like Hyacinth Robinson's, which prompts the further reflection that James's complex fate is not the American's alone but that of every man who lives in a state of tension with his historic past. In this, the American and the Communist in eastern Europe are one.

My illusions of a blanket American uniformity were effectively dispelled by a visit a year later. The things I most appreciated on my lecture tour were precisely those that seemed to contradict it. Two memories, as disparate as they could be, stick out in my mind. One is of visits to Roman Catholic women's liberal arts colleges. They were, so to speak, offshoots of nunneries. One was in Duluth, Minnesota. I was met at the airport by two nuns with a motor car. The elder said: 'Tell me, Mr Allen, are you familiar with nuns?' I got the impression that the way she phrased the question was deliberate but I resisted the temptation to be flippant and answered simply that I was not a Roman Catholic and had no occasion to meet nuns. I could truthfully have said that it hadn't been until the day before, in Toledo, Ohio, that I'd ever spoken to a nun.

I spent the best part of three days at the college in Duluth and if I say that the nuns clucked round me like so many hens I do not mean to imply anything more than that they were as little at ease in my company as I was in theirs. I was embarrassed by their solicitude and at the same time I seemed to be living in a kind of exile, for I took all my meals alone. Constraints did, of course, begin to break down and were evidently felt less by the younger nuns. I was fortunate in that we were running up to the mid-term elections and a television set was put at my disposal, so that I could look at the political broadcasts. Some of the sisters showed a lively interest in them. They were mostly Irish and overwhelmingly Democrat, and since my sympathies when I am in the United States are Democrat rather than not, this gave us common ground.

I taught two or three classes while there and the liberal outlook of the nuns who were professors took me completely by surprise. I had feared I should find I had to inhibit myself in exposition and discussion. I might have known better from experience in Toledo, where the question-period after my lecture developed into a discussion in which Lawrence's novels were the sole topic. This surprised me, for I had scarcely mentioned him. I commented on it later to the sister who was the professor. She explained that she was teaching *The Rainbow* and the students were very excited by it. It was the first time she had been allowed to teach Lawrence and she had had to fight hard to get permission. 'I won,' she said, 'by telling them that Lawrence belonged to the religious underground.' She was allowed to teach *The Rainbow* but not *Women in Love*. 'But I'll get permission to teach *Women in Love*,' she said, 'if not next year then the year after.' She was an impressive woman, and the enthusiasm of her students showed how successful she was as a teacher.

The other memory which gives me particular pleasure is of my visit to Montana State University at Bozeman. I was contracted to spend five days on campus meeting classes and making myself generally available, besides giving a lecture. Montana was by a long way the furthest west I had penetrated into the United States, and even the flight from Minneapolis seemed romantic. We touched down at places that seemed unimaginably remote, Fargo, North Dakota, for instance. It could have been any other small-town airport in America, and from the air the town seemed no different from thousands of others. Nor had it any specific associations for me. Yet in the strongest way it evoked the West; and when we came into Bozeman I found the West was there, all about me. It was at once novel and very familiar, for I had seen it scores of times before – in Westerns, though when I considered more carefully I realised the film country was hundreds of miles to the South. All the same, Montana *was* cowboy country, and it didn't seem to me affectation that even the reporter on the local newpaper wore high-heeled cowboy boots.

We were in the Rockies, on what was roughly a plateau five

thousand feet up and given over, it seemed, to grazing. It was no longer warm and there were occasional flurries of snow. At night it froze, and one was warned that in a week's time the snow would set in in earnest. Towns were few, widely scattered and small, scarcely more than a Federal post office, a couple of banks perhaps, a handful of stores and a cluster of houses on main street, which was the state highway. In its way, it seemed to me an idyllic country, less tamed than any I had known before. One felt that here life was governed by the seasons and by the nature of the terrain. For some men, I could see that it must offer the next best thing to paradise, and I could not think it was by accident that the academics I met were men of the open air and open spaces. Most of them seemed to have come from the East; they were escaped New Yorkers, Bostonians and Philadelphians who kept and rode horses, hunted and fished, and their talk was of these things. They seemed to have come to Montana consciously for the idyllic life and they did not seem to have been disappointed. I thought it entirely proper that the great topic of conversation while I was on campus was that the President of the University had only the other day shot a bear, which in local terms appeared to be the ultimate ambition of every man.

I knew that life at Bozeman would be no life for me but I could not rid myself of a grudging feeling of envy similar to that I have felt for athletes, for rugger players and boxers especially. The pleasure they had from their pursuits was unimaginable, though I could see they got something satisfying out of their bizarre practices. Ever since reading *The Marriage of Heaven and Hell* as a sixth-former I have been haunted by Blake's lines:

> How do you know but ev'ry bird that cuts the airy way,
> Is an immense world of delight, clos'd by your senses five?

I was envious of the worlds of delight others seemed to have and from which I felt debarred, and I often wondered whether our own individual specialisms amounted to much more than our own individual imprisonments.

The five days I spent at Bozeman were intensely enjoyable: they were so far removed from my ordinary life that they had the quality of pure holiday. The students at the classes I took were fresh and eager so that I was stimulated myself: American students, who are, by and large, considerably less well prepared than their English counterparts, are often because of this more keen and responsive, as though suddenly waking up to the pleasures of learning and anxious to make up for lost time. There were other, incidental delights. I recall the small museum devoted to the local Indian culture. Its curator was a retired professor of History in the University. He was learned in everything relating to the West, though, he said, the man who knew more than anyone else about this part of America was an Englishman, who was out that way every year. He wondered whether I knew him. I had to admit I didn't but I had met him, for he was Professor John Hawgood, of Birmingham University.

And then – it was the crowning event of my visit to Bozeman – I was driven for a day in Yellowstone Park, which was to close at the end of the week for the winter. In some ways, I was disappointed, for I saw no animals at all. Hibernation, I was told, had probably already begun, though at the cafés and restaurants we called at we were assured the bears had been round the night before, prospecting, raiding, turning over the trash-cans in the search for food. The geysers alone kept their promises. But I left Yellowstone full of admiration for the American national park service; and what should we see, once we were safely out of the park at dusk, but a herd of deer galloping across the cow pasture?

Within six months, I was in the United States again, and this time my wife and six-year-old daughter were with me. I was fulfilling a promise I had made while at Vassar to put in some time as visiting professor at the University of Kansas, at Lawrence, and I had agreed to go on, afterwards, to the summer session of the University of Washington at Seattle. We rented an agreeable ranch-style house about a mile from the campus and my small daughter settled down happily in second grade in the local school.

I was fortunate in seeing Kansas and Washington in such close proximity in time, for the one served to set off the other. In America, the adjective always applied to Kansas is 'corny', which according to the dictionary means 'out of date, old-fashioned; trite; sentimental.' This means only that Kansas is a rural, even a rustic state and it doesn't prevent the State University from being a notably distinguished one. The President of the University was accustomed in his speeches to refer to Lawrence as 'this Athens on the Kaw,' the Kaw being the name by which the Kansas River is known at that point. I had discovered that the University had celebrated its centenary a few months before we arrived, which was a salutary reminder of how relatively old American universities are compared with most of those in England. I had also discovered before I left home that the University and Lawrence had a surreptitious and dingy immortality in Frank

Harris's *My Life and Loves*. Harris, who had gone to America from Ireland at the age of fourteen, was a law student at the University in the early eighteen-seventies, having previously been a cowboy among other things. He put himself through the University by working as night clerk at the local hotel, which even now bears the same name as it does in *My Life and Loves*. Outside the Law School was a statue representing a man with a moustache standing with an arm round the shoulders of a younger man and gesticulating towards the frontier; a memorial to Horace Greeley's famous 'Go West, Young Man, Go West,' I imagine. I put it about that it was a speaking likeness of Harris in his student days and that he was obviously indicating to a neophyte in skulduggery where the pickings were. No one seemed much impressed, and when Harris's connection with the University was known I rather gathered it wasn't in the best of taste to refer to it. Harris, in fact, though no doubt a considerable scoundrel, was also a considerable journalist, and the short stories in his collections *Elder Conklin* and *Montes the Matador* are by no means negligible studies of life in the further Middle West and the South West in the last decades of last century. Though it is doubtless his own fault, he had not had justice done to him as a writer.

I could scarcely be in Kansas without making mental reference to Iowa, its northern neighbour. They shared the same rolling countryside, which had been prairie until a hundred years ago, and the people came from similar stock. Iowa achieved statehood in 1846, Kansas in 1861. But I felt one was considerably closer in Kansas both to the frontier and the past. Kansas was born in history, history standing for the spectacular and the bloody. In a way, it was epitomised in a mural in Lawrence City Hall, representing the firing of the city by armed raiders from Missouri, forty miles away. Not for nothing, indeed, was Kansas in its early days known as 'bloody Kansas'. It had come into existence almost as an equipoise to Missouri, which had been admitted to the Union in 1821. Missouri was a slave state from the beginning. The question of slavery was, of course, the great cause of tension between the states throughout the first half of the nineteenth century, and it was in an attempt to ease that tension that the Kansas-Nebraska Bill was passed by Congress in 1854. The bill gave settlers the right to determine whether slavery should be permitted under their governments, and one consequence of the bill was the founding by New England abolitionists of the Emigrant Aid Company. It settled as many as two thousand abolitionists as colonists in Kansas, the most famous being John Brown, he whose body lies a-mouldering in the grave. He was one of the great heroes and martyrs of the North; but he was also a great fanatic. He lived by the assumption that he had been chosen by God to destroy settlers who supported slavery. To that end, he murdered five of his neighbours. A year or so later, with a handful of followers he seized the U. S. armoury at Harpers Ferry, Virginia, for which act of insurrection he was hanged.

Thus, briefly, the historical background. Kansas was also the state into which emerged the Chisholm Trail, along which the grazing herds of cattle were driven up from the ranges of Texas to the railhead at Kansas City. It was a state in constant touch with frontiers even when it was no longer itself the frontier, and in Kansas I felt in the presence of the sort of history that is recorded in the border ballads. I saw Kansas, of course, entirely as enshrined in its principal university, and universities, American universities especially, are never representative of the values of the communities in which they have their being. Neverthless, I had the feeling that Kansas, by contrast with Iowa, was still unsure of itself, unsure of its identity and still searching for one, angrily certain, perhaps, of only one thing, the virtue of the Protestant ethic. At the very centre of the United States, it seemed nowhere specifically and could define itself only by taking sides, by aligning itself *against* somewhere else, most obviously, perhaps, against the state immediately across the river and its biggest city, Missouri and Kansas City, but also – and this seemed especially true of the English Department of the University even though many of the professors came from the East – against New York, New England and the eastern seaboard generally.

We were constantly visited by poets as they crossed the continent tirelessly from east to west and from west to east in the course of their itinerant reading, and I quickly realised how ignorant I was of the newer American poetry, how old-fashioned my tastes were. Or it may merely have been that, in terms of Philip Rahv's famous dichotomy, the poets who read at the University were redskins almost to a man, avowed disidents, militants against the war in Vietnam. They seemed to be either of the Black Mountain School or from San Francisco, though there was also Robert Bly, the Minnesota poet picturesque in poncho and the most fervent of them all against the war. I found him a stimulating extrovert who seemed a contemporary manifestation of the extreme romantic conception of the poet. He had been in England the year before, and he told me that he had liked England and the English much more than he had expected; a confession I found disarming. We were visited by Denise Levertov, too, who struck me as a woman of power and distinction. I did not know the poetry she was writing before she left England, but her affiliations now seemed entirely with the Americans and mainly with Whitman and the Black Mountain poets.

For me, our season of visiting poets came to a ludicrous climax near the end of the semester. I was taken aside by more than one of my colleagues and warned that the poet who was next to visit us was a notorious reactionary, a follower of Eliot and Auden. I was not used to thinking a liking for Auden the sign of a reactionary and I saw I was old-fashioned indeed, the more so when the poet in question was described to me as an Easterner who had had it soft all his life, freewheeling through prep. school, Amherst and Harvard to his Chair at Wesleyan University. He was presented to me as the acme of the effete, and the mere contemplation of him seemed to give rise to deep passions and complex hatreds. He could not have been more summarily dismissed if he had been English. He might indeed then even have been forgiven, for he could have been categorised as 'European and fancy,' in Thomas Wolfe's phrase.

He was, in fact, one of my favourite American poets, the wittiest and most elegant, and learned in his craft besides. I had met him in London and liked him. I was abashed by the reception he seemed about to receive and felt myself as in some way under sentence because I couldn't hide it from myself that he was almost my ideal modern American poet. Before his reading, a small dinner party had been arranged for him in a private room in the Union at the typically Mid-Western dining hour of six o'clock. He had not arrived at six-fifteen, and by then the denunciations of him had become simply irrational. He was not only a reactionary poet, he was indulging in characteristic Ivy-League behaviour towards the Middle West, condescending to us, high-hatting us. Everyone present knew perfectly well why he was late. That afternoon, he had been reading in Kansas City, and one of our colleagues had been deputed to drive there, pick him up and bring him back, after which it was understood he'd take him home first for a wash and a drink, since alcohol was not served in the Union.

He appeared at about six-thirty and we ate a hurried meal which passed without event; as indeed did the reading. He was treated, it goes without saying, most courteously, and he behaved similarly, though I detected irony in the running commentary he provided on his poems and in the way in which he was dressed. Tall, handsome, he was by a long way the best turned-out man in the room, the Brooks Brothers exquisite from a *New Yorker* advertisement. He was, I felt, taking some wry pleasure in conforming to his audience's preconceptions of him. He was Richard Wilbur.

At the end of the semester we left Kansas and in a leisurely fashion, by Greyhound bus, aeroplane and train made our way to New York, pausing at Des Moines, Chicago and Poughkeepsie to stay with friends. I saw my wife and daughter on to the *Queen Mary* and then flew to Seattle, where I was met by Henry Reed, who was my initial contact at the University of Washington. He had gone out there in 1963 as poet in residence after the death of Theodore Roethke, had held later appointments and was returning to England in a matter of days. It was he who had introduced me to the chairman of the English department, Robert Heilman, one of the best known and respected English teachers in America, a redoubtable scholar and an original 'New Critic'. We had become friends.

In Washington, I was again in territory new to me. It was the furthest I had travelled in America; indeed, if you travelled much further you would be in the Pacific Ocean. It was land's end literally, and I felt I was in Ultima Thule, so different did I find it from anywhere else I had lived in the United States. The difference was partly climatic. I had left New York on a day of appalling humidity with the temperature at 100 degrees and arrived in Seattle on a perfect afternoon fanned by a breeze off the Sound and the thermometer at 85. I knew that the climate of this section of the Pacific coast was always compared with that of southern England; it was better, as rainy but more temperate and balmy. And of course the scenery could not have been more different from that of Kansas. From the windows of the faculty dining room one looked east to Mount Rainier, the highest peak in the Cascades, over 14,000 feet high and permanently snow-covered. It looked perhaps twenty miles away but I don't doubt it was much further. The other way, almost underneath the windows it seemed, lay Puget Sound. And Washington is a state of great forests, almost, one might think, one huge national park.

The contrast between the two states illustrates beautifully, it seems to me, the effect of climate and landscape on people, for the racial stock in both Washington and Kansas is very much the same, indeed, the common American mix of peoples from the whole breadth of northern Europe, German, Scandinavian, Irish predominating, with dashes of Bohemian, Russian and other strains. But in Washington, one could not help thinking, it had been subjected to pressures more beneficent than Kansas knew. Washington, more than any state I had been in, seemed to be Walt Whitman's America. This, I do not need telling, is both a simplification and a sentimentalisation, the result, perhaps, of nothing more than six weeks in agreeable surroundings in a more than usually good summer. All the same, the feeling rested on some things that are real, that are matters of fact. One is that New York is too far away to be of immediate significance, and the eastern seaboard with its weight of history and traditions is remote enough to be ignored. The only city outside its frontiers it need concern itself with is San Francisco, and even San Francisco is the best part of five hundred miles away. The North West, in other words, of which Washington is the principal state and Seattle the chief port and metropolis, is virtually an autonomous region. In nothing is this more apparent than in its poetry, which goes its own independent way, owing nothing to Black Mountain or the Beats.

Another strong feeling the visitor to Seattle has is that the Ultima Thule in which he finds himself is very much the gateway to other worlds. I had not been prepared for the Japanese tourists I saw on all sides and it was not until I heard them talking to one another in demotic American that I tumbled to the fact that they were not tourists at all but native Americans, nisei, the descendants of Japanese immigrants. It is a reminder that, however far away it may be, Japan is the nearest foreign country westward from Seattle.

Seattle, then, is the port for what we with our local notions of the globe call the Far East. It is also the port for the Frozen North: Alaska is the next stop, and one has a sense of the close proximity of Alaska when one is in Seattle. It is many hundreds of miles away, but the number of people one meets who have been there or are on the point of going, make it seem a close neighbour.

The inhabitants of the North West seemed to me more free than those of Kansas, less hag-ridden by ancestral forces, more extrovert. They gave a greater feeling of being in control of their own destiny, a sense of being less trapped; it was as if they could take off at a moment's notice for somewhere else, Alaska perhaps or Japan. The difference between the North West and Kansas, I suspect, is probably the difference between peoples who are brought up and live on the shores of great oceans and those who live land-locked lives. And I must admit that notion of the North West as a country of what one might call psychological ease, grossly subjective as it is, may well have been influenced by the presence all round me of hippies. I walked through them twice a day, because part of the campus was given over to them. I was never particularly enchanted by hippy beliefs, but they did, at that moment of history and in that place, seem positively to have come into lotus-land. Those were the days of the Flower People, and it was disarming and surprisingly touching to be presented with a carnation as I walked towards or away from my classes, even though I never knew what to do with it and felt absurdly self-conscious carrying it in my hand.

During my last two weeks in Seattle I had a letter, forwarded from home, enquiring very cautiously whether I was interested in being considered for the Chair of English in the New University of Ulster. It was signed by the Vice-Chancellor. The University, which I had not heard of, was to open its doors to students in a year's time. I did not take the letter entirely seriously but I answered with commendable circumspection. I had one thing to do before returning to England, which was to look at literary New England. Accordingly, I stood on the bridge at Lexington, spent a day in Emerson's Concord and spat in Walden Pond. What particularly fascinated me was Melville's New Bedford, where I visited the chapel in which Father Mapple preaches the great sermon in *Moby Dick*. 'Delight, — top-gallant delight is to him, who acknowledges no law or lord, but the Lord his God, and is only a patriot to heaven'. Melville's description is astonishingly faithful to the chapel, which is still a seamen's chapel. I was thrilled by it, and moved; as I was by the whaling museum that faces it.

I caught the plane for London, not aware that I was thinking of the possible professorship in Northern Ireland. Then it dawned on me that Ulster was almost as easy to reach from London as Kansas or Seattle and I realised that the New Grub Street I had been wandering along for thirty years could all the time have been leading to the olive-grove of Academe, where, as we know, 'the Attic bird Trills her thick-warbled notes the summer long.'

Index

Ackerley, J.R. 63–4, 186
Aiken, Conrad 24
Allen, Charles 7
Allen, Donald 148, 200, 217
Allen, Frank 2, 6–7, 121
Allen, George 3–4
Allen, Walter ancestry 1–3; relatives 2–7; early reading of 6–7; and brothers 7; at King Edward's Grammar School, Aston 8–30; writes first articles 10; acts 10; and Gissing 10–11; sits School Certificate 13–21; studies Blake 13–14; and Shaw and Wells 14; and Bennett 14–16; and Desmond MacCarthy 15–16; and Birmingham City Public Library 16–17; and Robert Graves 16, 20–1; and D.H. Lawrence 17–19; and T.S. Eliot 19–20; passes Higher Certificate 22; and *Daily Express* oratorical contest 23–5; visits Poetry Bookshop 23–4; sits Balliol scholarship 25–7; and Oxford 28–30; wins Birmingham University scholarship 30; as undergraduate 31–45; and Ernest de Selincourt 33–4; and A.M.D. Hughes 34–5; and E.R. Dodds 39–42; and New Party 42–4; and W.H. Auden 44–5; 51–8; and Louis MacNeice 45–7, 91–5, 109; becomes a writer 48–50; and broadcaster 51; and John Hampson's wedding 55–8; and John Hampson 58–71; and J.R. Ackerley 63–4; and Graham Greene 64–5, 100–5; and Wiliam Plomer 65; and E.M. Forster 65–8; and Peter Chamberlain 68–9; and Leslie Halward 69–70; becomes a schoolmaster 72; at University of Iowa 72–80; visits Kansas City 80–1; visits Chicago 81; visits New York 81–6; and Robert Ballou 82–5; returns to England 86–8; joins Herbert Cater 89; completes *Innocence is Drowned* and moves to London 95–6; and Edward O'Brien 96–7; as reader for MGM 98–100; and Blue Moon Bookshop 105–7; and V.S. Pritchett 107–9; and Raymond Mortimer 109; and Margaret Gardiner 109; demonstrates 111–2; publishes *Innocence is Drowned* 113; completes *Blind Man's Ditch* 113; and Reggie Smith and Olivia Manning 116–7; and outbreak of war 116–7; publishes *Blind Man's Ditch* 118; and money problems 1939–40 119–21; and work in foundry 122, 130–1; and L.H. Myers 123–30; as air raid warden 131; and John Mair 132; becomes critic 133; and Henry 'Green' 133–9, 149–50; and wartime experiences 140–1; and George Woods 141–2; and Gwilyn James 142–4; and attempts to enlist 144–5; returns to Birmingham 144–5; marries 146; returns to London 147–8; and Roy Campbell 150–2; and Dylan Thomas 151–3; and Julian

MacLaren-Ross 153–8; and L.P.
Hartley 158–69; and Elizabeth
Bowen 166–7; and Edward
Sackville-West 167–9; and Anthony
Powell 169–71; and John Baker
171–2; and *New Statesman* colleagues
172–80, 186–8; moves to Lydd 181;
and Joyce Cary 182–6; and John
Raymond 188–94; visits
Czechoslovakia 194–200; and
Chun-chan Yeh 200–1; publishes
Dead Man over All 201; and *The
English Novel* 201–2; and Wyndham
Lewis 203–9; and Coe College
210–23; and *All in a Lifetime* 224; and
Hugh Gaitskill 225–6; visits Greece
226–9; becomes literary editor of *New
Statesman* 230; and Aldous Huxley
230–1; and Christopher Isherwood
231–2; and Richard Hughes 232–6;
and Vassar 237–53; and R.K.
Narayan 241–3; and architecture
253–4; visits Russia 254–8; and *The
Princess Cassamassima* 256–7; visits
Universities of Kansas and
Washington 265–71; becomes
professor, New University of Ulster
271
Allen, William 7
Allen, (father) 1–3, 6
Allen, (grandfather) 2
Anand, Mulk Raj 107
Arendt, Hannah 249
Auden, G.A. 40, 53
Auden, W.H. 21, 25, 34, 40–1, 44–5,
47, 51–8, 63–4, 66, 93–4, 101, 109,
209, 232, 240, 256
Aryton, Elizabeth 243–4
Ayrton, Michael 205, 243–4

Baker, John 171–2, 202
Ballou, Robert 82–5
Barbellion, W.N.P. 90
Barry, Gerald 50–1
Bates, H.E. 63, 70, 98
'Beaky' 9
Behan, Brendan 242
Bellow, Saul 249
Bennett, Arnold 14–16, 21

Bennett, Tertia 15
Beresford, J.D. 17
Bernstein, Sidney 194
Bishop, Elizabeth 85
Blackett, P.M.S. 225
Blumenfeld, R.D. 25
Blunden, Edmund 34
Bly, Robert 267
Bowen, Elizabeth 63–4, 162, 166–7,
181, 198
Bowra, Maurice 40
Breit, Harvey 217
Bridges, Robert 33
Bridson, Geoffrey 208
Brierley, Walter 18
Briggs, Asa 30
Brooks, Van Wyck 24
Brooks, Dr 81
Brophy, John 63
Brown, Francis 217, 222
Brown, Ivor 193
Burgess, Guy 194
Burnett, Whit 85

Campbell, Roy 150–2
Canetti, Elias 115
Carver, David 54
Cary, Joyce 35, 182–6
Cater, Herbert S. 89–91, 179
Cather, Willa 224
Caughlin, Father 79
Cecil, Algernon 166
Cecil, David 183
Chamberlain, Peter 68–9, 87
Chaplin, Charles 194
Charlton, Leo 63
Church, Richard 192
Clark, Kenneth 14
Connolly, Cyril 67, 192
Cooke, Alistair 243, 246–7
Cowley, Malcolm 85
Craig, Harry 231
Cummings, A.J. 90–1

Davenport, John 156, 175
Davin, Dan 185–6
Deeping, Warwick 207
de la Roche, Mazo 208
de Selincourt, Ernest 33–4

Divine, Father 83–4
Dixon, Pierson 196–9
Dodds, E.R. 30, 39–42, 63, 94–5, 107, 200
Dodds, Mrs 34, 40–1, 94
Doone, Rupert 94–5
Douglas, Norman 36
Driberg, Tom 90

Eliot, T.S. 19–21, 24, 33, 40, 50, 52, 63, 67, 82, 151, 194, 197, 205–7, 209, 216, 251
Empson, William 37–8, 250

Fairlie, Henry 192
Fiedler, Leslie 82
Fisher, Vardis 76–7
Fitzgerald, F. Scott 68
Florence, Philip Sargant 37, 92, 175
Foley, Martin 85
Forester, C.S. 68
Forster, E.M. 8, 60, 62, 65–8, 71, 114, 135, 176
'Frank' 9–13
Frost, Robert 223, 250

Gardiner, Margaret 109, 119, 123
Gardner, Helen 36, 182–3
Garnett, David 7, 17, 248–9
Giehse, Terese 55–8
Gilkes, Martin 11, 233, 236
Goodyear, Robert 105, 119–20
Graves, Robert 16–17, 20–2, 53, 222–3, 232, 234
'Green' (Yorke), Henry 26, 29–30, 49, 53, 67, 118, 133–9, 149, 217
Greene, Graham 15, 29, 54, 63–5, 100–5, 167, 187, 241
Gregory, Horace 82
Grigson, Geoffrey 13, 205–6

Haldane, J.B.S. 111
Halward, Leslie 69–70
Hampson, John 18, 52, 54, 55–71, 82, 91, 94, 101, 123, 135, 150, 168, 182, 231
Hanley, James 63
Harris, Frank 266
Harrod, Roy 29

Hart-Davis, Rupert 67
Hartley, L.P. 15, 124, 158–69
Hawes, Stanley 42
Hawgood, John 265
Heilman, Robert 269
Heller, Joseph 252
Hemingway, Ernest 68, 86
Heppenstall, Rayner 28
Herbert, A.P. 26, 29
Herickx, Gordon 42, 60, 63, 94–5
Hicken, Norman 11–12
Higham, David 118
Hobson, Thayer 182
Hopkin, Willie 18–19
Hopkins, Harry 79
Hore-Belisha, Leslie 25
Hughes, A.M.D. 34–5, 143
Hughes, Richard 17, 232–6
Hutchins, Robert 79
Hutchinson, A.S.M. 207
Huxley, Aldous 11, 19, 34, 36, 42, 96, 224, 230–2
Huxley, Maria 19

Isherwood, Christopher 41, 53, 66, 109, 231–2

James, Gwilym 142–4
Joad, C.E.M. 44
'Joe' 22–3, 27, 72
Johnson, Pamela Hansford 101
Joseph, Michael 96–7, 113, 118, 147, 182, 185
Joyce, James 34

Kauffmann, Stanley 252
Kennedy, Ludovic 243
Kermode, Frank 259
Knox, E.V. 26

Lahr, Charles 105–7
Lamming, George 217–18
Lane, Allen 202–3, 219
Lawrence, D.H. 17–19, 69, 248, 263
Lawrence, T.E. 66
Leavis, F.R. 13, 176, 250
Lehmann, John 67, 133, 231
Levertov, Denise 268
Lewis, Cecil Day 52, 116, 151

Lewis, D.B. Wyndham 17
Lewis, Froanna 206–7
Lewis, P. Wyndham 13, 17, 20, 94, 203–9
Lichtenstein, Vernon 214
Lindemann, Frederick 30
Linklater, Eric 1, 36–7
Lowry, Malcolm 24
Lusty, Robert 182

Macaulay, Rose 66, 107, 117
MacCarthy, Desmond 15–16, 151, 173, 178, 188, 199, 232, 246
McCarthy, Mary 55, 237
McCullers, Carson 249
MacDiarmid, Hugh 37
Mackenzie, Compton 179
Maclaren-Ross, Julian 140, 153–8, 169, 170–1
MacNeice, Louis 40, 45–7, 56–8, 63–4, 91–5, 109–16, 123, 150, 162, 167, 173, 217, 223, 237
Macrae, Elliott 202–3, 218–19
Mair, John 132–3
Malamud, Bernard 249
Mann Erika 55
Manning, Olivia 116, 149, 156, 237
Mansfield, Katherine 19
Martin, Kingsley 16, 50, 106, 174–80, 186–7, 198, 203, 224–5, 230
Maugham, W.S. 66, 97
Medley, Robert 94–5
Melville, John 42, 63
Melville, Robert 42, 63
Mercer, Caroline 237, 247
Miller, Arthur 242
Milne, A.A. 218–19
Mitchison, Naomi 51, 205
Monro, Harold 23–4
Moravia, Alberto 191
Morris, John 63
Mortimer, Raymond 109, 168, 172–3, 175, 177, 186, 258
Mosley, Oswald 43–4
Muggeridge, Malcolm 222
Muir, Edwin 128, 199
Mumford, Lewis 232, 262
Murry, John Middleton 19–20
Myers, L.H. 123–30

Narayan, R.K. 241–2
Newbolt, Henry 16
Nichols, Robert 11
Nicolson, Harold 42–4
Novemsky, Commissar 197–8, 200
O'Brien, Edward 85–6, 88, 96–7
O'Hara, John 68
Olsson, Halvor 37
Orwell, George 170, 187

Piper, Edwin Ford 79
Plomer, William 60, 64–5, 151
Partridge, Ralph 63
Plummer, Leslie 25
Potocki de Montalk ('King of Poland') 105–6
Pound, Ezra 16, 53, 208
Pound, Reginald 208
Powell, Anthony 30, 68, 99, 169–71, 176
Powell, Violet 169
Prescott, Orville 219
Pritchett, V.S. 64, 107–9, 172–3, 176, 186, 189, 208, 220, 249, 259–60

Rahv, Philip 218, 249, 267
Raymond, John 176, 178, 188–94, 224, 249
Read, Herbert 16, 28, 111, 206
Reed, Henry 28, 64, 269
Rees, Goronwy 118
Richards, I.A. 38–9, 68, 93, 109
Richardson, Maurice 173–5
Ricks, Christopher 259
Riding, Laura 17
Roberts, Michael 44–5
Roethke, Theodore 269
Romilly, Giles 173–4, 187
Rose, W.K. 207, 237, 240, 247
Rosenthal, M.L. 252
Ross, 76, 80–1
Rovere, Richard 247–8

Sackville-West, Edward 167–9
St John-Stevas, Norman 29
Sands, Ethel 15
Shaw, G.B. 22
Sheppard, J.T. 198
Sitwell, Edith 13

Sitwell, Osbert 13, 44
Smith, Janet Adam 186–7, 209, 225, 230, 249
Smith, Reggie 56–8, 91, 95, 110–11, 114–16, 146, 149, 152, 237
Snow, C.P. 225
Sonnenberg, Ben 243–4
Spender, Stephen 54, 66, 93–4, 115, 150, 239
Stanley, Eileen 93
Starkie, Enid 183
Stewart, J.I.M. 29
Stonier, G.W. 174, 178, 187
Strachey, John 43–4
Swaffer, Hannen 24–5
Swinnerton, Frank 15
Symons, Julian 205–6
Synge, J.M. 47

Tate, Allen 216, 223
Thomas, Andrew 4–5
Thomas, Dylan 151–3, 242
Thomas, Edward 5–7
Thomas, K.B. 2, 4
Thomson, Virgil 242
Titmuss, Professor 225
Todd, Ruthven 152
Trilling, Lionel 63, 213, 218, 248–50
Tugwell, Rex 79

Upward, Edward 53

Van Vechten, Carl 221
Ventura, Professor 198, 200
Verschoyle, Derek 97
Vocadlo, Professor 196, 200

Walker, Bernard Fleetwood 13
Walpole, Hugh 97
Warner, Rex 244
Warren, Robert Penn 244
Waterhouse, John 35–6
Waugh, Evelyn 1, 64, 135, 137, 170, 207
Weidenfeld, George 177
Wells, H.G. 15, 91, 108
Werth, Alexander 195
West, Nathaniel 224
West, Rebecca 205
Weybright, Victor 82, 219–20
White, Alan 207
Whiting, John 231
Whitman, Walt 216–17
Wilbur, Richard 268–9
Williamson, Hugh Ross 50
Wilson, Edmund 207, 259
Wilson, F.P. 60
Wolfe, Thomas 242, 268
Woodman, Dorothy 224–5
Woods, George 141–2
Woolf, Leonard 62, 176
Woolf, Virginia 34, 60, 62, 109
Worsley, T.C. 173, 178, 186–7

Yeats, W.B. 40, 44, 108